Harvard
Business
Review
Project
Management
Handbook

The Harvard Business Review Handbooks Series

HBR Handbooks provide ambitious professionals with the frameworks, advice, and tools they need to excel in their careers. With step-by-step guidance, time-honed best practices, real-life stories, and concise explanations of research published in *Harvard Business Review*, each comprehensive volume helps you to stand out from the pack—whatever your role.

Books in this series include:

Harvard Business Review Entrepreneur's Handbook

Harvard Business Review Family Business Handbook

Harvard Business Review Leader's Handbook

Harvard Business Review Manager's Handbook

Harvard Business Review Project Management Handbook

Harvard Business Review

Project Management Handbook

How to Launch, Lead, and Sponsor Successful Projects

ANTONIO NIETO-RODRIGUEZ

Harvard Business Review Press

Boston, Massachusetts

Copyright 2021 Harvard Business School Publishing Corporation
All rights reserved
Printed in the United States of America

10 9 8 7 6 5 4 3 2 1

No part of this publication may be reproduced, stored in or introduced into a retrieval system, or transmitted, in any form, or by any means (electronic, mechanical, photocopying, recording, or otherwise), without the prior permission of the publisher. Requests for permission should be directed to permissions@harvardbusiness.org, or mailed to Permissions, Harvard Business School Publishing, 60 Harvard Way, Boston, Massachusetts 02163.

The web addresses referenced in this book were live and correct at the time of the book's publication but may be subject to change.

Library of Congress Cataloging-in-Publication Data

Names: Nieto-Rodriguez, Antonio, author.
  Title: Harvard Business Review project management handbook : how to launch, lead, and sponsor successful projects / Antonio Nieto-Rodriguez.
  Other titles: Harvard Business Review handbooks series.
  Description: Boston, MA : Harvard Business Review Press, [2021] | Series: Harvard Business Review handbooks series | Includes index.
  Identifiers: LCCN 2021021693 (print) | LCCN 2021021694 (ebook) | ISBN 9781647821265 (hardcover) | ISBN 9781647821258 (paperback) | ISBN 9781647821272 (ebook)
  Subjects: LCSH: Project management—Handbooks, manuals, etc.
  Classification: LCC HD69.P75 N533 2021 (print) | LCC HD69.P75 (ebook) | DDC 658.4/04—dc23
  LC record available at https://lccn.loc.gov/2021021693
  LC ebook record available at https://lccn.loc.gov/2021021694

Hardcover ISBN: 978-1-64782-126-5
Paperback ISBN: 978-1-64782-125-8
eISBN: 978-1-64782-127-2

The paper used in this publication meets the requirements of the American National Standard for Permanence of Paper for Publications and Documents in Libraries and Archives Z39.48-1992.

Contents

PART THREE
Individual and Organizational Project Competencies

PART FOUR

A Better Future through Projects

Welcome to the Project Economy

The world is undergoing a massive series of disruptions. From the sustainability movement going mainstream to the rise of artificial intelligence (AI) to the maelstrom of the Covid-19 pandemic, tectonic shifts are reshaping businesses and societies. Projects are now the most important method we have to turn these challenges into positive change. Projects change the world. They make impossible dreams possible. In my quest to learn more about what really makes projects succeed—and fail—I have come across some incredible achievements.

In 1961, the prime minister of a ruined former British trading colony envisioned a project to build an economically sound country that would be robust enough for future generations. It included establishing the rule of law, efficient government structures, overall stability, and a continuous fight against corruption and the development of human capital as the country's key competitive advantage. The project set uncompromising standards for a universally accessible, top-flight public school system and applied rigorous meritocracy to education and hiring in the public sector. Today, Singapore is one of the most competitive economies in the world.

In 2010, a biotech company in San Diego began distributing the first commercially available body-part printer after a project conducted at the company transformed a breakthrough innovation into a revolutionary product. Regenerative medicine laboratories around the world have since relied on Organovo's printer to generate pieces of skin, muscle, and blood vessels.

An aging software giant made one of the most compelling turnarounds in recent history after a new CEO took over in 2014. The company had been unable to take the smartphone market from Apple, the cloud sector from Amazon, or search from Google. Five years after Satya Nadella's transformation project began, Microsoft's share price had tripled, restoring it to the position of world's richest publicly listed company. The list goes on: General Electric's spree of growth through six hundred seamless acquisitions in the 1980s and 1990s under Jack Welch's leadership; Amazon's introduction of Kindle, an affordable paperlike display device, with access to the world's largest bookstore in 2007; or the journey of DBS, the largest bank in Southeast Asia, to become the world's most innovative bank. All of these have been born from an extraordinary vision, clearly articulated, and methodically implemented through projects.

Think of the rollout of the euro in 2002 or the moment on the night on September 3, 1967, when Sweden switched traffic from driving on the left side of the road to the right. Or the small Danish city of Odense, which, through an ambitious project, transformed itself into a leading innovative robotics hub in Europe. Or Curitiba, Brazil's green capital and one of the most environmentally friendly and sustainable cities in Latin America.

Some remarkably fascinating technological achievements in the past hundred years have been brilliant projects: John F. Kennedy's vision to send the first man to the moon by the end of the 1960s; the creation of the Boeing 777, a technological masterpiece in the aircraft industry; and Project Purple in 2006, which built the first iPhone and transformed the telecommunications industry.

Finally, there are countless amazing personal projects—achievements reached under extremely adverse conditions or simply personal dreams that become reality through a project. Consider twenty-seven-year-old

Brazilian entrepreneur Elisa Mansur, whose startup won the 2018 World Bank Youth Summit project competition. Recognizing the chronic shortage of nursery care in her home country, which sees around two million infants and toddlers yearly denied access to this critical start in their lives, Mansur set up a network to provide community mothers with training, organization, daily schedules, and a rating system. In doing so, she established a process for improving early childhood education and created a brand-new Brazilian job market. Or Boyan Slat, who, as a sixteen-year-old from the Netherlands in 2010, took his first scuba dive off the coast of Greece and saw more plastic than fish. Three years later, he launched the Ocean Cleanup project with just €300 in seed money with the goal of removing 90 percent of marine plastic pollution by 2040. Stories like these show the impact that the younger generation can have through projects to transform their world.[1]

Project-based work is the engine that drives change and progress. Projects generate the major accomplishments of our civilization. They stimulate society to advance beyond what things are and how they are done and even to surpass long-established scientific and cultural limits.

Even so, until recently, projects have often been invisible, and project management has been unappreciated. This below-the-radar character changed in 2020, when the global pandemic brought projects to center stage (the most amazing of which was the development of Covid-19 vaccines in less than a year, a process that usually takes more than a decade). But closer to home, countless change efforts were taking place. At work, in our personal lives, and on the news, projects were suddenly everywhere, and we were part of them. Projects were hidden no more: the pandemic made clear that we are all project managers, and leaders are all executive sponsors.

From a world driven by efficiency to a world driven by change

Do you have any doubts? Are the various products, initiatives, and transformations just mentioned truly projects? They have more in common than meets the eye. Projects are limited in time; they have a start and an end.

They require investments, capital, resources, and human resources. They are made up of a series of activities included in a plan designed to generate a deliverable (a product, a service, an event) that will ultimately create value, benefits, and other impacts. Some elements of each project are unique—every project contains something that has not been done before.

Now think about how projects differ from operations. In 1908, Henry Ford transformed car manufacturing from mere skill to industry with the launch of the Model T, perfecting the mass production of automobiles. Three years later, mechanical engineer Frederick Winslow Taylor presented his theory of how to improve worker productivity by determining how a task could be performed more efficiently. Together, these are the landmarks of the beginning of the efficiency-driven world of operations. Higher volume, lower costs, increased speed, reduction through specialization and division of labor, and standardization determined how businesses were run throughout the twentieth century. The chief operating officer (COO) emerged as a preeminent leadership role in most organizations. According to Robert Gordon, US productivity grew the fastest between 1928 and 1950, a phenomenon he dubbed the "one big wave."[2] In the fifty years that followed, productivity in operations continued to increase by 2 or 3 percent each year.

Right after the turn of the new century, however, something flipped. Since 2007, productivity growth has been almost flat in the Western world, despite the explosion of the internet, shorter product life cycles, and exponential advancement in AI and robotics. Productivity stalled because *change* cannot be implemented with traditional efficiency methods. Change must be implemented through projects, and the world is starting to take notice.

The rise of the Project Economy

Projects are now becoming the essential model for creating value. Among German companies, for example, approximately 40 percent of the revenues and other activities are done as projects. Similar percentages can be found in most Western economies, and the figures are even higher in

China and other leading Asian economies such as Taiwan and South Korea where project-based work has been an essential element in their economic emergence.

Since around 2010, amid the increasing "projectification" of work, project management has grown into one of the United Kingdom's largest areas of business. With an estimated £156 billion in gross value added to the UK economy by project management and with 2.13 million full-time equivalent workers, this trend is likely to continue. Research carried out by PricewaterhouseCoopers and the Association for Project Management concluded that the profession makes a more significant contribution to the UK economy than does the financial services sector or the construction industry.[3]

The same trends are occurring in the public sector. In 2016, the US Senate unanimously approved the Program Management Improvement and Accountability Act, which was signed into law soon after.[4] The act aims to enhance accountability and best practices in project and program management throughout the US federal government and to reform federal program management policy. The following year, the queen of England awarded the Association for Project Management a royal charter, which recognizes the project management profession, rewards the associations that champion its cause, and provides opportunities for those who practice its disciplines.[5]

The pace of the Project Economy is only going to accelerate.[6] According to recent research, the value of project-oriented economic activity worldwide will grow from $12 trillion (in 2013) to $20 trillion by 2027.[7] Add to that the trillions spent on Covid-19 pandemic recovery projects. These are millions of projects requiring millions of project managers and executive sponsors per year.

Throughout industry, forward-looking companies and individuals are preparing for a massive growth of projects. One senior IBM talent executive told me, "Soon in IBM, we will no longer have job descriptions. We will have only project descriptions." Mohamed Alabbar, chairman of Emaar, the Dubai-based giant, announced that his company would abolish all the traditional job titles, as part of the company's shift to focus on "talent, not titles" and increase project-based work.[8] The decision was outlined to staff members in an internal email: "When you reach the end of this email, you will notice something different. I have no job title. And from this moment onwards, nor do you." The implication of this change is that individuals are no longer defined by the department to which they belong but on the projects on which they work. The Richards Group, the largest independently owned ad agency in the United States, removed almost all its management layers and job titles, leaving only that of project manager.[9]

A study from Microsoft, using "LinkedIn's Economic Graph," analyzed "all the data on LinkedIn that shows available jobs, their required skills, and the existing skills job seekers have."[10] The graph revealed the current ten most-in-demand jobs that, LinkedIn predicts, will have staying power into the 2030s. Among these jobs is project manager.

Executives are aware of the increasing importance of projects in their organizations. In a survey my colleagues and I conducted with 556 senior executives for this book, 78 percent of the respondents reported they plan to invest and build their project management competencies in their organizations over the next five years.* Soon, senior leaders, managers, and employees, regardless of their industry, will spend at least 60 percent of their time selecting, prioritizing, and driving the execution of projects. All of us must become project leaders—despite never having been trained to do so!

The path to becoming a project leader

The emergence of projects as the economic engine of our times has been little noticed but is incredibly disruptive and powerful. We are witnessing an unprecedented transformation with profound organizational and cultural consequences.

*During 2020, and in collaboration with HBR, we conducted the survey to help us better understand how organizations are using projects now, where people are finding success with projects, and where they are struggling. The survey had 1,284 participants: 556 senior executives and 728 project experts. Some of the findings will be shared throughout the book. The full results of the survey can be found at https://antonionietorodriguez.com/hbrstateprojectmanagement/.

Imagine the benefits, both for organizations and for society, if we could raise the current low success rate of projects. Consider the additional trillions of dollars and the social, environmental, educational, and other benefits this improvement would represent. And the impact could be almost immediate.

What's more, bold projects can give work meaning. Behavioral and social science show that working and collaborating on projects can be particularly motivating and inspiring for team members. When a project has ambitious goals, a higher purpose, and a defined deadline, people tend to remember them more clearly than they remember anything else in their careers. The moments they feel most proud of are the projects they work on—often the successful ones, but also the failed ones.

I hope you'll walk the path of becoming a project leader with me. The idea that eventually became this book first came to me more than a decade ago, when I was fired from my job as a project management expert. I soon realized that senior executives didn't understand or appreciate the value of project management. They saw it as a technical discipline for IT and engineers, one not worthy of their time and attention. *This attitude couldn't be more wrong.* When executives ignore project management, their projects are less likely to succeed. Products launch late. Strategic initiatives don't deliver. Business transformations fail. The key to project success is having executives and project managers sharing the same goals, working together, and speaking the same language. This realization set into motion my quest to simplify the methods of project management and bring them up to the leader's-eye view.

Throughout this book, I draw on my experience as a leading practitioner in several global corporations, such as PricewaterhouseCoopers, BNP Paribas Fortis, and GlaxoSmithKline. I am also a former president of the Project Management Institute and am an adviser and academic at several top business schools, where I have taught thousands of senior leaders, managers, and project managers. I have worked on and examined projects from every point of view, and I want to share that exceptional mix with you in this book.

I believe that anyone can learn to be a project leader and that people of any nature and background can persevere against the worst conditions to make their dreams a reality through projects. Projects inspire us all. My plea for society—and the purpose of this book—is that organizations, leaders, politicians, and everyone else will build the competencies required to transform and thrive in the new digital and project-driven economy.

The first project management book for everyone

As both a practitioner and an educator, I can do real-world testing to see what works and what doesn't. In my teaching, I have learned which concepts resonate with both executives and project managers. I've learned that if I wanted to keep everyone engaged and interested, I had to dispense with project jargon. I had to simplify the language and the project management tools and techniques to allow people to see how they could apply these approaches in their own organizations. This book not only provides you with a broad view of project management but also gives you practical skills you can use today to move your own projects forward.

Traditionally, books about project management have been complex and technical, developed by deep project experts and written for project management professionals, often ignoring the wider population that must deal with projects. The more arcane these books become, the more that project managers and executives retreat to their separate camps. This book, instead, addresses the topic from an outsider's perspective in a pragmatic, case-illustrated, and hands-on way. It presents a shared outlook, a simple framework, and a common language for every stakeholder, regardless of your role of any project. It teaches project managers to think like executives and executives to think like project managers.

Another shortcoming with the existing methodologies is that they tend to stop at the project's deliverables, assuming that the benefits, value, and impact will materialize when the deliverables arrive within the budget, on time, and per requirements. In many project management methodologies, how a project's deliverables are transformed into benefits is a black box. This book starts with a project's purpose and benefits as the foundation on which everything else is built.

I built this book on one more premise. Every project—regardless of the industry, the organization, the sector (public, private, or nonprofit),

FIGURE I-1

The Project Canvas

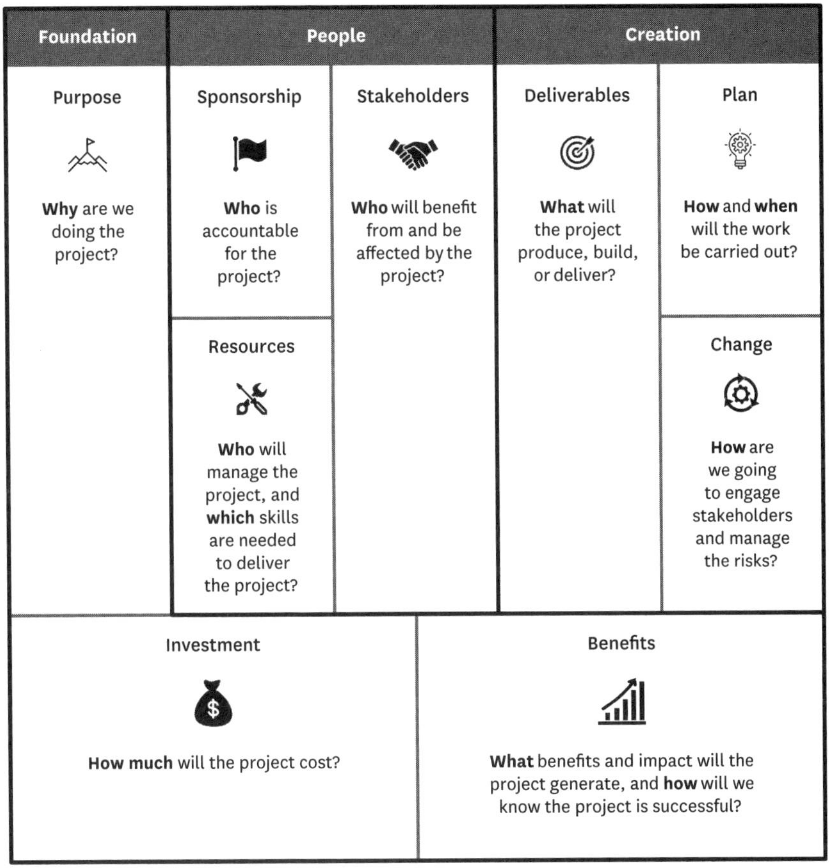

Foundation	People		Creation	
Purpose	Sponsorship	Stakeholders	Deliverables	Plan
Why are we doing the project?	**Who** is accountable for the project?	**Who** will benefit from and be affected by the project?	**What** will the project produce, build, or deliver?	**How** and **when** will the work be carried out?
	Resources			Change
	Who will manage the project, and **which** skills are needed to deliver the project?			**How** are we going to engage stakeholders and manage the risks?
Investment			Benefits	
How much will the project cost?			**What** benefits and impact will the project generate, and **how** will we know the project is successful?	

the methodology (agile or traditional), or whether it is personal or professional—is composed of the same elements that will determine whether the project is a success. These building blocks of projects are all captured in the central framework of the book—the Project Canvas (figure I-1). If organizations, leaders, and other individuals focus on these elements and apply the associated techniques, project success will be almost guaranteed.

This is the first project management book intended for everyone, no matter your level of experience with projects. The book addresses the challenges faced by both senior leaders and project managers, providing practical approaches and adapted tools for each role. It provides a new perspective on the Project Economy, shows you how to use some of the new opportunities offered by a changing world, and suggests how the future of work will be driven by projects.

If you are an executive or another leader, this book will help you better understand project fundamentals. You will learn how to ensure that projects have a strong foundation and the importance of your role as a project sponsor. You'll learn how to increase alignment and buy-in from project stakeholders and how to best support the project managers to deliver the projects successfully. If you are a CEO, this book will help you weigh the importance of the projects and strategically align and prioritize your project portfolio. You'll see ways to better support your project teams, to create a more agile and project-driven organization, and to be more successful altogether in a continuously evolving world.

Finally, if you are a project manager or if you work on projects, this book will teach you how to elevate your work to become more strategic and how to make senior leaders see the value of projects and project management. You will learn how to work with the Project Canvas to define projects more clearly. The canvas will also help you learn a less technical language to communicate about the project with the executive sponsor, the project team, and other stakeholders, increasing their buy-in and motivation. The canvas will also help you keep the project sponsor engaged, often a determining factor in project success.

The book is composed of twelve chapters in four parts. Part 1, "Project Fundamentals for Everybody," sets the context and provides universal basics and definitions. Chapter 1 explores the concept of organizational ambidexterity and how organizations are shifting from a world driven by efficiency to a world driven by change. In chapter 2, we'll look at what a project is—its definition, origins, and different characteristics and how to differentiate projects from the more traditional tasks. Chapter 3 describes the different techniques in project management (including agile methods, program management, and the megaproject approach) and explains how to determine which approaches and tools to apply.

Part 2, "The Project Canvas," is a step-by-step introduction to the main framework of the book. Chapter 4 introduces the Project Canvas and its three domains and nine building blocks. Chapters 5 through 7 cover the three domains in depth: the foundation, the people, and the creation. Finally, chapter 8 describes how to analyze projects using the canvas and how to adopt the framework in your organization.

Part 3, "Individual and Organizational Project Competencies," explores the capabilities needed to succeed in the project-driven world. Chapter 9 discusses project leadership, particularly the competencies for effective project management and sponsorship. Next, chapter 10 explores the selection and prioritization of projects through a process and a governance structure that help increase transparency and control in your organization's portfolio of projects. Chapter 11 examines why organizations must become more agile and project-driven and how they can do so.

Finally, part 4, "A Better Future through Projects," explores how project management will intersect with the megatrends that all organizations and societies are now facing: crisis management, AI transformation, diversity, and sustainability. As each of these trends asserts itself in the near future, the opportunities and challenges will be resolved in the world of projects.

Projects are designed to deliver benefits; that's the whole point. Every year, $48 trillion is invested in projects. Yet, according to the Standish Group, only 35 percent of projects are considered successful.[11] The wasted resources and budgets and unrealized benefits of the other 65 percent are mind-blowing. Imagine a world in which most projects deliver the outcome that is intended. Or imagine if we could just improve the success ratio by 25 percent. This improvement would equate to trillions of dollars of value and benefits to organizations, societies, and individuals. The purpose of this book and the framework it proposes is to close that gap and to increase overall project success for organizations, governments, and individuals.

Are you ready to take back some of that lost value? Are you inspired to launch a project to create to a better world? Or do you simply want a way to make better sense of the countless projects your organization is running? If you answered yes, read on.

PART ONE

Project Fundamentals for Everybody

1.

Projects Everywhere

From a World Driven by Efficiency to a World Driven by Change

A dramatic shift has taken place. We have left behind a century dominated by increasing efficiency, and we are living in an always-changing environment and a massive proliferation of projects. This chapter explores how *projects*, rather than operations, are driving short-term survival and long-term value creation today and tomorrow. Organizations of all kinds are running more projects than ever before. Project management can no longer be ignored, relegated, or misunderstood. Everyone involved in projects at all levels of organizations—employees, managers, project managers, senior leaders, and CEOs—must understand this shift as they select, prioritize, and execute these projects.

Operations run the organization, but projects change the organization

In a world driven by change, short-term survival and long-term results depend on **organizational ambidexterity**—a company's ability to exploit its current capabilities while simultaneously exploring new competencies.[1] Organizational theorist James March describes exploitation as actions such as refinement, choice, production, efficiency, selection, implementation, and execution. Exploration encompasses knowledge creation and analysis of emerging and future opportunities. Other scholars have described organizational ambidexterity as the balance between efficiency and flexibility, or between incremental and radical change.

Clearly, balance is key. Organizations that overcommit to exploration are likely to find that they suffer the costs of experimentation without gaining many of its benefits. They exhibit too many undeveloped new ideas and too little distinctive competence. A well-known example is Ericsson, the telecom giant that led to the development of the global system for mobile communications. At its peak, the company's R&D organization employed thirty thousand people in a hundred technology centers. Yet there was considerable duplication of work, and the company failed to capitalize on its many ideas. With its R&D results leading nowhere, Ericsson had to lay off around sixty thousand employees. Conversely, organizations that overcommit to exploitation are likely to find themselves trapped in a temporary equilibrium, prone to disruption, and wither away. Taken altogether, maintaining an appropriate balance between exploration and exploitation is a primary factor in system survival and prosperity.

Research has proven that ambidexterity leads to higher performance and better implementation of strategy, yet no clear solution has been found to keep the exploration and exploitation in balance over time.

Organizational ambidexterity in practice

Businesses are getting younger. The average age of an S&P 500 company in 2017 was twenty years, one-third of what it had been in the 1960s. Many organizations can no longer keep up with the pace of change.

FIGURE 1-1

Organizational ambidexterity

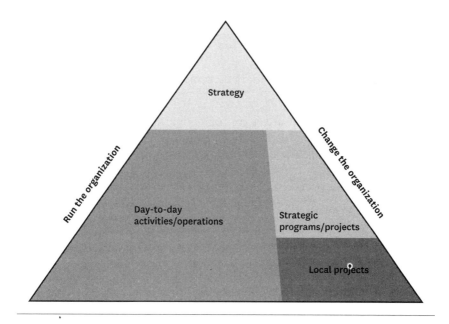

Part of the problem, I have learned in many conversations with leaders, is the abstract concepts and academic language of ambidexterity. Terms like *exploitation, exploration, adaptability, alignment, context,* and *organic systems* do not resonate in executives' minds.

We need simpler language that everyone can understand. In plain terms, this failure to keep up with change stems from the tension between two business dimensions (figure 1-1):[2]

- **Running the organization (operations):** This dimension makes up the core and legacy activities of the business. It includes processes such as sales, customer service, finance, manufacturing, and IT. Most of the revenues (and fixed costs) generated by firms are from running-the-organization activities. These activities keep the company alive; if they stop, the company will quickly die. The focus of running the business is short term. The objectives are mainly commercial, financial, and performance-driven; they are about efficiency, productivity, and speed. In academic terms, this dimension is *exploitation*.

- **Changing the organization (projects):** This dimension makes up the future of the organization. It includes all the organization's strategic and tactical initiatives, projects, and programs. Companies, including startups, and governments often have hundreds or thousands of initiatives running in parallel. Changing-the-organization activities create future value. The objectives are more strategic and closer to the vision, but the benefits are only achieved in the medium and long term and are less tangible and quantifiable than operational objectives. These targets aim at transforming the business to significantly increase growth and profitability. In addition, projects may be highly risky and there is no certainty that the projected benefits will be achieved at all. In academic terms, this dimension is *exploration*.

Focusing on both dimensions at the same time is a great challenge for senior leaders. Table 1-1 summarizes some key differences that leaders must consider. And to make it even more complicated, being successful in just one dimension on its own is extremely difficult. Manuel Hensmans, Gerry Johnson, and George Yip investigated 215 of the largest publicly listed UK firms from 1984 to 2003.[3] First they looked at how well the companies could run their business over a long period. Out of the 215 firms, only 28 were consistently top performers in their business sector over the two decades. Among these 28 firms, only 3 made major strategic changes while performing consistently over those twenty years. And this research is a few years old; the balance between running a business and changing its competencies is becoming progressively harder. What's more, you have much less time to do it.

Leaders are well aware of this challenge. One senior executive of Western Union—a market leader in the money transfer business—told me: "Western Union has been trying for a couple of years to change its business model to stay afloat (let alone grow) in a market which is facing

TABLE 1-1

Two competing models within every organization

Dimension	Efficiency driven (running the organization)	Change driven (changing the organization)
Period	Present	Future
Objectives	Generate revenues, survival	Create a vision, purpose
Culture	Command, control, discipline	Entrepreneur, collaboration
Focus	Efficiency, volumes, costs, products	Innovation, transformation, benefits
KPIs	Commercial, financial, performance	Strategic
Plans	Business, operational	Strategic, roadmap oriented
Skills	Deep expertise	Deep generalist
Key role	Chief operating officer	Chief project officer
Financial basis	Yearly budgeting cycle	Project based
Compensation	Operational results	Project results
Results	Predictable, tangible	High risk, intangible
Systems	ERP, APM, DevOps	MSP, PPM
Process	Standardized, automated	Unique, nonrepetitive, evolving
Structure	Hierarchical, rigid, silo based	Adaptive, project based, self-managed

Abbreviations: APM: Association for Project Management; ERP: enterprise resource planning; MSP: UK-based Managing Successful Programmes (a certification through an established program management framework); PPM: program and portfolio management.

increasing competitive, technological and regulatory pressures. The ability of our management to execute the strategies they present to shareholders, business partners, and employees is a make-or-break factor. They are all aware. Still, it so damn hard to make it happen."[4]

Simply put, the future lies with organizations that can manage and integrate both sides of *run* and *change*. Projects, initiative, programs—leaders understand that these are the tools they have for executing strategic change. But most of these executives don't understand why their change projects are underperforming.

The answer is simple: executives need to devote more of the right kind of attention to projects and change. The reason they have so much trouble with this solution began in the last century.

The proliferation of projects in organizations

How did we get to this state where projects are so essential to organizations' long-term success? An overview of the history of projects can help us understand this evolution.

Yesterday: The century of efficiency and operations

Since the 1920s, companies have been improving their running-the-organization dimension—operations—as a means of increasing productivity by becoming more efficient, reducing costs, and raising volumes and outputs. At that time, most companies were mainly producing goods, and growth was mainly organic. Companies grew by increasing production capacity, standardizing and automating processes, and entering new markets. Growth was achieved by increasing efficiencies and reducing costs. The management gurus of the day—Frederick Taylor, Henry Ford, Peter Drucker—focused on improvements in the running of the organization. Over time, since introducing changes required an effective way of managing them, improvements were carried out as one-off projects. The number of projects increased, marginally but steadily.

Many organizations, including publicly traded companies, operated on an annual planning cycle. Senior leaders collectively decided on strategies, budgets, and operating plans once a year and then managed operations in accordance with those goals and cost limits. Between annual planning cycles, few minor amendments were allowed. The yearly cycle shaped firms' processes, systems, and cultures. Companies organized themselves in hierarchal structures, creating departments along the value-chain elements. Department heads would be in charge of resources, budgets, and decision-making power. To ride the wave of efficiency, employees had to develop a deep specialization and sole dedication in one particular area. An in-depth understanding of one specific area or topic (this characteristic is variously described as deep skills, core competencies, deep expertise, and specialization) led to an individual's increased credibility, faster climbing of the career ladder, and growing income. Professionals would be trained in production, finance, marketing, sales, and quality, among other areas, and would spend their entire career there. Roles like generalist and project manager had no great career potential and commanded little appreciation.

Because of all these developments in the twentieth century, companies have made their operations extremely efficient. But efficiency at all costs has enormous downsides. In many cases, organizations focused on the headlines—results in terms of numbers—with little thought to the medium- or long-term impact this approach might have on organizational innovation or resilience. Companies have commoditized their processes, sacrificing elements of value for speed. They have grown their businesses through acquisition (often at the expense of organic growth or as an alternative to it) to accelerate their product-release schedules or just to produce more and more. But at some point, a strategy of more volume, more product releases, or more brand extensions simply runs out of road. Sustainable growth through further efficiency becomes impossible.

Today: The world driven by change and projects

Today every organization, public or private, operates in an environment subject to continual and sometimes disruptive levels of change. For example, political change can expose a business to new sources of competition. Markets may be opened or closed. New game-changing regulation might be introduced without warning. And there is, obviously, technological innovation, particularly associated with the internet and digital technology. To this can be added social shifts, with fluid customer attitudes to the environment, health or social responsibility. Growing the business, boosting its profitability, or securing its continuation depends on anticipating, managing, and driving change, which in turn depends on initiating and successfully completing projects.

Projects used to be temporary tasks, whereas operations were permanent. Now, changes are permanent, and operations are temporary tasks until the next change. Along with the increased digitalization of operations, it is much easier to find cheaper, better, or more competent partners to run them. Following this trend, Amazon Web Services (AWS) has become the world's most comprehensive and broadly adopted cloud platform, offering more than 175 fully featured operations and services. Millions of companies are using AWS to lower their costs, become more agile, and innovate faster. Even products themselves, now smart and internet-enabled, may develop new features and plug into new business models long after they are sold to end users.

In line with the increased focus on innovation, collaboration, and agility, more and more work is being executed as projects. In 1982, 33 percent of revenues and 22 percent of profits came from new products. Just ten years later, these figures had risen to 50 percent and 40 percent, respectively, according to Booz Allen Hamilton research. The shortening of product cycles inevitably leads to a faster sequence of development projects. From the introduction of the first generation of the Volkswagen Golf in 1974 to the market withdrawal of the Golf V in 2008, product life cycles have been shortened from nine to five years, a reduction of 45 percent.[5] A study carried out by GPM Deutsche Gesellschaft für Projektmanagement (German association of project managers) and the EBS Universität revealed that in 2019, up to 41 percent of the German gross domestic product was produced by projects and that there had been a steady increase since at least 2009.[6]

This extreme uncertainty generates a difficult operating environment for leaders and organizations. The yearly cycle that worked for almost a century no longer applies. The radically transformed circumstances call for new ways of working, more-agile operating models, and new forms of leadership. Crisis-tested leaders will need to develop a tolerance of ambiguity, a quickened operating pace, and a culture of constant change. Organizational structures, processes, and systems need to be adapted, too, to ensure the sustainability of the organization and to take advantage of new opportunities brought by the deeply changeable world.

Tomorrow: Projects on the march

In preparing to write this book, I examined how these worldwide trends are playing out in real companies. In a survey of 1,284 executives and project management professionals, the majority of senior executive respondents indicated that the number of projects in their organizations had exploded over the last five years. Some 87 percent of the respondents had seen an increase in the number of projects, and out of these respondents, 56 percent had seen an increase of more than 25 percent. A full 25 percent of respondents said that the number of projects had increased by more than 50 percent. In many cases, these project leaders are overseeing 50 percent more projects as well. Of course, this growth is a double-edged sword, as the correlation between the number of projects and success is by no means direct. Organizations that overstretch themselves will find their projects starved of human and capital resources. Organizations that overreach with their projects will find that their lack of experience and capability will compromise the value of what they can generate.

This meteoric growth of projects is affecting not only organizations but also our professional lives and the very nature of work. The traditional one-company career path of previous generations is now a distant memory. This approach was later followed by one in which a person developed a career in several companies, often in the same function. Today, people not only switch companies more frequently than ever but also switch functions; many becoming self-employed, moving to work 100 percent project based. Digitization makes the switch to skill-based self-employment or even to hybrid employment (combining traditional and independent work) much easier. According to recent research, the number of individuals working in project-based roles in the United States will increase from sixty-six million (in 2017) to eighty-eight million (forecast 2027).[7] This trend is likely to accelerate, and professional careers will become a sequence of projects.

Roger Martin is a business academic who early on wrote about the transition to project-based jobs in his acclaimed HBR article "Rethinking the Decision Factory."[8] He argues that one problem today is that careers and jobs are structured as if they were flat rather than spiky. He explained to me that in reality, they are filled with the peaks and troughs of projects:

> At least 80% and perhaps as high as 95% of jobs are an amalgam of projects. But instead of thinking, "My life is projects," the average person in an office building thinks that their life is some sort of regular job and that the projects get in the way of their regular job. And so projects are put off and mismanaged. In fact, in organizations

*the entire decision factory should be thought of as nothing but
projects. Managers should organize their lives around projects.
They should look more like professional service firms.*[9]

Projects are routinely marginalized throughout the corporate world. Over the years, I have found that the word *project* is extensively used yet largely misunderstood in private and public sectors. I have so often explored why companies have so many projects and why these companies often fail in delivering them or achieving any tangible benefits, that a senior executive once told me, "If you want to make sure that something is not done, make it a project."

Right up to the early part of the twenty-first century, the UK civil service was still largely staffed with highly intellectual people hired as "policy thinkers": people who rarely thought of themselves as being part of a business operation. Project management and the capabilities it required had rather sneaked up on the service. The UK Cabinet Office published a seminal report in 2000. *Successful IT: Modernising Government in Action* included the first mention of the term *SRO*, or senior responsible officer, to designate the senior civil servant with responsibility for a project.[10] Anecdotally, the genesis of this report was an enquiry that was thwarted by the government's inability to find any civil servant who appeared to be in charge of an expensive and failing project.

In the twenty-plus years since the report came out, the Cabinet Office has made great strides in increasing the professionalism of the civil service by bringing operations onto the same level as policy and by recruiting technical specialists to deliver projects. In 2018, an analysis by the UK's Institute for Government revealed that alongside the more than 160,000 operational delivery professionals (e.g., those who run the prisons or operate the job centers), there is a whole host of cross-departmental specialists in the UK government. In addition to the 12,500 people classified as project delivery specialists, there were more than 10,000 digital and data specialists, 4,400 legal specialists, 4,300 commercial specialists, and 4,300 analysts. Many of these professional will be making at least some contribution to government projects.[11]

Projects after the pandemic

On January 12, 2020, Uğur Şahin was having breakfast with his wife, Özlem Türeci, and discussing a paper published in the *Lancet* about the SARS-CoV-2 virus that was circulating in the Hubei Province in China. Both are doctors and cofounders of BioNTech, a German biotech company using mRNA technology to develop treatments for cancer.[12] Understanding that the current epidemic situation in China could potentially become a global pandemic, Şahin and Türeci decided that day to launch Project Lightspeed to use BioNTech's mRNA technology to develop a vaccine against this coronavirus within a year.

Their project, like other vaccine-development initiatives such as Moderna's, benefited from unprecedented support from governments and regulatory agencies around the world. For example, Operation Warp Speed provided the resources of the US federal government and the private sector to accelerate the testing, supply, development, and distribution of safe and effective vaccines, therapeutics, and diagnostics.[13] Partnering with Pfizer, a world-leading pharma company, not only brought additional funding but also provided expertise in late-stage clinical development, medical affairs, and regulatory aspects. Pfizer's expertise greatly facilitated interactions with the key stakeholders (governments, patient groups, regulatory agencies, the media, etc.).

Less than eleven months after BioNTech's launch of Project Lightspeed, and after several clinical trials with thousands of infected patients, the first regulatory approval for the BioNTech Covid-19 vaccine was given by the UK regulatory agency (Medicines & Healthcare products Regulatory Agency). A few days later, the first patient was injected with the first Pfizer-BioNTech vaccine for Covid-19, thereby bringing to governments, healthcare workers, and other citizens around the globe the hope that this was the beginning of the end of the worst pandemic since the influenza pandemic of 1918. (At the same time, Russia, with Sputnik, and China, with Sinopharm, had also developed vaccines at similar unprecedented speeds.)

The development of a vaccine in less than a year would never have happened if BioNTech had not taken a completely different approach to the development process, which traditionally takes around ten to fifteen years. BioNTech was the first vaccine producer to apply hybrid project management methods, mixing traditional and agile techniques (which we will examine in chapter 3) to blitz through the development phases and clinical trials. Consider some of the key reasons for the success of this project:

- The project had a clear and higher purpose: develop a safe and effective vaccine as soon as possible to help the world overcome the pandemic.

- The benefits of the vaccine were clear and much higher than the investment.

- The CEO of BioNTech took the role of the executive sponsor, fully committed and dedicated to it; he allocated most of the company resources to the project.

- The relatively flat company structure, the short communication lines, and the biotech startup environment allowed organizational agility during an unpredictable pandemic that required regular changes in scope.

- The project team took calculated risks (namely, using an existing mRNA technology and diverting it to a novel indication).

- The manufacturing capability of Pfizer allowed the mass production of vaccines before regulatory approval. The company's taking of this risk allowed immediate delivery to customers once approval was granted.

- Nearly all stakeholders had a high interest in, and a high positive impact on, the project; this level of engagement allowed for extensive coordination and collaboration.

- Procurement was facilitated by long-term relationships and partnerships (e.g., with glassmaker Schott for the glass vials).

For a time, the project legacy of the Covid-19 pandemic would seem to be the extraordinary feats of construction that saw hospitals, initially in China but then across the world, built from scratch in a handful of days. What may have a far greater and more sustained impact is the way individuals and organizations have learned to come together and collaborate in new ways to develop previously unimagined solutions to unanticipated problems, as demonstrated by the Pfizer-BioNTech vaccine-development project. The pandemic has shown the world how project managers can deliver new ideas and change infrastructure and systems at an accelerated pace.

In his 2012 TED talk Professor Eddie Obeng coined the phrase *the world after midnight* to describe the moment when everything changed in business.[14] For the majority of organizations, sometime during the first ten years of the twenty-first century was the moment when the speed of change (technological, social, and environmental) outpaced their ability to learn. This moment left them with a problem: How could they thrive in a world full of exponential change? How could they cut through complex challenges? And how could they pass that skill on to their leaders, colleagues, teams, and clients?

In many ways, the Covid-19 pandemic alerted us all that a new world after midnight had occurred. The new normal we sought for so long was in fact an ongoing state of continued disruption.

More is to come. Disruptive technologies will accelerate this trend. Robots and AI will take over almost all the traditional administrative activities and operational work. Some of these roles, such as travel agents, bank tellers, factory assemblers, packaging dispatching clerks, and call center agents, have already disappeared or been completely reshaped. Through robotic process automation, routine, repetitive, data-centric activities are automated. Today, bots are behind the scenes processing the majority of credit card applications. They can be programmed to easily handle all aspects of the process, including gathering information and documents, doing credit and background checks, and ultimately deciding if the applicant is worthy of receiving credit and issuing the actual card.[15]

Organizations will shift their focus more than ever to projects and project-based work. Projects are the new norm for creating value or, indeed, for simply staying in business. Projects are everywhere. We are now in the Project Economy. No matter your title or role, whether it's your first day on the job or you're the CEO, if you are concerned with how your organization creates value, then project management is now your concern.

2.

What Is a Project?

From Product Launches to Digital Transformations to Megaprojects

Everyone—students, business leaders, other individuals, and governments—uses the word *project*, yet it is largely misunderstood. There is confusion about what is and isn't a project as well as the nature of what project management is. Since projects drive more and more of the value that organizations create, everyone—from coders to project managers to executives—needs to understand what projects are and share a common language about what project management does. Let's start by defining some simple terms.

Definitions

Projects are limited in time; they have a start and an end. They require an investment in the form of capital resources (money, funds) and human resources (effort, time). Frequently they bring together people who have diverse expertise and backgrounds and who have never worked together before. **Stakeholders** are the individuals, groups, organizations, or other entities that are affected positively or negatively by the project. Projects are made up of a series of activities included in a plan, which is determined and designed to deliver an output or a solution (a product, a service, an event, etc.) that will ultimately create value. Some elements of each project are unique; a project is something that has not been done before.

Agile projects apply agile principles, which have their origins in software development. Agile approaches focus on enabling teams to deliver work in small increments, thus delivering value to their customers faster. Because the team evaluates project requirements, plans, and results continuously, it can make changes rapidly. In chapter 3, we will look at the most common types of agile project management.

Depending on their size, scope, or duration, projects can be categorized as programs or megaprojects. A **program** delivers a **capability**, that is, the organizational structures, processes, skills, or knowledge that enables new behavior. Programs are composed of several, sometimes hundreds, of projects and are long in duration. Digital transformation and mergers and acquisitions (M&As) are typical programs.

A **megaproject**, as defined by Naomi Brookes, professor of complex program management at University of Warwick, and Giorgio Locatelli, professor of project business strategy at University of Leeds, is a "temporary endeavor (i.e., project) characterized by: large investment commitment ($1 billion or above), vast complexity (especially in organizational terms), and long-lasting impact on the economy, the environment, and society."[1]

A **project management office** (**PMO**) is a department that defines, maintains, and builds project management competencies and standards across an organization. A PMO is meant to operate as a centralized and coordinated management hub for all the projects. The office aims to provide leadership with a clear overview of the status of its projects and to create efficiencies between projects. Organizations can have several PMOs at different levels to support local projects under the guidance of the central PMO. There are three main types of PMOs:

- **Supportive:** focused on best practices, templates, and capability building

- **Controlling:** focused on whether the project management standards and tools are being applied in the projects

- **Strategic:** focused on the delivery of the most strategic projects, either directly or through coaching and mentoring

Supportive and controlling PMOs have been traditionally seen as low added value and are often dismantled after a few years. We will look at the evolution toward strategy implementation offices in chapter 3.

Project portfolio management is the centralized management of the organization's projects. While projects and programs are about execution and delivery, project portfolio management focuses on selecting, prioritizing, and managing projects as a portfolio of investments. It requires completely different techniques and perspectives than does management of an individual project. Good portfolio management increases business value by aligning projects with an organization's strategic direction, making the best use of limited resources, and building synergies between projects. Organizations can have multiple portfolios of projects, usually one central portfolio encompassing companywide strategic projects, and several portfolios at the unit level. Project portfolio management has traditionally not been owned by one specific department; some organizations have it spread throughout, others assign it to IT or finance. More recently, the role has been added to the responsibilities of the PMO, making the positioning of this office much more strategic. In chapter 10, we will look in detail at this critical function.

Two additional, important definitions are the project manager and the project leader, terms that are often confused. Titles in projects are regularly misused; project managers often prefer to call themselves project leader, or even project director, to bestow themselves with higher status, yet the remit of the role remains the same. A **project manager** is a role with a set of responsibilities focused on the managerial elements of the project, such as the definition of the project plan. A leader, however, is not a title; it is a set of soft skills and a special mindset. In fact, to be delivered successfully, every project requires a mix of management and leadership competencies. Altogether, project managers and executive sponsors become **project leaders**

Operations and projects compared

Projects differ from daily operations in the following ways:

- Operations reflect an organization's day-to-day activities, which generally follow similar patterns and objectives every year (with some marginal improvements). Projects are one-off investments designed to achieve a specific objective.

- Operations are repetitive and easily automated. They operate according to a yearly budget and are staffed with dedicated team members. Projects are restricted in terms of time and budget and are staffed with temporary team members.

- Both project managers and operations managers require specialized skills, especially in people management, diplomacy, and negotiation. However, project managers need to work across the organization to bring different views together from people who often do not report to them. They must be good at managing uncertainty, because large strategic projects are partly unpredictable.

- After a project is completed, the end deliverables or outputs are often transferred to the operations side of the business, where the anticipated benefits of the project must be successfully achieved and sustained.

when they show the capabilities, competencies, and mindset of leadership. The most important characteristics of successful project leadership are described in chapter 9.

Finally, I will use the term *project* broadly in this book, encompassing all the different types of change initiatives described so far—initiatives that solve significant problems or generate something new or unique. I have found that when project management experts start debating the intricate differences between each term, everyone else's eyes glaze over.

As I explained in the introduction, the gap between executives and project professionals must be bridged. This bridge requires a shared lexicon—one that is simple and clear.

Classification of projects

Projects are not run in isolation. A company needs to have a good overview of its *project pipeline* of potential new ideas or investment opportunities and the value they might bring to the business. Management will decide to invest in some of the many ideas that are proposed, but it also needs to keep some unexecuted ideas in the pipeline. Monitoring and managing these ideas can help management react quickly to changes in the market.

The range of projects and change initiatives is vast, and different types of projects require different approaches. Projects should be analyzed and categorized according to two main criteria:

- **Complexity,** which is determined by several factors:

  - **Size:** How large is the project, its budget, and the resources required?

  - **Scope:** How many features does the project have? Which areas and locations are included?

  - **Stakeholders:** How many stakeholders (internal and external) are affected?

  - **Alignment:** Do key stakeholders and a majority of them agree on the project's relevance?

- **Uncertainty,** which is determined by these features:

  - **Novelty:** Has it been done before?

  - **Experience:** Do we have the knowledge?

  - **Clarity:** How certain are we about the features? Will they change?

  - **Budget:** Do we have enough budget and resources?

Using these criteria, we can classify projects. This typology, or categorization, connects naturally with the three innovation types proposed by Clayton Christensen.

- **Efficiency projects:** These projects keep the organization running efficiently. They include continuous improvement, process engineering, IT upgrades, and mandatory projects such as compliance and regulation. There is little uncertainty in terms of what these projects need to achieve. Complexity is usually low or medium when projects have an impact on large parts of the organization. Efficiency projects should be nearly 100 percent successful; anything lower, caused by such things as higher costs, more bureaucracy, or lower quality, will hurt organizational performance.

- **Sustaining projects:** These projects grow and expand the organization. They involve investing in areas beyond the core business such as new products, new services, acquisitions, new software, and new distribution and sales channels. Uncertainty of the project outcome is medium to high and at the beginning of a project, the organization doesn't necessarily know how to reach the desired outcome. Project leaders should take plenty of time to work on the business case, pin down the requirements, and build shared expectations *before* starting the project. Sustaining projects should be around 75 percent successful. Such difficulties as overreliance on the existing portfolio of products and services, erosion of margins, market share loss, or churn of talent, will decrease the medium-term viability of the organization. A 100 percent success ratio would mean that an organization is not taking enough risks.

- **Transformative projects:** These projects are radical innovations that build the organization of the future. They include developing new technologies, adopting new business models, or disrupting industries. These are the riskiest, most challenging, and most innovative projects. To flourish, they need complex conditions of collaboration, high creativity, and risk sharing. Business must absolutely adopt a fail-fast, learn-fast culture with transformative projects. The success ratio of transformative projects should be around 30 percent; higher would mean an organization is not taking enough risks.

Figure 2-1 shows the typology of projects that you can apply when looking at your portfolio of projects.

As a rule, the more complex and uncertain a project, the greater the likely cost and risk once the project is underway. You should make sure that the potential value and impact of your projects match their position in the chart and that your portfolio balances your organization's resources, capabilities, and capacity. Doing so will help you undertake the most sustainable and realistic mix of projects at any one time.

FIGURE 2-1

Project typologies

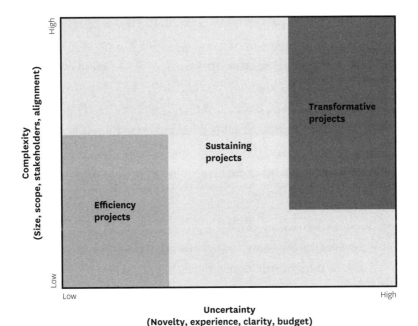

Examples of common projects

Here is an overview of some of the most common projects, from the least to the most complex:

- **Rebranding:** These efficiency projects might involve radical changes to an organization's name, image, logo, marketing strategy, and advertising themes. The objective of rebranding is to communicate a new primary message not only to clients and external stakeholders but also to employees. The benefits of rebranding are not always tangible, so these projects require strong senior executive support to be carried out successfully. An agile and iterative approach is recommended: build a fast proof of concept, and test it to obtain early feedback on the idea.

- **Regulatory and compliance:** All organizations must run mandatory projects to comply with relevant laws, policies, and regulations. These efficiency projects usually have a high priority in organizations, so rationale and senior executive buy-in of the rationale behind the project is guaranteed. Regulatory projects often have fixed deadlines, giving organizations less room to maneuver timelines than in business-driven projects. The main challenge in managing this kind of project is limiting its scope to purely regulatory matters. Because of their high priority, these projects often have more functionality added to them than is needed. Risk management—identifying and mitigating the risks that can hinder the project—is another challenge critical to avoiding failures and expensive penalties.

- **Outsourcing:** These efficiency projects are often related to IT initiatives, such as handing over the IT infrastructure maintenance or the software development to a third party. Outsourcing can also refer to contracting out such nontechnical services as the telephone-based customer service department and design, marketing, or accounting services. Procurement must be involved in the project if the right outsourcing partner is to be selected. The project manager needs to make sure that financial and relevant senior leaders have performed due diligence on the selected partner and that the business case is not driven by an optimism bias. Stakeholder management is a critical element, because the people being outsourced will often resist and try to derail the project.

- **Internal reorganization:** There are many types of reorganization projects, including mergers of divisions and decentralization or centralization of business units and functions. Reorganizations usually occur when a company changes strategies (particularly when a new CEO arrives). The rationale for a reorganization project must be clear and extensively communicated. Stakeholder management is also essential. Even if the project will have negative consequences for some employees, people resist less when they know the reason for the change. The project manager should focus on keeping the project on schedule. When a reorganization takes longer than foreseen to implement, employees become insecure and less committed.

- **Organizational capability building:** With these efficiency projects, organizations obtain, improve, and retain the skills, knowledge, tools, equipment, and other resources they need to do their jobs competently. These projects allow organizations to perform at a greater capacity. From a project management perspective, the main challenge is that the benefits are mostly intangible and take time to be achieved. Managers and leaders need to spend enough time clearly defining the purpose and expected benefits of these projects and to make them as measurable as possible. The role of the executive sponsor is critical to support the project manager and to keep people's faith in the project despite its lack of immediate results.

- **Downsizing:** In moments of economic instability, many businesses see cost cutting—in particular, downsizing—as a fast way to secure bottom-line growth and achieve efficiencies (despite research showing that downsizing does not guarantee performance returns). Downsizing efficiency projects are often difficult to manage from a stakeholder perspective; laying off employees can lead to distrust, reduced commitment, and low morale. As a project manager, you should expect high levels of resistance, especially from unions. As with any other project with high resistance from powerful stakeholders, one of the best approaches is to involve them in the project, for example, by giving them a seat and a voice in the steering committee. The executive sponsor should lead the negotiations in a fair and transparent way.

- **System implementation and process automation:** These types of efficiency projects include enterprise resource planning (ERP) and other software, sales force automation, customer relationship management, human resources management, help desk functions, and sales quotations. Whereas onboarding new technologies affects the nature of the organizations, systems implementation aims primarily at improving or automating existing processes. This type of project is notorious for being delivered late with budget overruns. To avoid these problems, consider using a hybrid approach, mixing traditional project management techniques to scope out and estimate the project as accurately as possible and an agile approach, like sprints (described in chapter 3), for the configuration and implementation of the software. As this type of project requires the engagement of external consulting and technology companies, and once you start a software development project it is hard to stop it, you should involve your procurement department to ensure that the contracting, scope of work, deliverables, and termination are clearly defined. This type of project usually has some resistance from stakeholders, especially from the users, who often don't like to change the way they work.

- **International expansion:** Entering a new market is a sustaining project and a complex one because of differences in culture, legislation, and other unknowns. From a project management perspective, the initial phase of the project is critical for its success; due diligence, market research, and the business case have to be done thoroughly before moving ahead with project implementation. The project manager selected should understand the region and its cultural aspects. Because of physical distance and local specifics and regulations, the selection of the team and partners is also critical. Risk identification and proactive mitigation *before* unknowns appear are two important additional elements. Finally, when several signs indicate that a project is not delivering its objectives as expected, or when unforeseen challenges become excessive, senior executives should be ready to cancel the project before too many resources are wasted.

- **M&As:** M&As are one of the most strategic types of sustaining projects and a fast way to generate significant profits (both by cutting cost and by increasing revenues). However, M&As also incur serious risks. More than half of mergers fail or don't deliver the expected benefits.[2] This kind of project tends to attract much attention from senior leaders early on, when the acquisition is announced, but once the integration is underway, their attention dissipates and leaders move on to the next big project. The project manager needs to keep the executive sponsor engaged throughout the entire project by scheduling regular and frequent progress reviews by the steering committee. Speed is another key element for successful integration; the rule of ten days to establish new leadership and one hundred days to have a detailed integration plan is well known.

- **New-product innovation:** These are transformative projects necessary for growth, maintaining market share, and responding to the competition and changing market conditions. There are two parallel paths involved in new-product development: one path involves idea generation, product design, and detail engineering; the other involves market research and marketing analysis. The first path constitutes a true project. Market research and marketing analysis are usually part of the activities involved in running the business. Most innovation projects fail; nonetheless, companies dedicate a big portion of their resources to introducing new products. When the idea has too many unknowns, avoid large-scale projects, and use prototyping and small, agile teams to test the concepts. Only when most of the unknowns have been solved and certain knowledge has been developed is it time to introduce a formal project.

- **New technologies:** Transformative projects such as digital transformations and adopting AI systems entail fundamentally changing how you operate and deliver value to customers. These projects have an impact on a huge number of processes, interactions, transactions, internal and external factors, industries, stakeholders, and so forth. Senior leaders must clearly define and agree on the rationale, purpose, and benefits of the project. Don't embark on a digital transformation just because everyone else is doing it. Project managers should usually apply a hybrid approach, combining traditional project management with agile methods. From a change management perspective, digital transformation projects should not be seen as the introduction of a new technology only. Rather, organizations should consider the transformation as a cultural change that requires them to challenge the status quo, experiment, and become comfortable with failure.

- **Business transformation:** These transformative projects involve changing from one strategy, business model, or culture to another. The main challenge for senior leaders is to know the right timing to leave the old business, which has often been successful, to move into the new one. Research shows that the failure rates of these projects are around 70 percent, often with such failure leading to the end of a business. Like new technology projects, business transformations need senior leaders to define and agree on the rationale and purpose. Starting a business transformation without a clear vision is a recipe for failure. The project manager should ensure strong involvement from the leadership team throughout, especially to make certain that leaders are first adopters of the changes and that the new business practices and models the adoption for the rest of the organization. Good transformations make companies live longer and be more successful overall.

———————

We now have a shared understanding of what is and isn't a project, the difference between operations and projects, and a common language to talk about them. This chapter has explored the wide range of initiatives that exist under the umbrella of projects. Next, we will start to look at project management. We are going to learn about the origins of project management, its essential characteristics, and how a wide range of projects requires organizations to gain dexterity in a wide range of project management practices.

Twelve principles of successful projects

1. Projects need a clear rationale, business case, and connection to a higher purpose before they are launched.

2. An active, ongoing, and fully engaged executive sponsor is critical to project success.

3. Projects change the status quo. Resistance should be expected and addressed from the early stages.

4. Effective project managers have to be true leaders. They must understand the technical aspects of the project while they lead and empower the team members to perform at their best.

5. People matter more than processes. Projects will always need motivated people to execute them.

6. Project failure is not always bad. Often, failure is an opportunity to learn, mature, and refocus on other more relevant projects.

7. Uncertainty is inherent in projects. Project management also means risk management.

8. Changes to initial project plans and requirements will most likely occur. Agility is essential.

9. Project-driven organizations work across silos, allowing greater flexibility and faster response time to competition and changing market conditions than do traditional hierarchical organizations.

10. Organizations need to prioritize projects to increase the success rate of project execution.

11. Project performance indicators should focus on outcomes (benefits, value creation, impact, opportunities, and risks) instead of inputs (costs, time, material, and scope).

12. Projects cannot go on forever; they have to be closed, even if sometimes not all tasks are fully completed.

3.

What Project Management Is Now

And Why It Needed to Be Reinvented

Project management is part art and part science. Before World War II, projects were managed on an ad hoc basis, mostly using informal techniques and tools.[1] The term *project management* that is in use today emerged amid the unprecedented period of abundant reconstruction projects in the postwar period. Governments started to request companies be more precise on their plan and cost estimates. The US Navy and some consulting firms, such as Booz Allen Hamilton, were some of the first contributors in developing modern project management. Over the second half of the twentieth century, project management started to be seen as a discipline different from engineering or architecture.

As is the case with definitions of projects, most definitions of project management are cumbersome and difficult for professionals not involved with project management to understand. For this reason, I'll use a simpler definition of project management, one that is clear and meaningful for all stakeholders. **Project management** is the collection of competencies, techniques, and tools that help people define, plan, and implement projects successfully to achieve a predetermined benefit.

Project management is not free; it always has a cost. It adds a layer of overhead and oversight to the implementation of a number of activities. It requires resources and time for an organization (in the form of extra documents, templates, meetings, and decisions). Studies show that total management costs for all phases of a project are generally somewhere between 7 and 11 percent of the project's total cost. If additional project controls, such as external audits, are added, costs increase to the 9 to 15 percent range. On small projects, project managers usually end up doing some or most of the project work. Blurring the lines between managing the project and completing the activities makes it difficult to identify the costs of management but usually allows for a pragmatic and economic approach to delivery. The larger a project, where the stakes rise along with the project's complexity and risk, the larger the cost of project management.

The reinvention of project management

Over time, what project management was and what it needed to be drifted apart. Organizations evolved fast, and although the number of projects increased exponentially for most groups, project management somehow stayed in the past. One of the goals of this book is to bring the two views of project management back together by redefining and expanding its scope. First, let's look at two areas where project management was failing.

Problem 1: Excessive focus on documentation, processes, and inputs

In the early years, project management focused on **inputs**—planning, estimation, cost, time, scope, and risk management. For decades, the most important advances of project management were in these areas. **Outputs**—purpose, rationale, value, benefits, impact, and strategy—were not part of the early definitions. This tendency to look internally is a large reason why the discipline of project management diverged from mainstream management, with its themes of leadership and strategy dictating the CEO agenda, over the past thirty years.

For example, most traditional project management theories start by presenting the life cycle of a project, which states that every project should be divided into phases or stages, basically a sequential model. You need to complete one phase (e.g., the definition) before you move to the next one (e.g., planning), and once you have finished one phase, you are not allowed to go back to the previous phase. In most cases, however, these phases are not how projects proceed in real life. Every project is different; there is always uncertainty in doing something new, and projects have unknowns, external factors, and human elements that can influence them. Many projects need smaller iterations in some areas and thus should be run in multiple phases in parallel, to adapt to the changing realities.

Traditional methods also tend to limit their scope to project deliverables. They assume that the benefits, value, and impact will materialize when the deliverables are produced within the budget, time, and requirements. In this view, how a project's deliverables are transformed into impact is seldom examined.

Problem 2: Rigid and one-size-fits-all methodologies

The original project management theorists and experts were influenced by the efficiency and standardization methods from operations management, which aimed at predictability and consistency in performance. These theorists believed that they could replicate and apply their philosophy to projects as well. A standard project management methodology, they thought, would ensure project success and, by extension, if applied to all projects in the organization, would guarantee the success of all the projects.

This thinking led most organizations and governments to adopt a standardized management methodology and apply it consistently to all their projects, regardless of the project's type, size, scope, and other criteria. In most cases, the methodology was based on traditional project management methods, also known as waterfall or predictive. In the past decade, a surge of agile methods—also known as adaptive methods, such as Scrum and kanban—have provided a fresh approach to implementing important change initiatives and projects with fewer constraints than exist with traditional project management methods. Agile methods originated in the tech world, where IT developers sought more flexibility and freedom to adapt the scope of the project without tight change controls from project managers.

Unfortunately, the emergence of agile methods has sometimes led to tribalism in the project community. Many consider these methods the antithesis of traditional project management: agile was cool and fresh; project management was old and obsolete. Seen as a dichotomy, organizations felt they had to adopt one or the other. In many instances, they drastically removed any references to traditional project management, including the role of the project manager, while they radically implemented agile systems throughout the entire organization.

Modern project management: A focus on benefits, an abundance of methods

In fact, the notion of a great schism between agile and traditional is totally wrong, and it has led many projects and change initiatives to fail. Instead, project success relies on applying the right methods to the right type of project. Some projects will need a predictive management approach, others an adaptive method, and still others a combination of techniques (a hybrid approach). And some change initiatives should be managed as continuous improvement rather than as projects.

The implementation matrix in figure 3-1 shows the three types of projects discussed in chapter 2 (efficiency, sustaining, and transformative) and the seven project management methods that fit best depending on the complexity (determined by the size, scope, stakeholders, and alignment) and the uncertainty (determined by the novelty, experience, clarity, and budget) of the endeavor at hand. Let's examine these seven methods in depth.

Continuous improvement

Most efficiency projects, such as process improvement, that fall under low complexity and low uncertainty on the implementation matrix should not apply standard project management methods. Although process

FIGURE 3-1

Implementation methods matrix

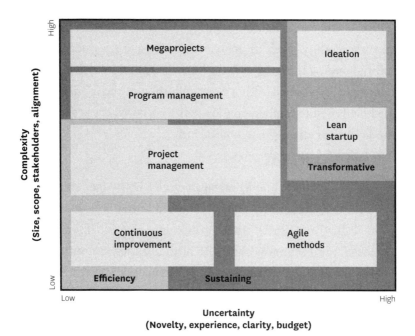

improvement efforts meet the criteria to be considered projects, the resources required to apply project management techniques and monitoring are often more costly than the benefits they deliver. The continuous-improvement designation allows organizations to significantly reduce the number of projects they have in their portfolio.

The following continuous-improvement methods can be used in place of project management:

- *The PDCA cycle* (plan, do, check, act) helps implement improvements to business processes, efficiency, or productivity throughout the organization using a simple yet structured approach.

- *Gemba* walks involve interacting with staff on an informal basis at the location where they do their work, allowing for problem-solving on a daily basis.

Project management methods (waterfall or predictive)

Traditional project management methods, also known as waterfall or predictive approaches, should be applied to projects of medium complexity and uncertainty, such as reorganizations, merger integrations, and capability-building initiatives. These kinds of projects require a predictive methodological approach with a clear definition of the requirements and detailed plans before implementation gets underway; these steps are then followed closely with progress monitoring.

The following methods can be used:

- PMBOK (Project Management Body of Knowledge), summarized in the *PMBOK Guide*, a book published by the Project Management Institute (PMI), is a set of standard terminology and guidelines for project management.[2] The publication states that five process groups are prevalent in almost every project. It includes best practices, conventions, and techniques that are considered the industry standard. The PMI regularly updates the guide to ensure that it echoes the most up-to-date project management practices.

- Prince 2 (Projects in Controlled Environments) originated in the United Kingdom and, thanks to the method's flexibility, has come to be accepted there as best practice for project management. With Prince 2, the outputs are clearly defined and there is a business justification for every project. This project management method is also characterized by well-defined roles for every team member and by products that are delivered on time and well within cost estimates.

Program management methods (hybrid)

Program management is the process of managing several related projects, often with the intention of delivering a strategic capability to improve an organization's performance. Program management emphasizes the coordinating and prioritizing of resources across projects, managing links between the projects, and the overall costs and risks of the program. It should be applied to projects with high complexity and low to medium uncertainty. Examples of such projects are industrial engineering, M&A, change management, and business transformation.

Program management uses mostly predictive methods, but if parts of the program have high uncertainty, some adaptive methods may be appropriate.

The following references can be helpful:

- *Managing Successful Programmes* (MSP), a method developed in the United Kingdom, provides a framework whereby large, complex change can be broken down into manageable, interrelated projects. MSP is very flexible and is designed to be adapted to meet different needs and circumstances. The method has been adopted by both public- and private-sector organizations.

- *PMI's Standard for Program Management*, fourth edition, provides clear, complete, relevant information generally recognized as good practices for most programs. It is principle-based, making it a powerful tool for a broad range of organizations.

Megaproject methods (hybrid)

Megaprojects are temporary endeavors characterized by large investment commitment (typically $1 billion or more), strong public-sector involvement, vast complexity, and long-lasting impact on the economy, the environment, and society. Megaprojects tend to be partnerships with multiple organizations, of which one or a few take the lead. These are hyper-complex projects with medium uncertainty. Examples include building a high-speed rail line, a mega dam, a national health or pension IT system, a new widebody aircraft, or staging the Olympics.

Megaprojects use mostly predictive methods, but in areas of the project with high uncertainty, adaptive methods may be appropriate.

The following references are helpful:

- *Oxford Handbook of Megaproject Management*, which provides state-of-the-art scholarship in the emerging field of megaproject management, helps the reader build competencies to manage programs the scale of which can transform a company, a city, or even a country. Some of the distinctive areas the book covers are systems thinking, commercial leadership, research methods, and performance management.

- *Industrial Megaprojects: Concepts, Strategies, and Practices for Success* gives a clear, nontechnical understanding of how organizations can prevent hazardous and costly errors when undertaking megaprojects.

Agile methods (adaptive or iterative)

Adaptive approaches should be applied when scope, requirement, or specifications are not known in advance; when they are likely to change throughout the life cycle of the project; or when there is much uncertainty about the outcome. Software and product development are two areas where adaptive techniques are essential.

The following methods are the most widely used (figure 3-2 compares professionals' use of these agile methods and more traditional methods):

- *Agile project management* is based on an incremental, iterative approach. Instead of in-depth planning at the beginning of the project, agile methods are open to changing requirements over time and encourage constant feedback from end users. Cross-functional teams work on iterations of a product over a period, and this work is organized into a backlog that is prioritized according to business or customer value. The goal of each iteration is to produce a working product. It uses six main deliverables to track progress and create the product: the product vision statement, the product roadmap, the product backlog, a release plan, a sprint backlog (see next paragraph), and an increment. It emphasizes collaboration, flexibility, continuous improvement, and high-quality results.

- *Scrum* was created by Jeff Sutherland in 1993, taking the term *scrum* from an analogy in a study by Hirotaka Takeuchi and Ikujiro Nonaka.[3] In the study, they compared high-performing, cross-functional teams to the scrum formation used by rugby teams. **Scrum**, a subset of the agile method and one of the most popular process frameworks for implementing this method, is an iterative development model used to manage complex software and product development. Fixed-length iterations, called **sprints**, lasting one or two weeks long, allow the team to produce software at a regular pace. Scrum follows a set of roles, responsibilities, and meetings that never change. For example, Scrum calls for four ceremonies that provide structure to each sprint: sprint planning, daily stand-up, sprint demo, and sprint retrospective. During each sprint, the team will use visual artifacts like task boards or burn-down charts to show progress and receive incremental feedback. What distinguishes Scrum from the other agile project management methodologies is how it operates by using certain roles, events, and artifacts.

- *Kanban* was inspired by the Toyota production system and lean manufacturing. The word *kanban* is Japanese for "visual sign" or "card." Kanban is a very visual method that aims to deliver high-quality results by painting a picture of the workflow process so that bottlenecks can be identified early in the development process. A kanban board, a tool to implement the kanban method for projects, is made up of different "swim lanes," or columns. The simplest boards have three columns: to do, in progress, and done. Kanban cards (such as sticky notes) represent the work, and each card is placed on the board in the lane that represents the status of that work. These cards communicate status at a glance. Because of its flexibility, kanban has gained traction in other industries and is one of a few project management methods that can be applied to any project that requires continuous improvement in the development process.

FIGURE 3-2

Usage rates of agile and traditional project management methods

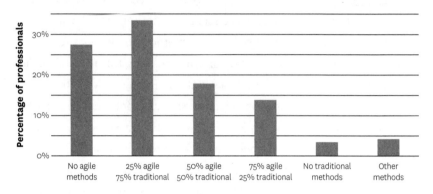

Source: *HBR Project Management Handbook* Project Expert Survey, July 2020, N = 728

Lean startup (adaptive or iterative)

When organizations intend to start up new ventures or radical new products, traditional project management methods don't apply. These projects have very high uncertainty and require significant amounts of testing, experimenting, and prototyping. Because they seldom work the first time, leaders should apply the fail-fast, learn-fast philosophy.

The following method can be used:

- *Lean startup* uses customers' desires rather than dictating what the organization will provide for the customers. The lean startup method aims to shorten product development cycles and to swiftly gauge the viability of a proposed business model. The methodology is driven by experimentation, iterative product releases to reduce risks, and validated learning.

Ideation

Applying project management techniques to projects (or, better, to *ideas*) that have high uncertainty and high to medium complexity is another recipe for failure. Innovation cannot be managed as a project; it requires other methods that foster quick experimentation and prototyping. Many projects fail because they are launched without being mature enough to be treated like a project. The right time to start a project will be covered in chapter 10.

The following method can be used:

- *Design thinking* has long been considered the holy grail of innovation—and the remedy to stagnation. It embraces the human-centered approach, and it offers startup businesses (and entrepreneurial ventures in organizations) techniques to get at the heart of a business problem and to obtain the right solutions.

Today, many organizations have broken out of the one-size-fits-all approach to managing all their projects. But as we saw in the results of the State of Project Management survey, too many companies remain rigid in their methods. Such rigidity is like trying to fix all your home problems with a single hammer. A lack of flexibility is a source of major risk, frustration, delays, and failure.

Pushing the reinvention further

A few organizations have already taken the leap to transform project management. They have advanced their practices and are now focusing on *outputs* and *benefits* rather than *inputs* and *scheduling*. A few other firms are flexibly basing project management on project needs rather than rigidly applying the same prescriptive or agile methods across their portfolios. Perhaps your organization is among them.

Nonetheless, there seems to be an unresolvable tension between the ever-increasing number of projects that organizations and governments are initiating, their growing scale and complexity, and the stubbornly poor performance of much of our project management. There is work to be done.

Since the early 2000s, we have seen an explosion in project management concepts, programs, certifications, and methodologies. The three major certification organizations—the PMI, the International Project Management Association (IPMA), and the Association for Project Management (APM)—are growing constantly. The number of certified professionals has reached significant levels. Consider the numbers of certified professionals by 2020:

- More than a million Prince 2–certified professionals

- More than a million PMI-certified professionals

- More than 300,000 IPMA-certified professionals

However, most of these methods and theories are based on the assumption of rationality, which doesn't consider the complexity of projects, their unpredictability, and human nature. Remarkably, stakeholder management wasn't included in the *PMBOK Guide* until its fifth edition, published in 2012. When it comes to how to create buy-in and commitment from multiple stakeholders, project management theories have so far provided few solutions.[4]

Despite the ubiquity of project management, the statistics are not encouraging. The returns projects deliver vary greatly. When we asked project professionals and senior executives to share the success ratios of their projects, more than a third of respondents said that more than half of their projects were unsuccessful (figure 3-3). These discouraging responses are compounded by the fact that 20 percent of these same

FIGURE 3-3

Project success ratios

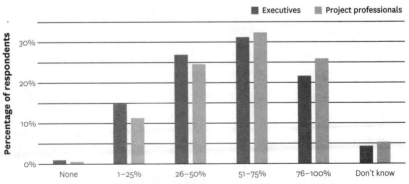

Source: *HBR Project Management Handbook* Project Expert Survey, July 2020, N = 728; and *HBR Project Management Handbook* Executive Survey, July 2020, N = 566

respondents indicated that they didn't know the return on investment their projects generated for the organization.

All the way back in 2003, Nadim F. Matta and Ron Ashkenas explained the problem in a *Harvard Business Review* article:

> *Managers use project plans, timelines, and budgets to reduce what we call "execution risk"—the risk that designated activities won't be carried out properly—but they inevitably neglect these two other critical risks—the "white space risk" that some required activities won't be identified in advance, leaving gaps in the project plan, and the "integration risk" that the disparate activities won't come together at the end. So project teams can execute their tasks flawlessly, on time and under budget, and yet the overall project may still fail to deliver the intended results.[5]*

This example is particularly disheartening because it suggests that many otherwise good projects that are apparently well managed still fail to deliver success.

Projects are designed to deliver benefits; that's the whole point. Every year, around $48 trillion is invested in projects. Yet, according to the Standish Group, only 35 percent of projects are considered successful.[6] The idea that 65 percent of projects result in wasted resources and budgets and unrealized benefits is mind-blowing.

It is even harder to quantify the losses in unmet benefits, social impact, and revenues from the massive delays or failures caused by poor projects and deficient project leadership—let alone whether the initial estimated benefits were actually met. As I pointed out in the introduction, a world in which most projects—or even an additional 25 percent—delivered their intended outcome would be a vast improvement in financial and other benefits to businesses, societies, and individuals.

What needs to change?

So how do we turn these statistics around, and which principles could set the foundations for success? There are seven key areas for improvement to break out of the outdated ways of traditional project management and reap the benefits of a modern approach.

1. A shift to project leadership

We don't simply need project managers and project sponsors; both of these roles must become **project leaders**: people for whom the skills and behaviors of project management are embedded and who are as wedded to the end goal as they are to the means of achieving it. Since the 1990s, there has been a steady shift in focus from the hard, technical elements of projects and project management (e.g., scheduling, scoping, finance, and risks) to the softer elements (e.g., people, behavior, culture, communication, and change management). In short, executives need to think more like project managers, and project managers need to think more like executives. Research proves that few people receive an education that teaches them the tools and techniques needed to both define and manage projects successfully.[7] Leading business schools don't teach project management as part of the core curriculums of their MBA programs. To increase project success, we need project management to be taught as a fundamental skill for strategists and leaders. Strategy and project delivery are mutually dependent and must become part of executive development.

To become project leaders, project managers must learn to feel comfortable with uncertainty. They must learn how to identify key information, when to make a decision, and how to make a sensible one: to posit an approach, move forward slowly, testing the water as they go and adjusting their direction to respond to what's working and adapting their activity to close down what's not. Chapter 9 looks at product leadership in depth.

2. Power to projects

We need to recalibrate all organizations by shifting power, resources, and budgets away from simply running the business toward changing the business, which is the remit of projects. This is no small shift. It means giving more resources, budgets, and decision-making power to projects and project teams at the expense of the traditional departmental hierarchy. Silos and the silo mentality are still very present in most traditional organizations, and when organizations challenge the status quo, significant resistance frequently appears throughout the organization and at every level.

The role of the COO, whose mission was to make organizational operations work efficiently and smoothly, with as few disruptions and mistakes as possible, is losing relevance. A new role, the chief project officer or chief transformation officer, will soon emerge. This person would be responsible for the coordination and successful implementation of all the projects and project-related work in an organization. In 2014, ING's Roel Louwhoff was appointed COO; two years later, he was appointed chief transformation officer, responsible for managing this bankwide transformation.

3. Simplifying project management methods

Project management methods must also become more holistic so that they can address more types of changes. Successful management disciplines are often linked to a few simple frameworks that are intuitive, quickly understood, and easily applied not only by executives but also by the majority of employees. For instance, the seven Ps in marketing, first proposed in 1960 by E. Jerome McCarthy (he originally proposed four Ps), is an easy framework that everyone can use to help determine a product's or brand's market offering.[8]

In contrast, project management methods have tended to be too complex to be easily understood and applied by nonexperts. These methods were developed primarily in the 1970s and 1980s by expert practitioners (at the beginning mostly engineers) for practitioners (also predominantly engineers). The pivotal assumption of the methods has been that documenting every aspect of a project in detail will provide a high level of control of the planned activities during the implementation of the project. Many project managers ended up producing massive numbers of documents and swaths of paperwork, leading to an overall feeling that the role was primarily administrative. Under these circumstances, not surprisingly, we saw the rise of the agile approach, triggered by the Agile Manifesto, written in February 2001 by seventeen independent-minded software practitioners. This movement has led most startups and many larger organizations to radically replace their traditional project management methods with agile practices. The project management methods I present in this book are a step toward simplification and wider access. The Project Canvas, which we will explore in depth in part 2, provides a simple framework for anyone, professional or not, to learn the fundamentals of projects.

4. Reshaping the project life cycle

Project methods, tools, disciplines, and competencies have been focused on what is known as the **project life cycle** (figure 3-4). Projects are composed of several phases. The most widely used sequence in traditional project management is as follows: initiation, planning, implementation (monitoring, reporting, testing), and closing (handover).

Traditionally, what happens before (ideation) or after the project is completed (run) is not the responsibility of either the project manager or the project. In many instances, the project manager is assigned after the idea has been chosen and the business case has been validated. The person is in charge of scoping, planning, and implementing the project deliverables, with little attention to the actual benefits of the project. Despite many advantages to limiting the scope of duty of projects and project management to the project life cycle, the limited scope has also diluted the potential impact of project leaders. For example, knowing when to start a project is a key factor in its success, yet it's a strategic talent very few companies have developed and there is currently no management framework available to help executives or individuals with this vital decision. This is just one of many critical areas that have been limited by existing methods.

To stay relevant and become a truly strategic discipline, project management needs to expand and focus in three areas: (1) innovation, (2) managing outcomes and deliverables after the project is completed, and, most importantly, (3) increase the focus on the benefits that the project will deliver. We will cover these aspects in more depth in part 2 of the book.

5. New measures of project success: From the inward-looking triple constraint to the outward-looking constraints

A vital tool in traditional project management, almost a holy grail, is the **triple constraint**—also known as the iron triangle or the devil's triangle (figure 3-5). The triple constraint addresses the challenges of trade-offs

FIGURE 3-4

Reshaping the project life cycle

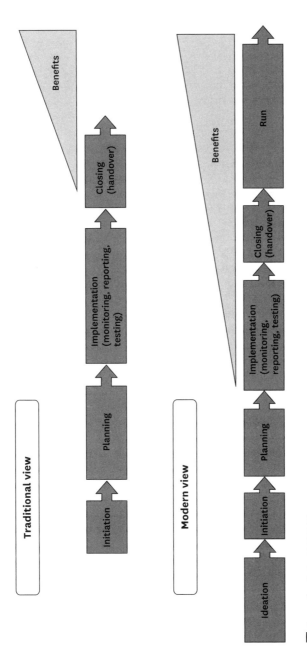

Traditional view

Initiation → Planning → Implementation (monitoring, reporting, testing) → Closing (handover)

Benefits

Modern view

Ideation → Initiation → Planning → Implementation (monitoring, reporting, testing) → Closing (handover) → Run

Benefits

■ Scope of project management

FIGURE 3-5

The triple constraint, or iron triangle

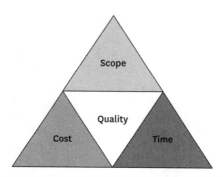

between scope, time, and cost—all of which affect quality—to keep things moving toward a successful completion (we will cover the details when we look at the Project Canvas). Project key performance indicators (KPIs) have been focused on these criteria since project management became a discipline. A project that finishes late, runs over budget, has a different scope than originally planned—is still today considered a poor quality project, or a failure. If you're managing a project, then you're working with the triple constraint. Some experts argue that this balance between scope, time, and cost is the single most important concept in the history of project management.

Of course, these are important aspects of any project, but they are limited measures—they are inwardly focused and miss many key elements of project success. There are plenty of projects that blew up their initial budget and were delivered years late but ultimately provided immense benefits. One famous case is the Sydney Opera House project. The construction started in 1959 and was originally scheduled for four years, with a budget of A$7 million. The project ended up taking fourteen years to be completed and cost A$102 million. From a traditional project management lens, it could probably be seen as one of the most disastrous construction projects in history. Queen Elizabeth II inaugurated the Sydney Opera House in 1973 after years of redesigns, underestimates, and cost overruns.[9] By 1975,

FIGURE 3-6

The new outward-looking triple constraints

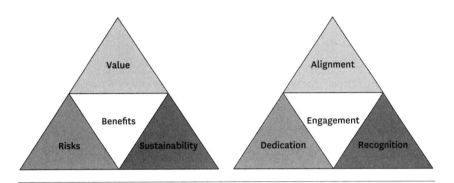

the building had paid for itself; today it has become a landmark not just in Sydney, but also around the world.

This example provides proof that in many instances the triple constraint alone doesn't determine project success. Despite its historical importance to project management, the concept remains internally focused at a time when project leaders must be looking at outward elements of project success, such as delivery of benefits and engagement of the project team, to measure performance. With this in mind, I have developed two new triple constraints, the benefits triple constraint and the engagement triple constraint (figure 3-6). We will look at these new tools in detail in part 2.

6. Transforming project management offices to strategy implementation offices

Because traditional PMOs have focused on processes, methods, and monitoring, they are often seen as highly bureaucratic, low-added-value units with little connection to what matters to the organization. In addition, PMOs have always been designed as a box in a hierarchy, which, as we will see in chapter 11, is an outdated structure for a world driven by change. The new version of the PMO will have a much stronger focus on value creation through driving change and strategy. Its role must evolve into a strategy implementation office, helping senior leaders with the prioritization, selection, and implementation of their key initiatives. The new office will also have a series of top project managers, who will act as CEOs of the most complex and transformative initiatives. They will be in charge of not only delivering the project but also ensuring that the benefits are achieved—and achieved faster than planned, when possible. We will also see new types of implementation offices that are more agile and often temporary, established to support portfolios of projects and agile initiatives, then disappearing when the projects are finished.

7. New technologies

The key systems that support the running of the organization are usually well established. Some of these applications are more mature than others, but the biggest improvements in automation have already been achieved. For more than three decades, companies have made the painful and costly transition to the present level of systems maturity. Many ERP projects failed or took much longer than foreseen, their costs were triple or quadruple the original estimates, and the promised benefits often came late or were never achieved. These large, troublesome projects left management with deep scars, which continue to be expressed by a lack of appreciation for project management and its value to IT and technical projects.

The projects side of the business is much less technologically mature than the operations dimension, and few tools related to managing this dimension have been in place for a long time. Microsoft Project, one such tool, is used throughout many organizations. This intuitive and flexible software can be used, although at only a fraction of its functionality, with less than an hour of practice. MS Project has had a positive impact on project management in helping project leaders manage their work more easily. The downside is that it is an end-user tool (and thus not centralized), and every project manager has a unique way of using it to plan projects. Consequently, individual project plans are not easily comparable and are difficult to consolidate for the purpose of reporting to management.

Businesses find companywide management of project portfolios indispensable for managing the change-the-business dimension. Without such a portfolio system, the management of hundreds of projects, thousands of resources, and millions of dollars with only such tools as Excel, MS Project, and PowerPoint would be a daunting task. Remarkably, this is what most companies are still doing. Until recently, companies had no control of their change-the-business dimension and had little idea of either the total costs invested or the expected benefits. I call this lack of control or understanding a black-box situation. Technology in this space, and its applicability to projects, has to drastically evolve for organizations to serve and improve how they and their project leaders implement their projects.

Other new technologies will also play a major role in modern project management practices in the coming years. We are on the cusp of seeing an AI revolution in the field. This transformation will dramatically change the role of project managers, automating many technical aspects and setting managers free to focus on soft skills and project benefits.

———————

This first part of the book has covered the fundamentals of projects and project management, looked at project proliferation that is now occurring everywhere, and explored how traditional project management is now giving way to more modern practices. It is time to start applying these concepts in your organization.

We are now moving into part 2, which introduces the main framework of the book, the Project Canvas. In the next five chapters, we will explore each of the nine building blocks that compose the Project Canvas, why using it will benefit your projects and your organization, and how to put the canvas into practice.

PART TWO

The Project Canvas

4.

Introduction to the Project Canvas

One Tool for Any Project: Traditional, Agile, or Hybrid

Some models do a wonderful job at simplifying business concepts. For example, Michael Porter's five-forces model and value-chain analysis help make strategy a key area for every organization to apply.[1] The Boston Consulting Group (BCG)'s Growth Share Product Portfolio matrix, developed by BCG founder Bruce Henderson, helps businesses easily grasp product mix.[2] These frameworks are some of the best known and most widely used in their domains, thanks to their ability to simplify complex matters.

In contrast, project management methods have been too complicated to be understood and applied by nonexperts. This state of affairs was never ideal, but in the world where more and more value is being driven by change and projects, keeping project management siloed and out of view of the rest of the organization is potentially disastrous. To rectify this problem, I present the Project Canvas, a single tool that enables you to examine any project rigorously and that is simple enough for everyone to use.

Simple, universal, and proven

Faced with the challenges of teaching project management to executives and other professionals (e.g., MBAs) who are not project managers, I developed the Project Canvas for two reasons. First, to keep them engaged and interested for days, I had to move away from the expert jargon—I had to simplify the language and the project management tools and techniques so that everyone could understand and apply them. Second, I wanted to reduce the staggering number of project failures that I had observed over years of research. Increasing the adoption of best practices would lead to a greater number of successful projects. I found inspiration in the Business Model Canvas.[3] This one-page framework, widely used by millions of people around the world, was developed by Alex Osterwalder and Yves Pigneur. If they could simplify the key elements of a business model into one page, I should be able to simplify the key elements of a project too. I've had the opportunity to meet and get acquainted with Alex and Yves, who have validated and endorsed the Project Canvas presented here.

The framework is based on another premise. Every project—regardless of the industry, the organization (profit or nonprofit), the sector (public or private), or whether it is personal or professional—is composed of common elements that determine the project's success. If individuals, leaders, and organizations focus on these elements and apply the techniques behind the elements, more projects will be successful. By using a more common language for its key elements, the Project Canvas helps project managers, project sponsors, and anyone else working on a project to easily relate to these elements and apply them.

The Project Canvas is not intended to refute the established methods of project management. On the contrary, the canvas should make them more universally accessible. It works with traditional, hybrid, and agile project management methodologies.

As an expert practitioner having held such project leadership roles as director of the Program Management Office at PricewaterhouseCoopers,

BNP Paribas Fortis, and GlaxoSmithKline, I have a unique competitive advantage over other management experts from academia and consulting. I can test what works in real life and what doesn't, and, not surprisingly, I have found that most of the standard project management theories are a long way from reality in most of today's projects. As the saying goes, "In theory, theory and practice are the same. In practice, they are not."

Outline of the canvas parts

The Project Canvas is composed of three domains, each made up of three building blocks. Each domain, or area of expertise, has a similar weight in the success of a project (figure 4-1). The three domains and their attendant building blocks are summarized as follows:

FOUNDATION DOMAIN

- **Purpose:** *Why* are we doing the project?

- **Investment:** *How much* will the project cost?

- **Benefits:** *What* benefits will the project generate, and *how* will we know the project is successful?

PEOPLE DOMAIN

- **Sponsorship:** *Who* will be accountable for the project?

- **Stakeholders:** *Who* will benefit from, and be affected by, the project?

- **Resources:** *Who* will manage the project, and *which* skills are needed to deliver the project?

CREATION DOMAIN

- **Deliverables:** *What* will the project produce, build, or deliver?

- **Plan:** *How* and *when* will the work be carried out?

- **Change:** *How* are we going to engage stakeholders and manage the risks?

FIGURE 4-1

The Project Canvas

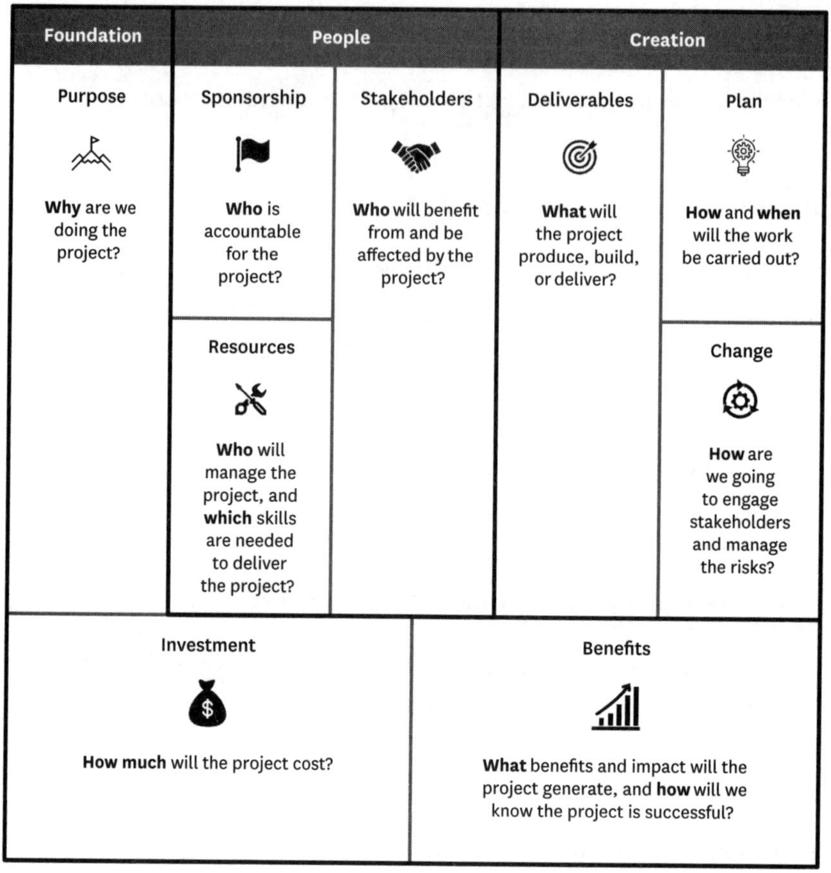

Foundation	People		Creation	
Purpose	**Sponsorship**	**Stakeholders**	**Deliverables**	**Plan**
Why are we doing the project?	**Who** is accountable for the project?	**Who** will benefit from and be affected by the project?	**What** will the project produce, build, or deliver?	**How** and **when** will the work be carried out?
	Resources			**Change**
	Who will manage the project, and **which** skills are needed to deliver the project?			**How** are we going to engage stakeholders and manage the risks?
Investment		**Benefits**		
How much will the project cost?		**What** benefits and impact will the project generate, and **how** will we know the project is successful?		

In some projects, one domain might carry more weight than others. But as a project manager, you need to ensure that all three areas are addressed in all projects.

What makes the Project Canvas, this new project management framework, different from all the other existing project management methods?

- It is simple and designed for all; it is valuable for executives, board members, managers, newcomers to the profession, and students.

- It can be applied to any project, whether the project is traditional, agile, or hybrid, as well as to programs and strategic initiatives.

- It focuses on value and benefits rather than processes and controls.

- It encourages you to focus on fast delivery of the elements of greatest value.

- It ensures that every project has a purpose and aligns with the strategy of the organization.

- It focuses on implementation rather than detailed planning.

- It expands the horizons beyond the traditional project life cycle, looking at the pre-project and post-project phases.

- It is fast and flexible, allowing changes to the project whenever they are needed.

Leaders should use the Project Canvas at the beginning of a project to assess how well it has been defined and whether it should be started right away or needs further refinement. The canvas should be applied throughout the project life cycle to keep track of the progress and ensure that all the critical elements remain valid until completion. The canvas also helps leaders assess whether the project successfully met all the identified benefits. Ultimately, the framework enables leaders to conduct a postmortem of the project to capture the lessons learned and to keep improving their internal competencies.

Chapters 5, 6, and 7 will look at each of the three domains and their nine building blocks. Besides providing descriptions and real examples, I will recommend questions to ask in each building block and an assortment of other tools to use. Chapter 8 will cover how to adopt the Project Canvas framework in your organization and put it into practice.

The canvas provides a unique opportunity for senior executives and project managers to start applying a method that is simple, universal, and proven, and will lead to better outcomes in their organizations. Greater success with your projects is now possible. It is time to take action.

5.

The Foundation

Purpose, Investment, Benefits

The **foundation** domain covers the essence and the actual meaning of a project while bringing it to a more strategic level. Before you commit to start any important initiative, the elements of this domain must be well defined and endorsed by the organization. Skipping this step will greatly increase the chances of project failure. The key elements you'll want to obtain for the foundation of a project include the following: clarity around the why (the purpose) of the project, buy-in and resources from the organization, commitment and time from leadership, and engagement from the project sponsor and members of the project team. Once the project is underway, you'll also want to win the support of stakeholders.

As outlined briefly in chapter 4, the foundation is composed of three building blocks (figure 5-1):

- **Purpose:** explains why you are doing the project, the problem you want to solve, and what you will achieve with it

- **Investment:** the total cost of the project including funds, capital, and all the resources needed to work on the project and achieve its purpose and benefits

- **Benefits:** the expected outcomes of the project; what the project will bring to your organization, your city, and your region, what success looks like, and how stakeholders will benefit from it

FIGURE 5-1

The foundation domain

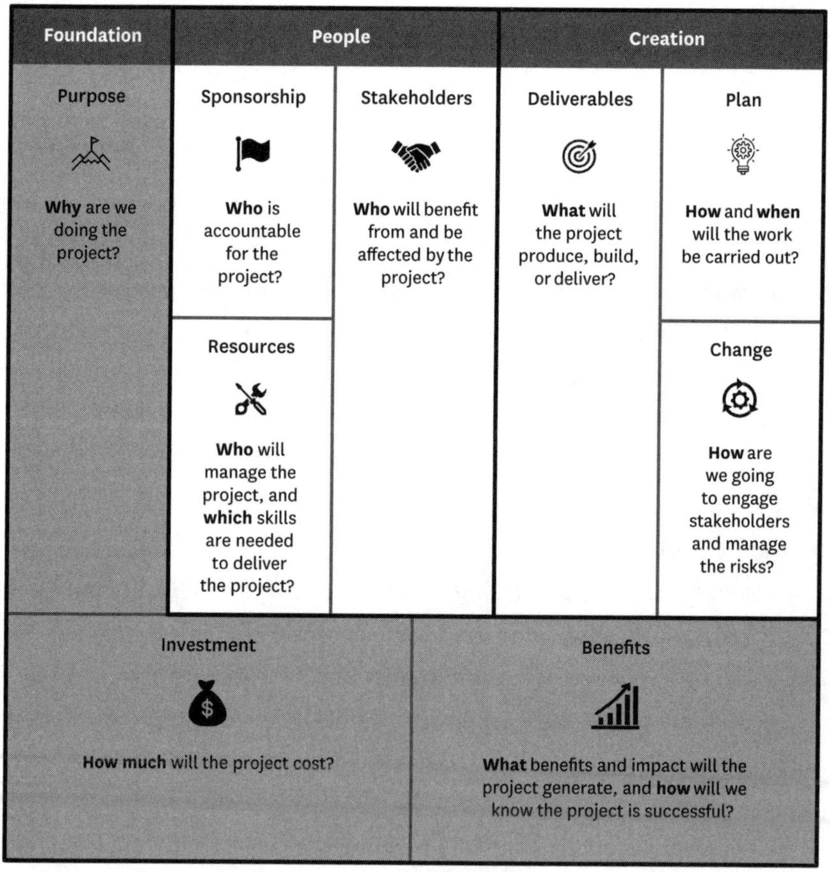

Foundation	People		Creation	
Purpose	**Sponsorship**	**Stakeholders**	**Deliverables**	**Plan**
Why are we doing the project?	**Who** is accountable for the project?	**Who** will benefit from and be affected by the project?	**What** will the project produce, build, or deliver?	**How** and **when** will the work be carried out?
	Resources			**Change**
	Who will manage the project, and **which** skills are needed to deliver the project?			**How** are we going to engage stakeholders and manage the risks?
Investment		Benefits		
How much will the project cost?		**What** benefits and impact will the project generate, and **how** will we know the project is successful?		

Purpose: *Why* are we doing the project?

Traditional project management theories usually focus on what the project will deliver, describing such outcomes as a new product or a new organization. Next, the project leaders would focus on defining how the team will produce the project outcome. But few organizations know how to articulate, or spend enough time articulating, the why of their project: its purpose, its reason for being, its connection with the organization's strategy, and, ultimately, why anyone should care. As Simon Sinek, famous for his book *Start with Why*, says, "People don't buy WHAT you do; they buy WHY you do it."[1]

Besides having a business case, a project should be linked to a higher purpose. Jim Collins and Jerry Porras, authors of the business classic *Built to Last: Successful Habits of Visionary Companies*, provide a useful definition of *purpose*.[2] We'll adapt their definition as follows:

A project's **purpose** is its fundamental reason for being. An effective purpose reflects the importance people attach to the project's work— it taps their idealistic motivations—and gets at the deeper reasons for a project's existence beyond just making money.

People have enormous strengths, and the best leaders know that it is possible to tap into these strengths through their hearts. When a project they work on connects to their inner purpose and passions, they can achieve extraordinary things. Remember that people don't have to be great at something to be passionate. Steve Jobs was not the world's greatest engineer, salesperson, designer, or businessman. But he was uniquely good enough at all these things, and he was driven by his purpose and passion to do something far greater. Conversely, lack of purpose or conviction about a project can quickly spread from one team member to the rest of the team.

Purpose-driven companies are 2.5 times better at driving innovation and transformation than are other companies, according to the EY Beacon Institute, while Deloitte says that on average, they generate 30 percent more revenue from innovations launched in the last year. These statistics

Beyond the business case

All project management methodologies demand that projects have a well-defined business case, which determines the Project Canvas building blocks of purpose, investment, and benefits. Unfortunately, when we are constructing a business case, even fundamentals such as cost or scheduling estimates are subject to bias. It's not human nature to present business cases that are likely to fail, and we tend to present our figures in a way that encourages success. Given the levels of uncertainty associated with most projects, overoptimism isn't necessarily wrong, but it's a habit you want to wean your people from if you don't want to find your all projects tending to overrun on costs or schedule.

An early study on project success, which I carried out while working with PricewaterhouseCoopers, found that only 2.5 percent of the companies successfully completed 100 percent of their projects. We reviewed 10,640 projects from two hundred companies in thirty countries and

are borne out in my experience: projects with a higher purpose have significantly higher chances to be successful than do ones that don't inspire people.

Understanding the purpose and its connection to the overall strategy is not just important for deciding whether to invest or whether the project makes sense strategically. It is also a key driver for engaging team members and the organization as a whole and motivating them to support the project.

The two main reasons for launching a project are either to solve a problem or to capture an opportunity:

- **What problem will we solve with this project?** For example, the Thames Tideway project might have given this answer: "London relies on a 150-year-old sewer system built for a population less

across various industries.[3] In many occasions, projects fundamentals were overly optimistic and based on wrong assumptions.

On the other hand, the Sydney Opera House, the UK's Millennium Dome, and even the Channel Tunnel are a few projects that had completely flawed business cases yet realized benefits that were never anticipated by those who originally conceived them. Over time, all these projects became extremely successful.

The thinking process, research, and analysis of options that go into constructing a business case remain helpful in developing a good understanding of the project and whether it is worth investing in. The Project Canvas recognizes that while the business case is an essential element of the foundation of the project, it's not enough. Our reality, which is increasingly digital and filled with volatility, uncertainty, complexity and ambiguity, requires that we look at the project foundation in a way that is more holistic, intrinsic, and prepared for change.

than half its current size. As a result, millions of tonnes of raw sewage spills, untreated, into the River Thames each year. We're building a twenty-five-kilometer super sewer under the Thames to intercept those nasty spills and clean up our river for the good of the city, its wildlife, and you."

- **What opportunity will we capture?** For example, the Boeing 777 project might have given this answer: "Airlines wanted a wider-fuselage cross-section, fully flexible interior configurations, short- to intercontinental-range capability, and an operating cost lower than existing models. The Boeing 777 will capture this huge opportunity in the commercial aerospace market."

If you cannot answer either of the two preceding questions easily and plainly, you should refrain from launching your project. You'll want to research it further until you find the real purpose behind the project.

Most projects have lengthy, technical, or deliverable-focused goals: a new software rollout, a new platform, an expansion program, a new set of company values, a reorganization, a digital transformation project. Other projects use financial goals such as a 10 percent return on investment (ROI). Neither of these goals is clear, nor does it inspire people to commit passionately to the project. Instead, projects should have at least one SMART objective (specific, measurable, action-oriented, relevant, and time-based; see further details below) reflecting the purpose of the initiative. The SMART objective should be clear, easy to remember, and, if possible, daring. Make the SMART objective your *elevator pitch*: a statement that is short, to the point, and highly memorable and that you can deliver in thirty seconds. That's what you want for your project.

TOOLS AND TECHNIQUES

Keep asking why to uncover your higher purpose

An easy method of finding the purpose of a project is to ask, Why are we doing the project? Usually leaders need to ask this question four to seven times to get to the essence of the matter. Think about a new HR system. Most project managers will say that the project is about implementing the new system, but that is not why we do the project. Instead, ask, *Why* do we want the HR system? The answer may be, To provide better services to our employees. You have just gone to a higher level. Next, ask yourself again why you want this outcome. Your next answer may be, To address our key issue of poor employee engagement. You just went to a higher level again, and a higher priority of thinking that is based on what is more important for you. Ask again, Why do we want to increase the engagement of employees? You might respond, Because we want our employees to be happy at work, which will lead to a higher performance of our business.

With this sequence of deeper and deeper questioning, you have now moved the purpose of your project from a new HR system to a project that will increase the satisfaction of your employees and improve your performance. What a difference, right? Now you have a project whose purpose connects with the organization's strategy and will motivate project team members. You can even add financial or any other value to it. Once you have gotten to the real reason, ask "by when" and "how much" questions. Your answer might be, We will increase the motivation of our employees by 30 percent on our next survey, in six months. (This exercise produces a SMART objective for your project—see the description of SMART in the next paragraph.) If after the exercise you don't reach something relevant— something that will motivate people to work on it—then I strongly recommend that you do not start the project.

SMART objectives

Since George T. Doran coined and popularized SMART objectives in 1981, they have become an essential tool to select the most valuable goal, while focusing people on what really matters and remove distractions. SMART is an acronym for the following five elements:

Specific: provide the "who" and the "what" of the project.

Measurable: focus on "how much" the project will produce.

Action-oriented: trigger practical actions to achieve the project objective.

Relevant: accurately address the purpose of the project.

Time-based: have a time frame indicating when the objective will be met.

Every successful project needs at least one clearly articulated SMART objective. An iconic example is John F. Kennedy' moon-landing project: he wanted the US to be the first country to put a man on the moon, before the end of the 1960s.

Thinking 10X: Making your purpose exponential

Alphabet's X, the innovation lab, famously champions the idea of seeking solutions that are "10X not just 10%" better. Mark Bonchek, an entrepreneur and adviser, says, "To create exponential value, it's imperative to first create an exponential mindset. The incremental mindset focuses on making something better, while the exponential mindset is something different. Incremental is satisfied with 10%. Exponential seeks 10X."[4]

Imagine, for example, that you launch a project with the purpose of reducing the plastic waste in your organization. Currently, five tons of plastic is generated per year. Team members on most projects would be happy to achieve a 10 percent reduction, or 0.5 tons less plastic waste. Applying the 10X thinking would mean you want to eliminate the plastic waste. This exponential goal forces the team to think differently, to take a leap in imagination, and to try new approaches. Even if the 10X goal is not ultimately achieved, the selected solution will most likely bring a breakthrough.

Developing and sharing stories

Strategies are not enough. We need something more human and personal. As Jeroen De Flander explained to me, "Stories make messages stickier. Wrap a story around your message, and it becomes twenty times easier for the listener to remember."[5] Stories put information in a context that people can relate to. Narratives bring a future vision to life, inviting team members to imagine it with you, exploring its ultimate benefits. Because stories are more memorable than a recitation of facts, they can be retold from person to person. With their deep understanding of human emotions, motivations, and psychology, stories facilitate an emotional connection—they reach for the heart.

As Anders Inset, a world-leading business philosopher, once told me, "Bezos is not using PowerPoints; he's using storytelling, and people are tapping into that, getting an understanding of the topics, trying to visualize how to explain it. And that's how a project succeeds, and I'm a strong believer of that."[6]

Back to our HR system example, we can develop a story around one employee, Clarisse. Although Clarisse had been one of the most joyful and committed employees, she had not been motivated for a while now. She didn't understand where the company was heading and if her work was having an impact. With the new HR system, Clarisse will be able to chat with other employees and senior management about her challenges and understand the new strategy around making a healthy planet—a strategy she will relate to and connect to her daily work. Clarisse will again be proud of going to work and helping the organization achieve this new goal.

Putting this building block into practice

Psychologists have done extensive research on the impact that positive thinking, including believing in success, can have on individuals. Success is a self-fulfilling prophecy. When we expect to succeed, we automatically mobilize our internal resources to achieve the outcome. When others believe in us, the dynamic is reinforced. That is why project leaders need to create a positive environment, where successes are applauded and the difficulties of a project are downplayed, to cultivate a can-do spirit in the team. People need someone who believes in them so that they can believe in themselves.

Key questions to ask

Defining your project's purpose effectively requires clarity and alignment with both team members and the organization's goals. The purpose should not be fancy or embellished—it has to be genuine, and it has to feel meaningful. These questions can help you determine your project's purpose:

- What makes the project great and unique?
- Does the project have an emotional element?
- What will be remembered about the project ten years from now?
- What aspects would make people volunteer to participate and to contribute to the project?
- What problem will we solve with this project?
- What opportunity will we capture?

Investment: *How much* will the project cost?

Project costs include the time spent by the people working on and supervising the project plus all the other investments (consultants, capital, material, software, hardware, and so on) required to deliver the project. Project managers usually refer to all these costs as the **project budget**, which together with time and scope, make up the triple constraint in traditional project management. Without budget, there is no project.

The accuracy of the cost estimates depends on clarity and stability of the scope (requirements and specifications) of the project. The clearer and more stable the scope, the more accurate the estimates will be. Unfortunately, given the fast-changing world and the ambitious nature of organizations and of the projects they initiate, stability and certainty over a long period has become a rare commodity.

Projects need sufficient resources to succeed. An alternative way of expressing this observation is the admonition "Cut your coat according to your cloth." Only a few projects are so time-bound that you need to deliver everything up front. For the remainder, the mantra should be this: deliver what your budget can afford; you can always go back and deliver some more, if you are successful.

A handful of projects have the luxury of an unlimited budget. This financial freedom allows greater resources for the project, accelerates it, and can assure delivery against an often-tight or even fixed schedule. Unlimited budgets are often the case for projects that are launched and supported by top officials. Some of the majestic projects built in the Middle East in the past decade—for example, the Burj Khalifa, at 828 meters the tallest building in the world, was sponsored by the sheikh of Dubai and was built on an unlimited budget.

In smaller organizations, the concept of an unlimited budget may be reflected in certain high-priority projects that may call on the whole team to drop its other work and focus 100 percent on the project. These projects are usually a response to an external imperative such as a sudden crisis, a software failure, or a regulatory compliance issue, and they cannot be sustained over a long period.

Even so, an unlimited budget is no guarantee of success. If some of the key elements described in this section are missing, there are chances that the project will fail. A clear example is the project to launch the Obama administration's Healthcare.gov website. When the website was launched on October 1, 2013, it promptly collapsed, causing tremendous reputational damages. Yet budget was not a constraint.

TOOLS AND TECHNIQUES

Top-down, bottom-up budget estimation

Most of the cost in a project is the time spent by the team to perform the project activities. This is one reason why schedule overruns are often so costly. The best and most accurate way to create a budget is by first having an initial high-level (top-down) orientation on the total project cost. Identify the potential budget available, and look at the costs of similar past projects. Remember to factor in people's availability. You can't include in a budget a resource you don't have.

Once you have established the broad requirements and broken the project down into activities (we will see how to do this in chapter 7), start from the bottom up by estimating the cost of each activity. This exercise should be carried out with the main contributors to the project. External parties will need to provide their cost projections. Consider activities or extra costs that could be incurred after the project has been completed. Adding the costs of all the activities will provide an accurate view of the total investment required to carry out the project. Large projects usually include a contingency amount (5–10 percent) of the total estimated cost to handle unforeseen expenses.

Then compare the bottom-up estimate with the initial top-down estimate. If there is a big gap, and if there is an important budget constraint, consider reducing the scope or even reevaluating whether the project should be carried out. Beware the temptation to massage the figures or make overoptimistic assumptions in an effort to shoehorn the project into the budget. The project will either fail entirely, fall well short on the value you intend to deliver, or face substantial cost overruns. In any event, the project—and your reputation—will take a hit, and these results will then have an impact on subsequent projects.

Putting this building block into practice

The budget is derived directly from the requirements of the project and the urgency of delivering them. The more detailed our definition of the requirements and the more fixed they are, the more accurately we can estimate the budget. To reduce the risk of budget overruns, never allocate the total amount of the budget to the project at the beginning. Break it down into portions. Establish stage gates and quarterly review cycles to check status and budget consumption. If the project's original business case is still valid, release another portion of budget. If the project is having serious problems, ignore any sunk costs and seriously consider canceling it.

One way to provide flexibility and resilience in uncertain projects is with take and put options. With these options, you invest minor quantities in multiple ideas and commit to larger investments once the idea has been converted into a viable prototype and is ready to be developed. This incremental approach allows you to adapt your spending according to the progress of the project, the value it generates during delivery, or both these results.

If you are unsure about certain risks and you have already planned or anticipated ways to reduce the scope or delay aspects of the project to a future phase, then the decision to introduce these measures can be triggered by preset criteria. On the other hand, if your project starts with cautious assumptions and a limited budget and appears to be delivering increased value ahead of schedule, then you can add in or accelerate planned requirements.

Key questions to ask

- Does the project have a fully dedicated budget that has been well estimated?

- Could the project's budget absorb overruns?

- What options might you include in your budget for reducing the scope or slowing the project (in the event of setbacks) or for accelerating the project or adding scope (if you are ahead of schedule in terms of delivery and value creation)?

Benefits: *What* benefits and value will the project generate?

Benefits and value, such as ROI, growth, sustainable practices, or social impact, are the reasons why we do the project and how we measure its success. Since the turn of the new century, much has been written about these types of benefits, and they have been included in such project management methodologies as benefits management and benefit realization. However, not all businesses apply this lens to their projects as a standard practice. Most projects continue to be planned, and milestones set, according to deliverables, artifacts (objects produced), and outputs when project planning should instead be planned based on the expected benefits.

The relevance of benefits

Project benefits have historically been considered an outcome of delivering a project on time, on budget, and within scope. There are a couple of reasons for this assumption. First, it stems from the tendency to focus on the project simply as a process for planning, designing, initiating, and delivering an asset. When you do this, project success is defined very simply as delivery of the asset. But however you define value, whether in social or financial terms, it is what people *do with the asset* that matters, not the mere fact of its existence. For this reason, the majority of the benefits will accrue *after* the project has completed.

The second reason why benefits have been assumed has been the singular focus on financial benefits. While a financial emphasis may seem prudent, such a focus on the hard measures of how much money the project generates or how much it saves is often nonsensical. If we build a parking lot next to a patch of national forest to encourage people to walk, run, and bird-watch there, the lot will require an investment of cash. The value that it generates, on the other hand, is in the mental and physical well-being these activities bring to the citizens who use the parking lot. Good luck putting a coherent financial figure against that benefit.

Instead, we should focus on positive impact. Stakeholders should be able to point to something—anything—and say, "See that? Before our project, it was bad. Now, because of the project, it is good (or at least better)." You may be able to show whether a positive impact has been considerable, medium, or small. If a project brings a useful invention to the market, that is a positive impact. If it turns a previously fetid swamp into a lovely park, that is a positive impact.

The challenge of measuring benefits

Still, benefits are easy to claim and far harder to validate and measure, especially when they accrue over a long time. Because projects don't happen in isolation, efforts to define a straight-line, cause-and-effect relationship between what you have done and how people have benefited are also difficult.

Take the example of the parking lot next to the forest. Mary may achieve happiness by walking in the forest, but tracking this benefit is complicated because everything happens after the parking lot is built and the project is delivered. Certainly, the parking lot has now brought Mary to the forest to walk, but how do you measure the value of the wellness this generates in her? And to what extent is Mary's increased wellness attributable to her walks in this forest rather than another forest? You'll certainly need to track lot usage and some socioeconomic measures relating to health and well-being in the region. Also, beware of project leaders who claim "orphan" benefits for their projects. Asserting that Mary's improved ability to recognize different bird species is a project benefit doesn't work unless you can link this improvement directly to your strategic objectives, in this case, people's well-being. Finally, don't forget that your parking lot has generated disadvantages, such as the traffic caused by all those vehicles now making their way to the forest.

Best ways to focus on benefits

There is a three-stage process to improve the focus on the project's benefits:

1. **Identifying and agreeing on the intended benefits:** Since the success of the project will be measured by benefits achieved, the process you use for identifying and mapping the benefits must be inclusive and transparent. Involve your stakeholders so they will know what is expected of them once the project is completed. Use the benefits card (at the end of this chapter) to allow the key stakeholders to define which benefits they expect from the project. Show a clear link between your project, its benefits, and your strategy to help reassure your investors of the project's credibility.

2. **Planning the benefits:** Using the input from key stakeholders, the project manager should develop a benefit plan that shows when the project will deliver value. This is a critical step in benefit management, yet it barely exists in today's project management practices. The benefit plan should be approved by the steering committee.

3. **Tracking and realizing the benefits:** Realizing the benefits of the project has generally fallen under the remit of the executive sponsor, but the project manager should be responsible as well. Keeping an eye on the benefit plan and tracking the progress toward delivery of your benefits is essential. The sooner the benefits can be captured, even if the project captures just part of the expected value, the better. Benefits milestones should be announced and celebrated—stakeholders care more about knowing when benefits are achieved than when deliverables are. On the other hand, if the benefits are no longer important, or if your likelihood of delivering them is shrinking, it could be an indicator that a project should be canceled. At the end of the project, the steering committee should verify the benefits achieved, assess whether the project has been a success, and ensure that the follow-up of the benefits beyond the project are tracked and have an owner accountable for continuing to realize them.

Project benefits in complex systems

Complex systems and systems thinking are now well recognized in most modern organizations. Many projects that change businesses, launch new products, or introduce new infrastructure have consequences and impact that extend far beyond their original scope. While you may be tempted to frame your project benefits in strictly commercial or financial terms, many of your stakeholders will apply their own value judgments on your project. These may be an equally powerful driver for success or failure.

In *Systems Leadership*, Ian MacDonald, Catherine Burke, and Karl Stewart identify six principles of behavior for managing complex systems:[7]

1. **People need to be able to predict their environments.** In project terms, this principle means that your stakeholders need to be able to see clearly how your project will affect their lives (ideally for better).

2. **People are not machines.** Beware of language that advocates *efficiency improvements*, *performance enhancements*, or *productivity gains* when you are framing a rationale for business transformation.

3. **People's behavior is based on six universal values.** Consciously or unconsciously, people will assess the benefits of what you are proposing through the values of honesty, trustworthiness, courage, respect for human dignity, fairness, and love.

4. **People base some aspects of their culture on mythologies.** These make up the lens through which they will be making sense of your project. So remember that not all rationales will be seen through cold logic; some benefits that stakeholders value are intangible.

5. **Change is a result of dissonance.** For individuals or groups to shift their behavior and how they interpret the world, there needs to be a significant and sustained tension between their views and the emerging reality.

6. **It is better to build relationships on the basis of authority rather than power.** As opposed to power, authority is something given to you by the organization. Just because you *can* make a project happen doesn't mean you should if you don't have stakeholder buy-in.

TOOLS AND TECHNIQUES

The benefits triple constraint

As explained in chapter 3, a well-known concept in project management is the triple constraint, or iron triangle, which is composed of the scope, the time, and the cost of the project. The principle behind this triad, however you name it, is that if any of these three critical factors changes throughout the project, the other two will have to be adjusted if quality is to be maintained. This book proposes two new triple constraints that better reflect the potential success of a project: the benefits triple constraint and the engagement triple constraint (see chapter 6).

The benefits of a project have three constraints (figure 5-2):

- **Value delivered:** both tangible (financial return, etc.) and intangible (social impact, new capabilities, etc.)

- **Risks:** usually, the higher the risks, the higher the benefits, but also the higher chances of failure

- **Sustainability:** whether it will continue delivering benefits in the long term or is just a onetime thing

FIGURE 5-2

The benefits triple constraint

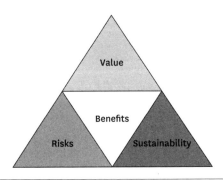

As with the iron triangle, the three constraints on benefits affect one another. So, for example, if the executive team members suddenly want to try to increase the value of a project, then they will need to take higher risks, which will have an impact on the long-term sustainability of the project.

Considering the project, results, users, and benefits (PRUB) model

In his 2014 book, *Validating Strategies*, Phil Driver introduced a simple but compelling model for understanding the role of benefits in project management. The model helps validate what you are doing and check whether indeed a given project can be delivered and, if so, whether it is likely to generate the value that is anticipated.

He calls this the PRUB model (for projects, results, users, and benefits), and the premise behind his model is powerful: "only end-users can create benefits." Table 5-1 presents some examples of the PRUB model applied to a few projects.

One strength of the model is that it can be used in reverse. You can, for example, start from the position of "improved health in mothers and babies" and work backward to identify projects and a strategy that will drive these benefits.

Benefits are the basic currency of value associated with a project. Although they should always be quantified through recognized methods or

TABLE 5-1

PRUB (projects, results, users, and benefits) model examples

Projects	Maternity ward renovation	Parking lot construction	New HR system
Results	A modern maternity ward	A parking lot near a forest	A new way to communicate with employees
Users	Obstetricians and nurses	Forest visitors	Organization's employees and management
Benefits	Improved health in mothers and babies	Mental and physical health	Employees who are more engaged; improved employee performance

other evidence, they can be both financial and nonfinancial. For example, people's well-being has both psychological benefits and financial benefits (in terms of reduced health-care costs).

The UK Office for National Statistics now includes happiness as one of the measures in its dashboard of national well-being.[8] As a performance measure, happiness is solidly nonfinancial, and yet, through the use of careful polling and market research, increases or decreases in national happiness can be tracked as a measure of progress.

Many project benefits are realized after a given project has been delivered. In construction terms, the value and the benefit of a building depends on its use and operation once the project is completed.

Accelerating project benefits

Today, organizations need to change and create value fast. They often cannot wait until a project is completed to start generating benefits. For example, if you are an expanding hotel chain constructing a new building, you might, with a standard approach, only start generating benefits after eighteen months, when the hotel is ready to open. Or instead, to capture benefits earlier, you could plan the development in such a way that you build a casino on the ground floor in six months and start operating it while the rest of the building is still being constructed. Accelerating benefits requires thinking differently at the planning stage.

Benefits card

The **benefits card** (see the appendix) is a checklist that will help both the executive sponsor and the project manager identify the main benefits and key impacts of their projects. Each project will bring different benefits to different stakeholders. Project leaders should identify the main benefit expectations for each key stakeholder early in the process, formally validate them at the project steering committee, and agree on the top three benefits for the project. The main benefits should be included in the benefits plan, discussed in the next section.

Benefits plan

Since its inception, project management has focused on basing its plans on deliverables, outputs, and artifacts, even though what really matters to most key stakeholders is the impact and value the project will bring. The **benefits plan** describes the benefits of the project and when they will be delivered. The inputs to the benefit plan come from the benefits card and the business case of the project. It is much more difficult to define and plan benefits than to do so for deliverables. Break down the project benefits in smaller, quantifiable milestones, such as 10 percent of expected users on the new application, or a thousand new customers (out of the target of one hundred thousand) signed up. Each benefit milestone should have an owner accountable for delivering it. Some benefits are delivered over a period long after the project has been completed. Project managers need to ensure that the benefit plan covers this post-project phase, and the owner of the benefits continues to track them through this period. By developing this new type of plan, we move the focus from outputs to outcomes and, at the same time, increase the visibility of the project's benefits and accountability for ensuring they are realized.

Quantifying the unquantifiable

Numbers communicate variable ideas more effectively than do words.[9] For example, *extremely fast* is entirely relative to an individual's perception and expectation of speed. But *a hundred miles per hour* is an absolute measure. The same holds true when we talk about greater productivity. Unless everyone is clear about how productivity is expressed and agrees on the current level of productivity and the impact of improved productivity, then the concept is vague and open to misinterpretation.

According to systems engineer Tom Gilb, you can quantify everything, even love. He suggests you make a list of all the aspects of love—a deconstructed view of love based on its component parts. Even though we recognize that it's a subjective view, we can share and discuss it nonetheless. Pick any element of love you like, for example, trust. Then break it down into its constituent parts (truthfulness, reliability) to get a better understanding of

TABLE 5-2

Impact estimation example

The importance of each attribute to individuals is rated numerically between 0 and 100, with 0 being the lowest importance. Value is the sum of the first three attributes divided by cost.

	Pears	Mangoes
Taste	50	70
Nutritional value	40	60
Look	30	70
Cost	40	50
Value for $	120/40 = 3	200/50 = 4

what trust is, how it manifests itself, and which aspects of love operate on trust. For each of these parts, define a scale of measure.

Of course, we can't compare pears and mangoes. Or can we? A little tool called **impact estimation** can be used to solve and quantify complex problems. Here is a simplified version of how it works: Take several qualities that interest you about fruit (e.g., flavor, nutritional value, shelf life). Rate these qualities numerically for different fruits. You'll end up with a figure of merit for how good each of these types of fruits is for your particular purposes. If we now add the element of cost, you can work out the value for money (see table 5-2). Using our subjective rating, we learn that mangoes have more monetary value than pears. Impact estimation is a powerful tool for looking at complex systems and making goals quantifiable.

Financial viability

There are both simple and sophisticated ways to assess the financial viability of your project. Without a thorough and appropriate financial analysis, there is a great chance the project will end up losing money. To ensure accuracy, have any estimates validated by your finance department. The most common metrics are these:

- **ROI:** measures the project's gross financial return on the investment, expressed as a percentage of the total estimated cost.

- **Net present value (NPV):** helps you assess what that future money is worth in today's dollars. If the NPV is positive, it means that the money you are investing today will generate future cash flows that are earning the required amount of return (above the discount rate). A negative NPV means that the project may not be worth doing.

- **Internal rate of return (IRR):** the annualized and compounded interest rate that the project will return as a percentage. IRR is perhaps the most difficult to calculate but arguably gives the most accurate financial assessment of a project. A good IRR will be at a minimum more than what you can get by putting your money in the bank.

- **Payback period:** how long it takes to earn back the investment made in the project. You decide on an appropriate period (e.g., two years), and if the project earns back the investment within that period, it's good. If it takes longer, then it's not a good idea.

- **Opportunity costs:** the other initiatives that will be missed out on if you decide to carry out this project. If the value of other projects is higher, then you should reconsider which projects you invest in.

Putting this building block into practice

Common best practice is for the project sponsor to be given the responsibility for delivering benefits. The sponsor can then help steer the project according to how the team and stakeholders have agreed to define the benefits (using the benefits card). While basic controls such as cost, time, and quality can be checked at the project management level, clarity on the benefits allows the sponsor to make sure that the project *should* still be delivered in its current form and be successful, or whether it should be curtailed or even stopped. A sponsor's ability to make these decisions depends greatly on access to a clear and up-to-date progress report on the state of the benefits for the project as well as a good understanding of how any decision might affect those benefits.

Given that the benefits for many projects largely accrue after the project is completed, you need to ensure that your organization has someone who can take on the responsibility to deliver benefits at that point. In the medium to long term, the person should build feedback systems to reflect the lessons from the use of the project deliverable (whether it's the operation of a building, the piece of infrastructure, or the effectiveness of a business change). This is a substantial undertaking, particularly when the organization responsible for delivery of the project is a different organization from the one that is operating the asset.

Benefit management remains a challenge for many projects and organizations, not least because of the time that passes between a project's initiation, delivery, and then realization of the benefits. The value of a project can also be seriously undermined if the business case overestimates the value of the benefits or the likelihood of delivering them.

Key questions to ask

In its *Guide to Developing the Project Business Case*, the UK Treasury offers three useful questions for assessing the value of a project:[10]

- By how much can we allow benefits to fall short of expectations, if the proposal is to remain worthwhile? How likely is this?

- By how much can operating costs increase, if the proposal is to remain worthwhile? How likely is this to happen?

- What will be the impact on benefits if operating costs are constrained?

We have seen in this chapter the three building blocks that form a solid foundation for projects. Having a clear purpose, or the why of the project, is the first stepping-stone. Next, a comprehensive view of the investment, in terms of costs and capital resources, is required to carry out the project. And finally, the leaders and stakeholders need clarity about the benefits delivered by the project: how and when they can claim that the project has been successful. In the next chapter, we look at another essential area for project success: the people domain.

6.

The People

Sponsorship, Resources, Stakeholders

Projects don't exist without people. People's competencies and behavior are among the main drivers of successful project management. The emotional and individual expectations of team members and key stakeholders must be addressed to bring about the best in them. Across the project life cycle, engagement levels of individual team members should be monitored. Today, virtual project teams, often not colocated, are commonplace. In this environment, project managers and executive sponsors must well understand behavior, emotions, and culture. The **people domain** covers three building blocks that are connected by the human factor (figure 6-1):

- **Sponsorship:** the conduit between the organization funding the project and the project team delivering it; the executive sponsor is also accountable for delivery of the benefits

- **Resources:** the human resources—the people delivering the project, from the project manager to the project team to consultants—and the particular capabilities they require to make it all happen

- **Stakeholders:** all those involved in, affected by, or benefiting from the project

FIGURE 6-1

The people domain

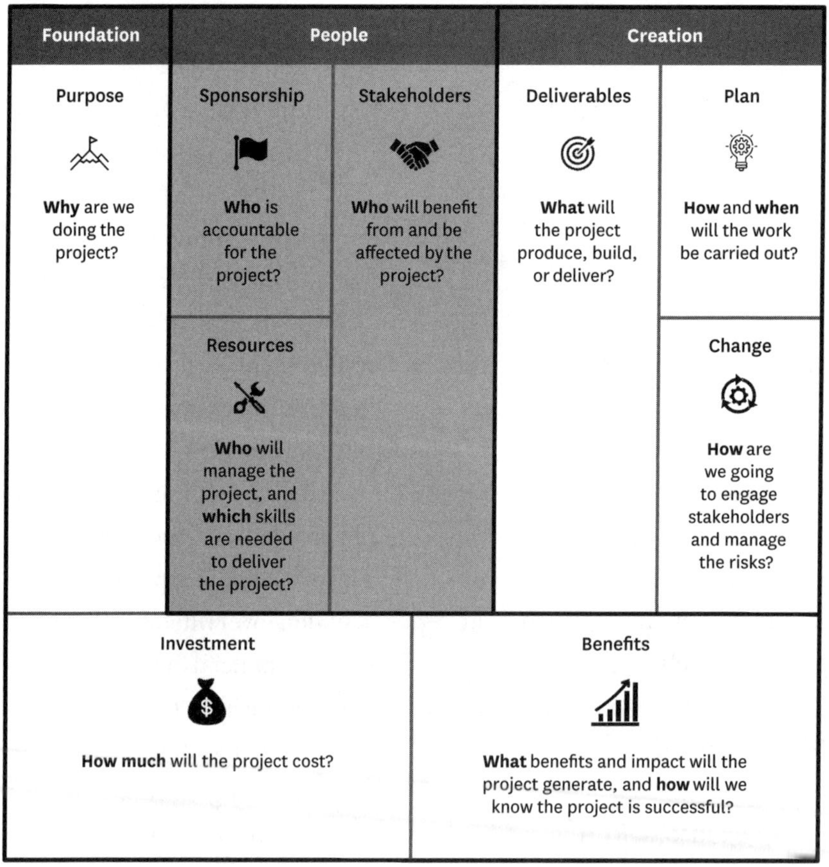

Foundation	People		Creation	
Purpose	**Sponsorship**	**Stakeholders**	**Deliverables**	**Plan**
Why are we doing the project?	**Who** is accountable for the project?	**Who** will benefit from and be affected by the project?	**What** will the project produce, build, or deliver?	**How** and **when** will the work be carried out?
	Resources			**Change**
	Who will manage the project, and **which** skills are needed to deliver the project?			**How** are we going to engage stakeholders and manage the risks?
Investment			**Benefits**	
How much will the project cost?			**What** benefits and impact will the project generate, and **how** will we know the project is successful?	

Sponsorship: *Who* will be accountable for the project?

Many projects start without clarity about who is ultimately accountable for their successful delivery. As projects tend to span across departments, business units, and even countries, they are often prone to shared accountability and collective sponsorship. Often, many executives may feel responsible for delivering the project, yet no one is truly accountable for driving it to successful completion—or is on the hook if it fails.

In many projects, organizations choose the executive sponsor haphazardly. They often see the role as something symbolic or a reflection of authority: *The more projects I sponsor, the more powerful I am.* This casual approach to sponsorship is one of the most common errors that lead to systematic project failure.

In reality, the executive sponsor holds an incredibly vital and influential role in any project, especially strategic and complicated ones. The more complex the project, the more critical the executive sponsor's role and the more time it demands. Although executives commonly sponsor a dozen projects at once, such an approach is fraught with problems. These executives lack sufficient bandwidth to provide meaningful support for each project. One CEO of a large global telecom company bluntly admitted to me, "Currently, I am the executive sponsor of eighteen projects. The five projects to which I dedicate time to follow through—where I support the project leader and team, and chair the steering committee—go much better than the thirteen that I sponsor but don't dedicate any time to."

Let's look at an example of ineffective executive sponsorship. In August 2007, Fortis Private Bank's shareholders overwhelmingly backed one of Europe's largest takeovers ever in the financial industry. Fortis, Royal Bank of Scotland, and Banco Santander made a €71 billion offer for the largest bank in the Netherlands, ABN AMRO bank. But after just over a year, Fortis Bank was broken up after experiencing extreme difficulty financing its part of the joint acquisition. Even after receiving a round of bailouts, Fortis was nationalized by the Dutch government and renamed back to ABN AMRO. Fortis's Belgian banking operations were disposed of in a fire sale to BNP Paribas.

Over the fourteen months that the project lasted before it collapsed, the ultimate executive sponsor, Fortis's CEO, was seen in Amsterdam on only two occasions. Splitting and integrating the newly acquired ABN AMRO bank was a tremendous challenge that generated great resistance and required fast decision-making. The old ABN AMRO directors and employees saw the CEO's absence as a sign of weakness, which they exploited by not supporting the separation project and avoiding sharing vital information. Critical decisions that needed to be made quickly ended up taking weeks or months. In the end, the lack of executive support for the bank's most important strategic initiative became a primary reason for the acquisition's failure and the destruction of more than €20 billion of shareholders' value.

This meager sponsor involvement is a common pattern. Despite the importance of executive sponsorship, too many senior leaders dedicate far too little time engaging with their projects. Our research confirms this observation. Executives lack either the practical experience or the capability

FIGURE 6-2

Executives' time allocation

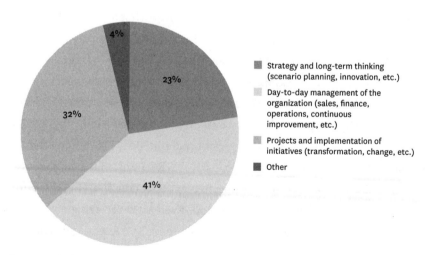

- Strategy and long-term thinking (scenario planning, innovation, etc.)
- Day-to-day management of the organization (sales, finance, operations, continuous improvement, etc.)
- Projects and implementation of initiatives (transformation, change, etc.)
- Other

Source: HBR Project Management Handbook Executive Survey, July 2020, N = 566

for the role of sponsor, or they simply do not understand the importance of their own engagement. Executives say they spent they largest amount of their time in managing the day-to-day operations of their organization, and one-third on projects (figure 6-2).

Most project managers understand the importance of the role of the executive sponsor, especially on initiatives that have an impact on, and require involvement from, different areas of the organization. However, project managers rarely ask the sponsor to become more involved in the projects. Some managers are afraid of putting their job on the line by calling out executives on their responsibilities. Even so, I strongly recommend that project managers not hesitate to engage the executive sponsor. Let these leaders know the importance of their roles, and remind them of their ultimate accountability for the project.

This dynamic may be on the verge of changing. In a recent discussion I had with a group of project managers, one manager proposed that to obtain the best-qualified and most committed executive sponsor for a new project, the team should be invited to interview candidates for the role on the basis of what it, the project team, needs. Sponsors without the experience, skills, and, most importantly, empathy for the team's needs or the willingness to commit the requisite time would speedily be weeded out. Unfortunately, I have yet to see any organizations brave enough to take such a radical step to mitigate the imbalance of power between project team and sponsor.

Ron Ashkenas provides good insights on the expectations for the role in his article "How to Be an Effective Executive Sponsor."[1] He suggests two steps to take: First, before launching the project, the executive sponsor and the project manager should meet to set, clarify, and align expectations. Second, these leaders should define realistically how much time and effort will be required from the executive level. It takes a strong emotional commitment to do what is necessary to help see the projects through. Executive involvement can be rewarding for the sponsor, too, since it provides an opportunity to work with senior colleagues and be viewed as an enterprise leader.

When I am asked by an executive sponsor to lead a project, I first ask for time to briefly study the purpose of the project. I let the sponsor know

Responsibilities of the executive sponsor

- Ensure the project's strategic significance.
- Establish approval and funding for the project.
- Secure support from key stakeholders.
- Resolve conflicts and make decisions.
- Be accessible and approachable—on-call support for the project manager.
- Participate in periodic reviews.
- Chair the steering committee.
- Encourage recognition.
- Support closure review.
- Be ultimately accountable for the project.

that if I accept the role, I need to have this executive's ongoing support throughout the project. I request that the person commit thirty minutes every two weeks to discuss the project. Right after we agree on these issues, I send the executive a meeting invitation for the same day and time (e.g., Mondays from 11:00 to 11:30 a.m.) every two weeks until the end of the project. That way, I ensure regular access to the executive sponsor, creating a good habit in this leader to review the project as well (see "The power of habits" in the Tools and Techniques section).

Steering committee and project governance

The executive sponsor, together with the project manager, should define how the project is governed. According to the *PMBOK Guide*, the project management guidelines mentioned earlier in the book, project governance refers to "organizational or structural arrangements at all levels of an organization designed to determine and influence the behavior of the organization's members."[2] **Governance** represents a series of transparent undertakings around the project: the basis for decisions, the roles and responsibilities of those involved, stakeholder engagement, and how the project will be managed. It is multidimensional and considers people, their roles, and the structures and policies of the project, and it provides direction and oversight to the project team. There also needs to be an understanding of the project's environment to ensure a good fit with the established organization's governance.

Governance translates on the project organization chart into a hierarchy of decision-making and delivery roles explaining who has accountability and responsibility for what. A central body in a project is the steering committee, which is chaired by the executive sponsor and run by the project manager. The members and the frequency with which the committee meets are often determined by the importance of the project in the organization. One steering committee I sat on for a project integrating two large European banks was chaired by the CEO and met every day at 5 p.m. It was evident to all that the integration project was the company's number one priority, and we had to show progress daily. In contrast, I have also worked on a project whose steering committee met every three months. Most senior leaders didn't show up, because they had other priorities, and those who were present hardly remembered what the project was about. The first project was extremely successful, the second a complete failure.

These examples show the importance of a high-performing and involved steering committee in the success of a project. The committee is usually made up of high-level stakeholders, such as the CEO, department heads, business-unit leaders, and experts. Their main duty is to endorse the project and to provide guidance throughout the life cycle of the project. The steering committee addresses the bigger issues that appear during implementation of the project, such as delays, additional cost, significant scope changes, risks that put the project's benefits at stake, staffing issues, and resistance from key stakeholders. The steering committee also gives the green light to a project if stage gates are being used. If some members of the committee disagree about the project or its value, these issues should be sorted out immediately.

Strong project governance will address three organizational challenges:

- **Resources have other responsibilities on top of the project.** For example, a developer whose main job is to keep the website up and running is asked to join a digitalization project. Because her current responsibilities are not modified, her contribution to the strategic project will be in addition to her day-to-day job. The developer's not being fully dedicated will have an impact on the speed of the project.

- **Resources have different reporting lines outside the project.** For example, a legal expert is part of a regulatory compliance project, which is led by the vice president of the business. The legal expert is not participating in the weekly project team meetings. The vice president has tried to convince the legal expert to join, but as she doesn't report to him, she doesn't feel obliged to follow his instructions.

- **Departmental objectives differ from project objectives.** For example, a finance controller is required to participate in the development of the business case of a large companywide project. However, his direct boss, the chief financial officer (CFO), is under pressure to finalize the annual accounts, a key objective for the finance department. Despite tight deadlines, the project is at the mercy of the CFO's willingness to cooperate.

Without strong and clear governance, projects may cause battles for resources and attention, leading the project to delays and, eventually, failure.

To address these forces, senior leaders need to play a key role in supporting the project, through the steering committee, and providing the means and time required to complete the work. For the success of large, complex projects, senior leaders must liberate the selected team members from their day-to-day responsibilities as much as possible, preferably completely. If the project is of outmost importance, then senior leaders should not hesitate to dedicate their best and most talented resources.

TOOLS AND TECHNIQUES

Checklist: How to select the right executive sponsor

Usually the executive sponsor is selected organically, according to where the project originates—it can be marketing, IT, finance, a business unit, regulatory, strategy, and so forth. However, a few criteria may override the project origins when you are choosing the right person. The sponsor should have the following attributes:

- Has the highest vested interest in the outcome of the project

- Is owner of a budget, both in financial and in human resources

- Is high enough up in the organization to be able to make budget decisions

- Is ready to dedicate at least one day each week to support the project

- Preferably has a good understanding of the technical matters of the project

Checklist: Best practices for establishing and running a steering committee

- Does the project require major investments and affect large segments (or the entirety) of the organization, region, or country?

- Have you identified which resources, departments, suppliers, partners, and so on, need to contribute to the project? If any of them have an involvement of 10 percent or more of the total project budget, they should be part of the steering committee.

- Are the members of the steering committee budget owners (of resources, capital, etc.) with enough decision-making power?

- How much momentum does the project need? The greater the pressure for progress, the more frequently the steering committee should meet.

The power of habits

There is no doubt that projects are agents of transformation, but a good project manager should establish habits for the projects and team. Film director David Lynch told Charlie Rose, "Some people have heard the story that I went to Bob's Big Boy for seven years every day at 2:30 and had the same thing."[3] For example, establish project team meetings at the same time, on the same day of the week. Follow a similar habit for the meetings with the executive sponsor. Or hold weekly communications at the same time, on the same day. When you put some order in lives of people working in your team, they will be free mentally to go find the best solutions.

Eleven tough questions to ask yourself as a project sponsor (or steering committee member)

1. **Accountability:** Who's responsible for the project?

2. **Competencies:** Do we have the competencies to sponsor the project (and do you know what they are)?

3. **Commitment:** Can I dedicate enough time to support the project team (two to four hours per week)? If not, why?

4. **Alignment:** Is the executive team 100 percent supportive of the project? If not, why not?

5. **Purpose:** Why are we doing this project?

6. **Benefits:** What are the benefits, and what is the impact?

7. **Value:** Have the benefits been quantified? If not, why not?

8. **Belief:** Are we certain the project will achieve the benefits? If not, why not?

9. **Prioritization:** Are we going to do the most consequential or profitable things first?

10. **Project manager:** Have I selected a project manager who is well prepared and a good fit for the purpose? If not, why not?

11. **Resources:** Have we dedicated enough resources of an appropriate quality to the project? If not, why not?

Putting this building block into practice

A project should have the most appropriate executive sponsor—one person, not many. This person will be accountable for the outcome of the project; it should become a priority for the sponsor.

As leaders, you and your colleagues need to define and agree on a strong governance structure to ensure the commitment of the organization. You should also establish clear roles and responsibilities. All contributors must know the role they play and how much time and resources are requested from their teams.

Finally, you need to appoint the right hierarchical level of decision makers—senior roles, often budget owners—to the steering committee and determine the frequency of their meetings. A steering committee should meet at least once a month. For a strategic project, meeting every two weeks will create momentum. The more frequent the meetings, the greater the pressure.

Key questions to ask

- Has a capable executive sponsor been appointed?

- Does the executive sponsor believe in the project? Is the person ready to dedicate sufficient time for support and oversight?

- Is the executive ready and able to dedicate enough time (for a strategic project, between two and four hours per week, depending on the project phase) to drive the project to success?

- Has the project's steering committee been established, including the frequency with which it will meet?

- Are the appointed and selected members committed to participate?

Resources: *Who* will manage the project, and *which* skills are needed to deliver the project?

Projects are delivered by people. Ensuring that the organization has the requisite resources—with the right skills, expertise, and experience to implement the project—is an essential responsibility of senior management.

Project managers need to develop strong leadership skills, especially for complex and cross-functional projects. These require pulling resources from across the organization and changing the status quo. In fact, the best project managers are not only leaders but also entrepreneurs and owners—they are the CEOs of their projects.

Marshall Goldsmith, the world's number one executive coach, told me, "Executives tend to see project managers as technical experts: very tactical people, focused on the detail challenges of the project. Modern leadership is moving into facilitation. The best CEOs I have coached are great facilitators. Therefore, the project managers of the future will have to become project leaders, strong in facilitation, rather than technical experts."[4]

Since around 2010, we have seen the focus shifting from the original hard skills of project management (scope, planning, scheduling, and estimation) to soft skills (leadership, stakeholder management, and communication). A good project manager can navigate the organization, motivate the team, sell the project's benefits to the key stakeholders, and deliver within scope, on time, and within budget. A successful project manager needs to be proficient at other skills:

- Understanding the strategic and business aspects of the project

- Influencing and persuading stakeholders at all levels

- Leading in a matrix organization

- Creating a high-performing team from a group of individuals

- Motivating and providing feedback to the project team

- Monitoring the progress of the project work

Unfortunately, good project managers are scarce, and since companies have many strategic projects, such projects are often led by managers lacking some of the necessary qualifications.

It is up to the executive sponsor or the project selection committee, preferably with the support of the PMO, to appoint the project manager. Selecting the right individual with the right skills and experience to lead a project team is a critical success factor. Yet many organizations struggle to understand and recruit on the basis of anything more than technical skill or to differentiate between different styles of project manager and different projects. Moreover, executives often see leading a high-profile project as a development opportunity for high-potential managers. Managers may be assigned to lead a large strategic project to get exposure to top management. While they may build complementary skills not required in a line function, the problem is that they don't see projects as a long-term career, and they are usually uninterested in learning about project management in more depth.

Resources and project staffing

The goal of project staffing is to make certain that the project has sufficient staff with the right skills, relevant experience, and enough availability required to carry out the project successfully. Project roles, responsibilities,

Public-sector procurement

In the public sector, the importance of recruitment is well recognized. Projects carried out by governments rely heavily on external experts: contractors, engineers, consultants, and so on. Increasingly, however, government civil service is recognizing that it is very difficult to be an *intelligent* client on many of these projects without a substantial internal resource of knowledgeable individuals. Without these key individuals, how can you identify what you need, contract it from the private sector, oversee what the contractor delivers, and assure good quality and value for the money in the outcome?

Smart governments are modernizing their procurement practices. The UK government's publication "Project Delivery Capability Framework" provides a common language to describe job roles and the knowledge, skills, and abilities needed to perform project work across all areas of public projects.[5] In 2018, the European Commission published its project management methodology guide to enable project teams to manage their projects effectively and deliver solutions and benefits to their organizations and stakeholders in both the public and the private sectors.[6]

The problem of procurement in public-sector projects is so widely known that it hardly needs to be illustrated with an example, but a brief

and skills are the key elements to be considered. Surprisingly, many organizations launch projects without doing a capacity check before confirming the initiative.

If the right resources and competencies are not available in the organization, they can either be developed through training or be acquired externally. Often, the best and most experienced staff (e.g., developers) are booked on other tasks and projects. If their contribution is not suitably planned, the project is going to suffer. Lack of availability of required resources leads to delays and frequently to project failure.

one might provide some insight. Construction of the Elbphilharmonie Hamburg reached a level of complexity that was apparently too much for the state to handle. In 2007, the construction was scheduled to be finished by 2010, with an estimated cost of €77 million. Construction officially ended in October 2016, at a cost of €789 million. As this example shows, slimmed-down administrations are barely capable of efficiently controlling construction projects, and supervisory boards staffed according to the proportions of political power fail when it comes to monitoring projects. Power and decision-making end up in the hands of the vendors of the project, who can take advantage of the situation by charging significantly more than what was initially planned for their work, at the cost of public funds.

On the other end of the spectrum, the Sichuan-Shanghai Natural Gas Pipeline Mega Project in China is an amazing example of how to successfully run a large state project. The Chinese authorities established strict bidding and qualification processes to select the best contractors. All documents related to bidding were issued and reviewed by experts. The state prioritized securing quality of resources. Eighty-nine external supervisors were hired just to train all 4,079 project members on quality, health, safety, and management. This megaproject was delivered in only twenty-seven months.

Beyond availability, a key aspect of project success is team commitment. As mentioned earlier, project team members often have other responsibilities besides their contribution to the project. Commitment to the project is never a given, especially because employees are often asked to join in such a way that it is difficult for them to refuse (we have all received an email that asks us to "kindly" agree to something but where in reality we have little choice). Team members are often working for free or giving up some of their private time—they will only contribute at a high level if they believe they're part of an amazing project.

Procuring external resources

Do not overlook the importance of your recruitment and staffing strategy in projects. Projects are temporary and tend to have novel components that drive the need to hire external capabilities. Consultancies can provide advice and resources to organizations carrying out projects. It is usually cheaper to engage external people for a project rather than permanently hire internal staff. Important projects, such as M&As, require significant involvement of consultants and third parties, often reaching up to 30 to 40 percent of the total resources in the acquisition project. The larger the amount or the higher the dependency on external resources, the more attention the project manager needs to pay to procurement.

The number of external parties a project uses should be determined by the competencies needed to deliver the project. No matter how many outside people are brought in, the key is to ensure that they feel part of the team and are overseen by the project manager rather than being treated as independent workers with little commitment or stake in the project.

High-performing project teams

One of the most overused words in organizations is *teams*. Very often, what is referred to as a team is a group of individuals working occasionally on the project with different degrees of commitment and dedication. Research shows that if you look at various individuals working on a given project, the best worker will be ten times more effective than the worst. Ten times better sounds good until you learn that the highest-performing teams are *two thousand* times more efficient than the worst. We often assume the secret to an incredible project team is a group of superstars, but the good news is that this isn't the case. Research shows that "real teams" allow normal individuals to do extraordinary things.

Charles Duhigg, author of *Smarter Faster Better*, talks about five key items that help to make real teams:[7]

- **Purpose:** Does the project have a strong purpose? And does it mean something important to each member of the team?

- **Contribution:** Does everyone have a role in which they perform at their best?

- **Psychological safety:** Can anyone in the team take a risk or speak up openly without feeling insecure or afraid to be punished?

- **Camaraderie:** Can everyone count on one another to do high-quality work on time?

- **Recognition:** Does everyone get recognition for their contribution?

The project manager and the executive sponsor must understand what goes into making a high-performing team. Effective teams don't just happen: group performance is based on instituting shared trust and respect, an understanding of the individuals and their different backgrounds, and agreement on a common purpose.

Project teams often miss the mark on high productivity because their leaders don't build this foundation in the early stages of project. The best project leaders set aside time for the team members to become acquainted with one another, participate in setting project goals, hold each other accountable for meeting these goals, build trust across the team, and establish the ground rules for team behavior. An important aspect to consider when forming the team is that the most engaged members of a project often joined the project voluntarily. Take advantage of these members' enthusiasm; it will be contagious.

TOOLS AND TECHNIQUES

Dedication and commitment

As an executive sponsor, you can ask the project manager two questions to help assess whether the project is in good hands:

How much of your time do you dedicate to this project? Strategic projects require 100 percent dedication. Anything below that can lead to distraction and to a reduction in the pressure on the project. Project managers are often asked to lead several projects simultaneously. In my experience, it is hard to lead more than three important projects at the same time, and it is difficult to manage an important project while having a full-time position in the day-to-day activities of the organization.

How committed are you to the success of the project? Since every project faces some challenges, if the project manager and team members are not committed, the project will most likely be a total failure. A great example of this positive thinking is Alan Mulally, the project manager in charge of building the Boeing 777, a massive undertaking in the worst circumstances, after the terrorist attacks of September 11, 2001, and with Boeing struggling to survive. Yet his strong commitment and full-time dedication drove a project of ten thousand team members to create one of the most advanced aircraft in the world.

FIGURE 6-3

Dedication and commitment matrix

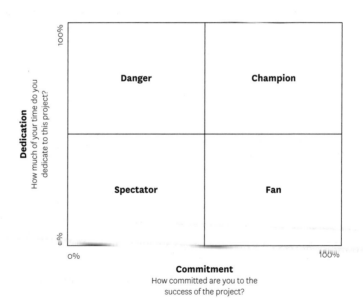

The steering committee can use the dedication and commitment matrix to assess how engaged the project manager and the executive sponsor are (figure 6-3). If either of them is a fan or a spectator, the lack of commitment to a project can quickly spread to the rest of the team. When conviction or morale drop significantly, the sponsor should intervene and find ways to restore confidence, either by taking corrective actions or, eventually, by replacing the project manager. When the project manager and the executive sponsor don't dedicate enough time to the project, to be available for the team and to follow up on progress, the pressure and focus needed to deliver the project will vanish.

Eleven tough questions to ask yourself as project manager

1. **Competencies:** Do I have the competencies to lead the project (and do I know what they are)?

2. **Commitment:** Will I dedicate more than 50 percent of my time to lead the project? If not, why not?

3. **Sponsor:** Have I ensured that the executive sponsor is committed and dedicates enough hours per week to the project? If not, why not?

4. **Purpose:** Why are we doing this project?

5. **Believe:** Are we 100 percent sure the project will be successful? If not, why not?

6. **Benefits:** What are the benefits, and what is the impact?

7. **Value:** Have the benefits been quantified? If not, why not?

8. **Prioritization:** Are we going to do the most consequential or profitable things first?

9. **Resources:** Have we dedicated enough internal or external resources of an appropriate quality to the project? If not, why not?

10. **Completeness:** Have we forgotten anything critical?

11. **Evidence:** How can we be sure if the plan is working? How can I check it out?

High-performing team

A high-performing team is a group of talented and motivated professionals working together to achieve the project's goal. They assure the top levels of performance and productivity. Here is a practical checklist you can apply to create a high-performing team for your project:

1. **Introduction:** The team has the time to meet and get to know each other.

2. **Goal-setting:** All team members participate in establishing the project and team goals.

3. **Ground rules:** The team has defined expectations about team behavior and values, which have been written down and shared.

4. **Team identity:** The team can describe its primary purpose and expected goals. Wins and losses will be team wins and losses, not individual wins and losses.

5. **Contribution:** The members have responsibilities in their area of expertise and are aware of how they can actively contribute to achieving the goals of the project.

6. **Problem-solving and risk-taking:** The team has a problem-solving culture and is encouraged to take risks. Individuals are not blamed or punished.

7. **Joint decision-making:** The team is capable of making decisions that are backed by the entire team in a timely manner.

8. **Conflict-handling:** Team members feel free to voice conflicting points of view, including disagreement with the project leaders. Conflicts are resolved in a timely and direct fashion, without damage to relationships.

9. **Feedback:** Both the team and the individuals receive feedback regularly, and there is a mindset of continuous improvement.

10. **Leadership:** The project manager and executive sponsor embody and model the high-performing team rules.

Responsibility assignment matrix

A responsibility assignment matrix is a simple tool used to cross-match key activities with the various roles in a project (see table 6-1).[8] It assigns the following levels of responsibility:

- **Responsible:** person responsible for carrying out the activity

- **Accountable:** the ultimate owner of the activity

- **Consulted:** individuals or groups that need to be consulted and provide input

- **Informed:** individuals or groups that ought to be informed

The matrix has several uses. It helps ensure that things are done, because tasks and activities are assigned to particular individuals. It underlines the difference and the significance between the person who does each task (is responsible) and the person who makes sure that the activity (or the project as a whole) meets the required standard. Finally, the matrix helps keep communication and decision-making lean by keeping the right people involved in the right ways.

TABLE 6-1

Example of a responsibility assignment matrix

	Laura	Alexander	Selma	Lucas
Define project purpose and business case	A	R	I	I
Appoint project manager	A	I	I	I
Define scope and requirements	C	R	C	I
Create project plan	I	A	R	C
Test solution	I	A	C	R
Launch solution	I	A	R	C
Track benefits	A/R	R	I	I

Abbreviations: A, accountable; R, responsible; I, informed; C, consulted.

Putting this building block into practice

At the beginning of a project, both the executive sponsor and senior management need to implement several steps:

- Assess and confirm that the organization has the people and budget capacity to work on the project.

- Ensure that the competencies and knowledge required to develop the solution are there.

- Anticipate potential bottlenecks by freeing up people or by engaging external capacity and expertise.

- Establish a standard process to appoint the best-prepared project managers to lead the project.

Organizations must also develop a framework for building project management competency and an official career path to help project managers grow in the role and to encourage the best project leaders to remain in the organization. Organizations should also find ways to motivate external parties to stay committed and engaged to deliver according to the specifications of the project within budget.

Key questions to ask

- Does the organization have sufficient resources with the required skills, and will it dedicate them to the project?

- Has a professional, qualified, and committed project manager been appointed to lead the project?

- If the project needs external experts, are there incentives and penalties in place to ensure they deliver the project successfully?

Stakeholders: *Who* will benefit from and be affected by the project?

Stakeholders are those who have a stake or an interest in the project. Or they will be affected in some way by the project and so usually have an interest in influencing it.

As we saw in chapter 5, key stakeholders should be asked about their expectations on the project outcomes. In the end, stakeholder satisfaction is the ultimate success criterion: if the project brings benefits to the key stakeholders, it will be considered successful. The expectations of all stakeholders, however, will rarely coincide. Sometimes, if they have the power to do so, some individuals or groups will seek to influence the project to align with their own expectations or even bring it to a halt. There's a common aphorism in the project world: "There is always someone who will be happy if your project fails. Find them and understand why."

Pressure from stakeholders can lead to change in the project scope and increase the complexity of the management task, jeopardizing cost and causing uncertainty. Even if you have a well-defined project with a clear implementation plan, if the views of the stakeholders are not properly addressed, the project is likely to eventually face resistance. The larger the project, the more stakeholders there will likely be. On a sizable, publicly funded project, it is easy to identify more than a hundred stakeholder groups, all with different levels of involvement, expectations, and power to influence the project. The more stakeholders, the more communication and change management activities are required of a project manager.

The executive sponsor and the project manager must be able to identify, engage, and communicate with stakeholders of varying degrees of influence and interest. Stakeholder influence is often weak in the early stages of the project, when the project's purpose and objectives are still in development. When the project kicks off and starts to be planned, stakeholder influence increases. When the project goes into implementation and the changes introduced become visible and start having an impact on some of the stakeholders, resistance reaches its peak. The executive sponsor should influence the other senior leaders and other senior external stakeholders affected by the project; meanwhile, the project manager should take care of the rest, involving the sponsor when required. The project steering committee is one of the best places to discuss stakeholders' influence, expectations, and measures to tackle resistance.

Internal and external stakeholders

There are two groups of project stakeholders: internal and external. Identifying and managing internal stakeholders is often more challenging than the same tasks for external groups. Most commonly, the internal stakeholders are the employees directly affected by the project outcomes, but they can also be the senior leaders of business units, departments, or functions or anyone else in the organization. Not surprisingly, when you are gathering input on the different needs and expectations for the project, it is difficult to find a solution that satisfies everyone. Some of the toughest projects have an impact on working relationships, involve restructuring, or have unions as significant stakeholders.

TABLE 6-2

Common internal and external stakeholders of projects

Internal	External
Project team	Suppliers
Project manager	Vendors
Project sponsor	Consultants
Steering committee	Customers
Employees	Regulators
Management	Financial institutions
Executives	Unions
Board of directors	Media
Company owners or investors	Communities
	Local governments
	Nonprofits
	Citizens
	Society

External stakeholders are the individuals or organizations that are not part of the organization but take part in or have an interest in the project. Often they do not participate in the day-to-day activities of the project, but their actions could eventually influence the outcome.

The stakeholders in a project vary with the type of project and the industry. Table 6-2 presents a list of the most common stakeholders.

Stakeholder analysis and stakeholder management can be time-consuming. In large and complex projects, such as M&As, you cannot talk to everybody touched by the project or involve each person all in the project activities. Therefore, to successfully implement a project and achieve its goals, the executive sponsor and the project manager must strike the right balance between keeping stakeholders involved and making unbiased decisions.

Neglect key stakeholder groups at your peril

The Cross City Tunnel project in Sydney, Australia, is a painful case study in project failure due to mismanaging stakeholders. As with many large projects that run into trouble, a whole smorgasbord of issues undermined the feasibility and the financial business case, but stakeholder management clearly stands out. Faced with significant cost overruns, the Roads and Transport Authority found itself boxed in. To maintain its original pledge of "no cost to the government," it opted simply to increase the toll charges for the planned users, thereby immediately undermining the likely volume of traffic and the economic model for the tunnel. The New South Wales auditor-general's audit of the project was less than enthusiastic: "By the time the tunnel opened, the toll had reached nearly $35 [Australian] a week for a commuter using it in both directions. It is reasonable to assume that a significant proportion of potential users will have been put off. This may detract from the objective of removing traffic from the surface streets."[9]

Protecting one group of stakeholders at the expense of another may solve an immediate crisis but is also likely to store up trouble for later in the project. Stakeholder management, which always requires compromise, depends on transparent and equitable sharing of both pains and gains.

The key benefit of stakeholder analysis is to bring clarity to complex situations and a better understanding of the expectations of those interested in, or affected by, the project. The added value very much comes from the discipline of undertaking the process. The results of the stakeholder analysis are key inputs to the change management building block described later in the book.

TOOLS AND TECHNIQUES

The engagement triple constraint

The last triple constraint concerns engagement in the project. It should be used by the project manager and executive sponsor to assess the impact of changes to any of the three elements of engagement (figure 6-4). The tool will help them plan possible corrective measures to maintain a high level of engagement around the project among both the team and the stakeholders.

The engagement triple constraint is composed of the following elements:

- **Alignment:** the emotional connection of the people—the project team and stakeholders—with the project, determined by the project's purpose and the team's passion for it. The lesser the alignment, the more likely people will see the project as just another job.

- **Dedication:** the time dedicated by the team and stakeholders to the project; it is always better that resources are 100 percent dedicated to stay focused on getting it done, however, this is often the exception.

- **Recognition:** a critical element for keeping the individuals and teams engaged. They need to feel that they are contributing to the project, that they play a role in its development, and that they are recognized for it.

FIGURE 6-4

The engagement triple constraint

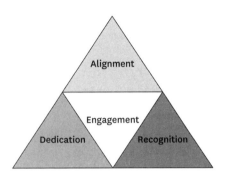

As with the iron triangle, every time one of these factors changes in the project, the other two must be adjusted if the level of engagement is to be maintained. So, for example, if the project team disagrees on the project purpose or if the purpose is unclear, this alignment element will probably affect the dedication of the team. These conditions influence the engagement and performance of the group, which will be reflected in the performance of the project.

Stakeholder analysis matrix

This matrix is most frequently used for weighing and balancing the interests of stakeholders. Whenever possible, the project manager should address their needs to meet the project's objectives. Unlike the risk appraisal (covered later in the book), which should be carried out with a larger group, stakeholder analysis should be conducted in a smaller group— usually just the project sponsor and the project manager—because some of the discussions can be quite sensitive. This group should initially assess the stakeholders during the preparation phase. After identifying the major stakeholders, the group categorizes each one according to three dimensions. The first is the level of impact or interest in the project or its outcome. The second is the level of power or influence that the stakeholder

FIGURE 6-5

Stakeholder matrix

Mapping stakeholders can help project sponsors and managers visualize opportunities and risks for the project. In this case, the sponsor may want to focus on engaging Alex more in the project, or persuading Jim or Anna on the benefits of the project.

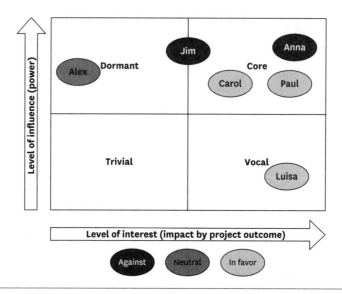

could have on the project. This dimension is usually linked to the power of the individual or group in the organization. The third is the stakeholder's current position toward the project.

The analysis can be done regularly to track the changes in stakeholders' attitudes over time. Figure 6-5 is an example of a stakeholder matrix that you can use.

The following are some communication and persuasion strategies that you may wish to adopt to deal with the various groups.

- **Core (high power, high interest):** When a core stakeholder is in favor of the project, you must keep the individual informed and provide regular updates on the project. Core stakeholders are great ambassadors of your project; use them to lobby other groups, make sure they voice their support, and consider including them on your steering committee. On the other hand, core stakeholders who are against the project present an important risk. Don't avoid them, however; instead, pay attention to them. Find out what is important to them, help them out, and win their favor. Use favorable stakeholders to try to convince resistant ones of the benefits of the project and to counter any negative influence that dissenting stakeholders may have on other groups. Sometimes just by listening to people and involving them, you may turn detractors into promoters of the project.

- **Dormant (high power, low interest):** High-powered stakeholders with low interest can be an opportunity or a threat in waiting. Depending on the project's outcome, they could become sudden opponents or supporters of the project. Meet with these dormant stakeholders and find out what is important to them. If the project is likely to have a positive effect for them, make sure they are aware of this possibility. Monitor that changes to the project do not suddenly increase the level of unfavorable interest.

- **Vocal (low power, high interest):** Although vocal stakeholders are less dangerous to the success of the project, it is important to consider them. If they are in favor of the project, they can become strong allies. They can help promote the project with other stakeholders. Keep them informed of the progress and involved where possible, and ask for their advice. If the stakeholder looks at the project unfavorably, you can always talk to them, but don't spend too much time trying to convince them. Eventually you can ask the executive sponsor to take a firm line.

- **Trivial (low power, low interest):** Trivial stakeholders are the least relevant and risky for the project. You can always keep them informed, but don't waste much time and resources on those with little power and little connection with the project.

Role-based and agenda-based stakeholders

Another effective way to analyze stakeholders comes from project management expert Louise Worsley. She describes two distinct types of stakeholders:[10]

- **Role-based stakeholders:** described according to function, whether the stakeholder is an individual (sponsor, team member) or an organization (client, contractor, investment company). Managing role-based stakeholders effectively involves clear lines of responsibility and communication, effective contracts, and well-understood processes for change management and dispute resolution.

- **Agenda-based stakeholders:** largely external to the project (elected officials, competitors, end users, others connected to the work of the project or the final asset). These stakeholders' attitudes and behavior may strongly influence how the project needs to be conducted and its subsequent success.

A project with numerous role-based stakeholders will definitely be manageable even if it requires considerable brainpower, time, effort, and attention to detail. A project with numerous agenda-based stakeholders, on the other hand, is more complex; predicting the outcome of actions or decisions of these projects will be challenging. These complex projects still require planning, time, effort, and attention to detail, but you also need to be ready to respond to the unexpected, to compromise, and to recognize that success is partly out of your control.

Putting this building block into practice

As a project manager, start by identifying the key stakeholders and categorizing them using the stakeholder matrix. Understand their needs and expectations for the project. While categorizing stakeholders is useful and important for planning different communication and management strategies, beware the danger of stereotyping individuals, and never forget that their attitudes and behaviors can and will change throughout the stages of the project. Champions may become opponents, and vice versa, if they are not managed consistently and sympathetically. Aligning stakeholders to actively support the project throughout its entire life cycle until completion is paramount to project success but can be a daunting task. The project manager needs to engage the executive sponsor, who plays a major role in stakeholder management.

Key questions to ask

- How many key stakeholders does the project have?

- Can you identify any major resistance that might bring the project down? How would you address it?

- Can you identify any significant support that you can leverage to increase buy-in of your project?

- How will you adapt your stakeholder strategy to the different stages in the project?

In this chapter, we have learned how to address the three building blocks connected by the human factor. You are now aware of the importance of the executive sponsor in overseeing and supporting the project and what is expected from such a crucial role. Then we looked at how to staff your team, including the project manager, the project personnel, and the external contractors, and the importance of creating a high-performing team. Last, we learned how proactive stakeholder management is one of the most important tasks for today's project managers and executive sponsors. Project beneficiaries, the executive sponsor, the project manager, and the project team members are all individuals and groups driven by values, personalities, ethics, perceptions, and personal interests. To different extents, these unique people bear greatly on the implementation of the project and determine if the project has been successful. Seek to engage them in the project at every turn.

In the next chapter, we will look at the third and final domain, the *creation*, which is what people usually think of when they imagine project management. It is the visible part of the project iceberg—scope, requirements, deliverables, outputs, plans, risks, and change management.

7.

The Creation

Deliverables, Plan, Change

We have seen that projects today are often large and complex, carried out in an uncertain and fast-changing world, and subject to many forms of execution risk. Failure to define what is (and isn't) included in the scope of the project leads to unplanned or unnecessary work, schedule and budget overruns, or benefits that go unrealized. Failure to plan the project carefully, or the wrong planning approach, leads to rework and delays. Failure to precisely communicate the plan and address stakeholder needs leads to confusion about, and resistance to, the project. In this chapter, you will gain the tools to overcome these pitfalls and to develop a successful project.

The **creation domain** covers three building blocks that build the "visible" part of the project (figure 7-1):

- **Deliverables:** what the project will produce, build or deliver; the deliverables are defined by the key stakeholders and project team and will generate the benefits of the project

- **The plan:** how the deliverables of the project will be developed; the plan determines when the work will be carried out and who will do it

- **The change:** how the project will engage stakeholders to support the project and how the risk of the project will be managed

The creation includes both the hard aspects of project management (definitions, scope, designs, schedules, plans, milestones, costs, and risks)

FIGURE 7-1

The creation domain

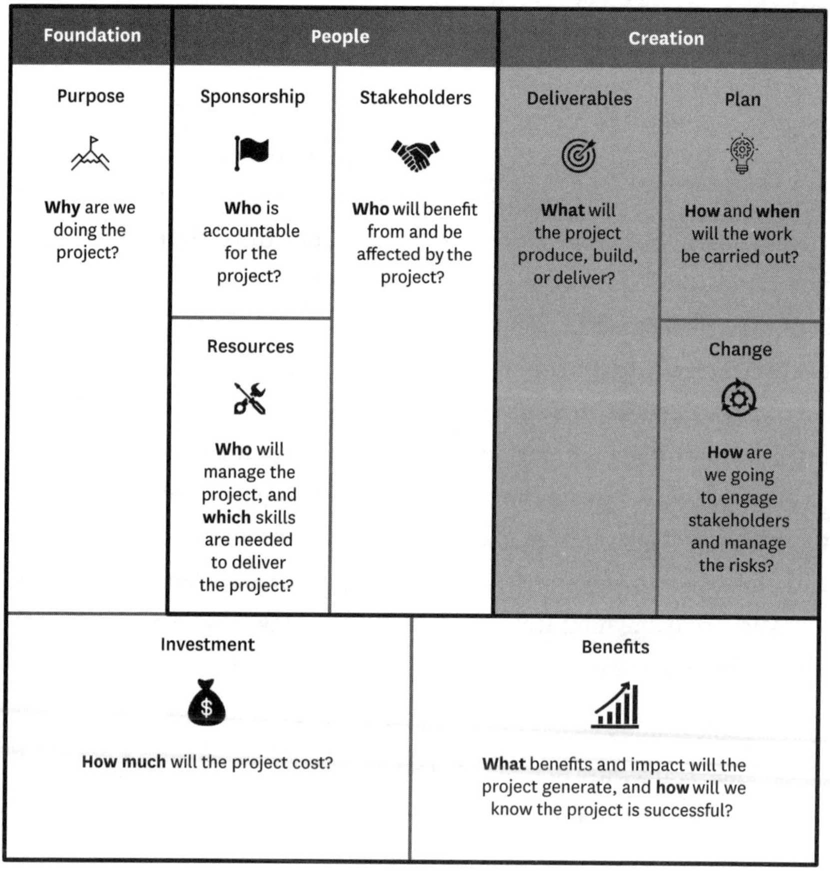

Foundation	People		Creation	
Purpose	**Sponsorship**	**Stakeholders**	**Deliverables**	**Plan**
Why are we doing the project?	**Who** is accountable for the project?	**Who** will benefit from and be affected by the project?	**What** will the project produce, build, or deliver?	**How** and **when** will the work be carried out?
	Resources			**Change**
	Who will manage the project, and **which** skills are needed to deliver the project?			**How** are we going to engage stakeholders and manage the risks?
Investment			**Benefits**	
How much will the project cost?			**What** benefits and impact will the project generate, and **how** will we know the project is successful?	

and the soft aspects (motivation, empathy, training, coaching, communication, and change management). Addressing all the elements at the right time and with enough depth will increase the chances of project success.

Deliverables: *What* will the project produce, build, or deliver?

Projects exist to develop something—often something new—in the form of outputs and deliverables. These deliverables should lead to the achievement of the project's purpose and benefits. Although they are related, a project's deliverables (e.g., the design and features of a new company website) and its benefits (e.g., capturing additional business) should be distinguished.

Imagining, defining, understanding, and agreeing what the project will consist of and deliver is one raison d'être of project management. It is also one of the main challenges.

The what of the project is also known as the *scope*. Other commonly used terms include *solution*, *specifications*, *detailed requirements*, *design*, *functionality*, or *stakeholder expectations*. Defining scope involves setting the boundaries (what is included in, and excluded from, the project) so that all activities within the project's scope (and only those activities) are included in the project plan.

A project's scope should not be confused with the project's benefits. For example, the scope of a new university auditorium will entail the dimensions, the seating capacity, the building materials, the technology, and so on. The benefits, however, might be an improved learning experience and, ultimately, an increase in the number of enrolled students.

Development of scope is an important step in all project management methodologies. For projects whose ultimate outcome is clear (those with a low level of uncertainty, such as a property development initiative), project leaders can define the scope accurately and in detail in the early stages of the project. For projects with more uncertainty (e.g., a digital transformation initiative), the scope will only emerge fully once work has begun. For the most uncertain projects, duration and costs estimated at the beginning of the project will need to be limiting or emergent. *Limiting* implies that the senior team will agree on a budget for the work and expect the project team to deliver as much functionality or as many elements of the asset as they can for that budget. *Emergent* denotes that the senior team will agree on a budget to cover a period, say, twelve months, and then revisit the project both during that initial period and again near the end of the period to set a further budget for the next defined period.

As we saw in chapter 2, there is always uncertainty when you are starting a project. The level of uncertainty about the scope is the key criterion in the decision to use traditional predictive project management methods or agile approaches.

Traditional project management: Imagining and defining the outcome you want to create

Traditional project management methods involve defining the scope as a prerequisite for drafting the project plan, estimating the time and costs, and starting the implementation. This approach makes intuitive sense: let's not start rolling out the new organization until we know precisely how it is going to look. Or let's not start building a house until we know the detailed floor plan and the materials that will be used. But when levels of uncertainty are high, determining the project scope is an educated guess. This decision remains one of the most difficult tasks in project management.

Usually, the work and analysis around the scope is collected in the **scope statement**, which describes the details of the project outputs. Start with the purpose. Ask yourself, What concept is going to solve our problem? What product will help us capture the opportunity? Is it a new process, a new system, a new culture, or something else? Deliverables are typically included in the scope statement, as well as the acceptance criteria the deliverables must meet. It also sets out assumptions, constraints, and project exclusions, which identify and explicitly state what is out of the scope of the project.

A clear and comprehensive scope statement is useful in managing stakeholder expectations. Its level of detail will be a factor in how well the team can subsequently control changes to the scope; we cannot easily control something that has not been adequately defined. The more precise we can be with our definition at the highest level, the easier it is to undertake the next step: splitting the scope into the work breakdown structure.

A **work breakdown structure** (**WBS**) is a comprehensive, systematic means of defining project work. The PMI defines the WBS as a product-oriented "family tree" of project components; this structure organizes and defines the total scope of the project. Each descending level represents an increasingly detailed definition of a project component.[1] The lowest level of the chart will describe an element of work that can be defined and the responsibility allocated to a single person. The project scope consists of the total sum of all the elements of the WBS. Conversely, an element that is not contained in the WBS is not a part of the project and is referred to as *out of scope*.

Generating a WBS is a consensus activity, ideally involving (as appropriate) the executive sponsor, the project team, key stakeholders, suppliers, external experts, and, possibly, key customers. You're aiming to deconstruct the project into discrete component activities that are small enough to be assigned to a single responsible person (the owner) and for which you can meaningfully measure progress. The WBS looks like a family tree, with each generation being called a level (figure 7-2). The top level is usually designated "level 0," the next one down "level 1," and so on.

Each task owner is responsible for defining the task completion criteria, determining who should participate in the task, and making sure that it is completed successfully. Once you have defined the WBS of your project, each task owner will estimate the time and duration that each element will take to be developed, and this information will be the main input for the project plan.

Of course, while the WBS is an essential element to provide stability to a project, change in the project is usually inevitable as activities are happening in a dynamic environment. Consideration should also be given on how to introduce changes to the WBS (see the section titled "Managing changes to the *what*").

FIGURE 7-2

Work breakdown structure (WBS): Renovation of Notre-Dame Cathedral

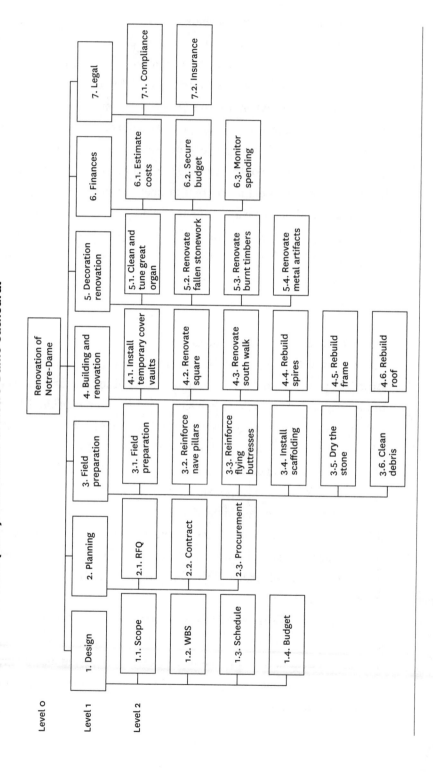

Steps to build the WBS of your project

1. Gather the executive sponsor, project team, experts, key stakeholders, suppliers, and, if appropriate, some key customers for a detailed design workshop. It should not be rushed; for small projects, you should take at least half a day.

2. Prepare a whiteboard, and distribute Post-it notes for everyone.

3. Write down the project concept at the top of the board, and let everyone define elements, one per Post-it note, and place them on the whiteboard.

4. Group the notes according to categories. If several people come up with similar elements, that is a good sign: there is alignment on what the project should produce.

5. Under the top line, which lists the project concept, write down each of the main categories. Place the already-grouped Post-it notes below the appropriate category.

6. More levels of detail are generally required for projects that are larger or more risky.

7. Continue to break the work down until one owner can be assigned to each of the lowest-level elements. For each of these elements, the owner should estimate costs and be responsible for completion.

Agile methods: Developing the product backlog

When a project's scope is uncertain, adaptive project management methods are better suited than traditional project management methods. If you are creating a system from scratch, or if you have many uncertainties about your value proposition and functionalities, or if you don't know what to prioritize or what the customers want, then agile is a better choice.

Agile methods were created for software development. IT projects come with a unique set of uncertainty challenges because not only do the deliverables need to work, but also nobody knows which parts of the IT project are going to be the most valuable to users or customers until they try them out. If a traditional project is the equivalent of a journey from Cape Town, South Africa, to Washington, D.C. (for which the traveler can be provided with an itinerary and an arrival time), then an IT project is the exploration of a new region of jungle for which the explorer measures progress by how much ground is covered in a day.

Let's look at how the *what* is defined in a popular agile method, Scrum. The Scrum framework consists of three roles: the product owner (the client or sponsor), the Scrum master (similar to project manager, but that role is not recognized in the agile methodologies), and the developer (the engineer or the builder). Included in this method are four rituals: sprint planning, where *sprint* represents a period of work (e.g., one day's exploration of the jungle); daily Scrum (which bit of the jungle are we going to do today, and how far will we get?); sprint review (how much of the jungle have we now managed to cover?); and sprint retrospective (how effectively did we explore the jungle today?). The Scrum method also includes three artifacts (product backlog, sprint backlog, and potentially releasable product increment). As explained earlier, the product is the deliverable (e.g., an events management functionality added to an existing website). The **product backlog** is the product's parts that have yet to be developed (e.g., you have built the booking function but you still have to add the payment process). The **sprint backlog** is the list of features to be developed by the project team through sprints. A **potentially releasable product increment** is an improvement to the product that will allow the team to release the product to customers and users.

The product owner is responsible for defining the *what* of the project. This person describes, together with the team, the scope of the project in the form of the product backlog. One of the best rules of Scrum is also one of the simplest: a clear separation of scope (product backlog) from work (sprint backlog). Items in the product backlog can be anything: ideas, features, requirements, prototypes, documents, pictures—whatever you like. At some point, the team will analyze all the items, grouping them into user stories, which is a combination of features that describes the type of user, what they want, and why. Once the product backlog is determined, the developers decide which work gets done during each sprint, and how.

Managing changes to the what

Even if the scope has been defined well at the beginning of the project, there is a good chance that it will change during the life cycle of the project, thereby altering the duration, cost, plans, and benefits of the project. The more the scope changes, the more challenging it is to deliver the project successfully and according to the initial plan. In research my colleagues and I conducted, project professionals highlight "frequent changes in the requirements (scope) and timelines" as the number one challenge they face when implementing projects (figure 7-3).

Scope creep describes the tendency of stakeholders to increase an originally agreed-upon scope one element at a time without agreeing to a corresponding change in schedule or an increase in investment. Project leaders should resist scope creep. It will undermine your budget or force you to cut back on other aspects of the scope that were part of the original plan. In extreme cases, scope creep can leave you delivering an outcome that is completely out of balance with the original business case.

In rare cases, scope creep can operate in the opposite direction—when cost issues or political concerns slowly remove scope from a project until it loses its value. That was the case with the UK identity card scheme launched as a project in 2002. After the project began, other government departments as well as civil liberties groups whittled away at such features as iris scans and chip and PIN capabilities until the card offered little more than what a driver's license already did.

Traditional project management treats changing requirements as a sign of failure in up-front planning, but a change of scope is sometimes inevitable and should be treated as an opportunity. Try to lock down the scope as early as you can, but the project sponsor, acting on reasonable requests from stakeholders or intelligence and advice from the project manager, may sometimes decide to expand the scope if the added benefits outweigh the additional costs. You will need to accommodate other changes, with their requisite costs, if they substantially increase the chances of project

FIGURE 7-3

Top challenges to implementing projects

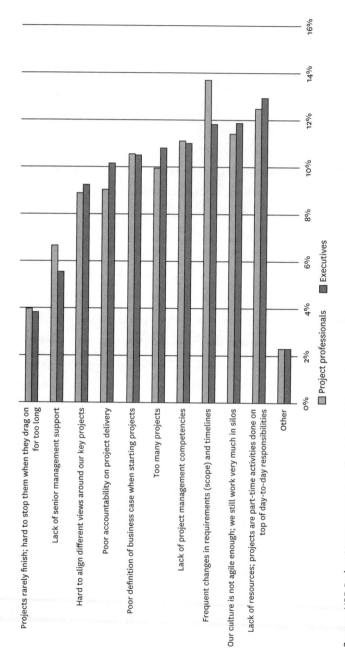

Source: HBR Project Management Handbook Project Expert Survey, July 2020, N = 728; and HBR Project Management Handbook Executive Survey, July 2020, N = 566

success, offer additional benefits, or are difficult to refuse, for political reasons. While scope creep is something to resist, managing the ongoing discussions of scope with stakeholders is an unavoidable and essential part of project management.

TOOLS AND TECHNIQUES

The **BOSCARD framework** (for background, objective, scope, constraints, assumptions, risks, and deliverables) was created in the 1980s by French multinational Capgemini. The framework consists of the following seven prompts to help you define the scope of your project:

- **Background:** Describe the relevant facts to show an understanding of the environment, political, business, and other contexts in which the project will be carried out.

- **Objective:** State the goals of the project, and demonstrate an understanding of its business rationale.

- **Scope:** Describe what the project will develop, and break its various stages down into milestones. Describe the resources that will be made available and the corresponding external partners, if applicable.

- **Constraints:** Describe the key challenges and roadblocks to be addressed in planning the project.

- **Assumptions:** State the key hypothesis that has been used to define the project rationale, objectives, plan, and budget. If assumptions change later, it might justify a renegotiation of the project.

- **Risks:** List the risks that may affect the realization of the objectives, the project's impact, or its timeline and finances.

- **Deliverables:** Describe the key elements that will be produced by the project and how they connect to each other and to the project objectives.

By addressing each area, you can be clear on what should be done (and what should not be done). Have an up-front discussion with the executive sponsor and key stakeholders about the boundaries of the project, and consider the following key components:

- **Scope description:** Is the scope clear, and does it include all the features and functions required to create the project deliverables?

- **Acceptance criteria:** Are you confident that the project team and stakeholders share the same criteria for determining the success of the project?

- **Deliverables:** What specific outputs are required at different phases of the project for it to progress?

- **Exclusions:** What functionality or outputs have you and the stakeholders agreed will be specifically excluded from the scope?

The traditional triple constraint, or iron triangle

As briefly described earlier, the triple constraint has historically represented the three major limitations on a project. The concept is widely used by project managers to keep projects on course and protect them from failure.

The traditional triple constraint is composed of these three considerations (figure 7-4):

- **Scope:** what the project will deliver. Requirements, functionality, specifications, and deliverables are all elements of the scope. As we have seen, the challenge is in defining the scope precisely in advance while knowing that it is likely to change over time.

- **Time:** how long it will take to complete the project. The time can also be referred to as the schedule or plan. Sometimes, the length of time is determined by a hard, predefined deadline.

- **Cost:** also known as budget. The budget is determined by the amount of work and investment needed to carry out the project. There may be an upper limit on how much can be spent to achieve the desired or defined results.

FIGURE 7-4

The traditional triple constraint

The triple constraint says that cost is a function of time and scope and that these three factors are related in a defined and predictable way. Ultimately, all three factors come together in the middle of the triangle to determine quality (figure 7-4). If we want to shorten the time while maintaining the scope and quality of a project, we will increase the cost. And if we want to add more functionality to the scope, we will increase the project cost or time. Every time a project manager is asked to change one or more of these three elements, the manager should analyze the consequences and present the trade-offs to the executive sponsor for validation before introducing the changes.

As mentioned in chapter 3, there are some flaws in this triple-constraint concept, which is why this book presents two additional triple constraints, one on benefits, and one on engagement.

Putting this building block into practice

At the beginning of the project, you as the project manager should gather the main stakeholders and key contributors together to define and agree on the scope in as detailed a manner as possible. Don't be afraid of taking extra days to address major uncertainties. A delay of one week during the scoping phase can avoid longer delays during implementation, when glitches may derail the whole project altogether.

Involve experts, stakeholders, and members of past project teams in early discussions to identify the key risks of the project. Don't forget to assess risks that the organization will bear if it invests in the project—or any risks that arise if the organization does *not* take on the project.

Some projects will have thousands of risks, so you don't want to make risk management too bureaucratic. Even if it is important to start broadly with the identification of risks, the focus should be on the most likely and most severe ones.

Once the project is underway, a regular discussion about emerging or changing risks can help you manage what's on the horizon.

Key questions to ask

- Has the *what* of the project been clearly defined? Do you know precisely how the outcome of the project should look?

- From zero to 100 percent, how certain are you that the scope will not change? Have you adapted your approach accordingly?

- Is there a clear process for managing changes to the *what*?

Plan: *How* and *when* will the work be carried out?

Project planning is the building block in which we define the *how* and *when* of the work, which will ultimately lead to the project deliverables and benefits. As mentioned in the previous section, the better defined the *what* of the project, the easier it will be to define the project plan.

Project planning dictates the time frames in which the project will be completed, the budgets and costs in terms of resource requirements, and the sequence of tasks to be completed. The plan specifies when activities should start or end in light of the project's expected duration, resource availability, target dates, or other time constraints. The complex and iterative task of planning a project typically involves several duties:

- Identifying all the tasks necessary to meet the scope and the WBS of the project

- Identifying and selecting the resources required to carry out the work

- Estimating the effort and cost of completing each task

- Balancing completion dates against the availability of the appropriate resources to complete all tasks within the available time

- Identifying dependencies between tasks so that they are scheduled in the correct sequence

- Identifying realistic start and end points for each given task

- Using critical-path analysis to identify tasks that are required for the success and timely completion of the project and that must begin and be completed on time

Moving from the WBS to the Gantt chart

Once completed, the project plan will be represented in the form of a Gantt chart. Named after Henry Gantt, who invented this tool in the 1910s, a Gantt chart illustrates a project schedule derived from the WBS. These charts, a useful way of showing what work is scheduled, can be used for planning projects of all sizes. Included in Gantt charts are several important pieces of project information:

- The start date and end date of the project

- Project tasks, their duration, and who is working on them

- Interdependencies between the tasks

- Milestones and deliverables

Today, most Gantt charts are created in Excel or with project management software. Figure 7-5 shows an example of the relationship between a WBS and a Gantt chart.

FIGURE 7-5

From work breakdown structure (WBS) to Gantt chart

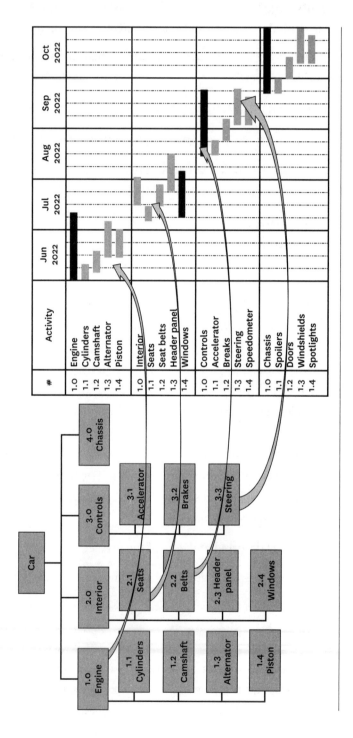

Life cycle phases of projects

The life cycle of a project varies with the industry and the organization, but most cycles have at least the following distinct phases: (1) initiation and conception, (2) planning, (3) execution and monitoring, and (4) handover and closure. Each phase will typically have a different level of cost and risk associated with it and will involve different teams or individuals. Thus the initiation and conception phase—the process of imagining and framing the project—will carry a far lower cost and represent a far easier process to pull the plug on than with the execution and monitoring phase, when teams are building or creating the asset. Project phases can be broken down further to reflect discrete elements in these main phases. For example, the mechanical and electrical phase of a construction project is the stage at which the main shell of the building is ready to receive the electricians, plumbers, and painters.

Don't imagine that the team members' work starts at launch; increasingly, project planners and designers include project delivery people or contractors in the initiation and planning phases to make sure what the planners are designing is actually buildable. The transitions between the phases are also often a source of risk because one team is likely to be passing the project over to another. The boundary between the execution and the handover phases—when the output or asset is handed over to the new owners, users, and operators—is particularly problematic.

Milestones and stage gates provide important and visible markers that a phase has been completed or that a new phase is about to start. The milestones enable you to generate and assure progress against your schedule, and the stage gates identify significant moments in the project's life when a go/no-go decision is made against an agreed-upon set of criteria. If used well, both these indicators provide useful opportunities to continue the health and the economic imperative of the project. If used poorly, they add cost and bureaucracy to the process but no benefits. Beware the achievements of milestones in name only, when the reality is that parts of the project marked as complete are actually far from it. And be wary of a stage-gate process that is so laborious and time-consuming or so dependent on absent decision makers that it simply adds time and cost to the endeavor.

Time in projects has peculiar qualities. A week at the beginning of a project is the same as a week at the end of the project, but they don't feel the same. Closer to the deadline, people tend to become nervous and make mistakes. The role of the project manager is like that of an orchestra conductor. They set the tempo and intermediary deadlines, which vary throughout the project life cycle.

Defining good plans

Different people and teams may be responsible for various project phases (and even within phases). Project sponsors change; key personnel leave or retire. In spite of this churn, the ongoing questions for any organization should always be these: Can we still deliver our project and produce the required outcome for the agreed-on investment within the agreed-on periods? Is what we are planning to deliver still relevant and valuable in the context of the world outside the business?

Good planning should keep these questions in mind. You need an overall time frame and the key phases in it to measure your progress against your plan. You also need time to stop and ask, Are we in a position to go to the next phase?

In addition to the project you're working on, your organization is likely to be running multiple other projects, each of which is drawing on resources at similar or different times. For this reason, organizations of a certain size normally run PMOs. These offices (also sometimes called portfolio or program management offices) can report on, and provide oversight across, the phases of the project or the projects in a portfolio (see chapter 9).

The detail and sheer scale of a plan depend entirely on the project's size, complexity, cost, and time frame, but several questions can be asked about all plans:

1. Does the plan make sense? Is it realistic? Is it transparent? In other words, does everyone understand what needs to be done, by when, and by whom and how the different activities combine to create the finished product?

2. Is the plan available in appropriate detail for the varying levels of those involved? For example, a project manager will want to know exactly when and how the 153 licenses needed for a given software will be procured.

3. Does the plan give the leaders the information they need to make decisions? For example, the consequences of delaying an important milestone should be clear. Decision makers need to understand what should happen, what is happening, and why.

4. Does the plan adequately distinguish between certainty and uncertainty? Think about how boats' radar systems work. Ships navigating the sea will have one radar system for when they are approaching port—a system of very limited range but with considerable detail of not only the geographical hazards but also such mechanical or human hazards as other ships or people on Jet Skis. The ships will have another system alongside this for when they are at sea—a system that can cover a far wider range but will include far less detail. This dual technique, then, is how you should construct and update your plan. It will enable you to make the big long-term decisions and the much smaller immediate decisions, and just as importantly, it will not include details that are highly uncertain and liable to change. Overly detailed plans for the future may lull you into a false sense of security or cause you to ignore events or risks because they do not appear in the details of the plan.

From plans based on deliverables to plans based on benefits

As we have discussed, project management has been too inwardly focused. Traditionally, project plans included deliverables, outputs, resources, and timing—but all these components fail to describe when the benefits and purpose will be delivered. Seek to shift from plans based on deliverables to plans based on benefits (see the "Benefits plan" section in chapter 5).

Testing and quality assurance

Ensuring that the outcome of the project meets the quality expectations is an integral, often overlooked part of project management. Teams tend to focus on doing the work and leave quality assurance until the end of the project, when adjustments are most expensive.

Project managers are responsible for ensuring that a project meets or exceeds the expected quality. Lack of quality suggests that the project is no longer fit for the purpose for which it was initiated and should be canceled. At a simple level, quality in a project has two distinct but interrelated aspects: the quality of the output and the quality of the process. You can deliver an asset that is fit for purpose, but if you have incurred significant additional costs through rework and delay, these drawbacks can undermine the value of the project just as much as a substandard asset can.

Some projects require official and significant quality validation tests before commercial production is started. This is the case with many infrastructure, production, life science, and engineering projects.

In IT, developers commonly perform user testing and other simulations to ensure that the product satisfies stakeholder needs. Traditionally, new systems were tested toward the end of the project, a practice that often led to additional work and delays in the schedule. With agile development methods, quality is checked on an almost weekly basis.

Project Glass was Google's effort to develop augmented-reality glasses. The product was introduced in April 2012, but because of numerous quality failures, and privacy and security concerns, the project was canceled. It ceased production in January 2015. When Glass was released, Google cofounder Sergey Brin suggested that the glasses should be treated as a finished product when Google started selling it to the public, even though everyone in the lab knew it was more of a prototype with significant kinks to be worked out. The product faced serious quality issues on its release, such as unappealing and uncomfortable design and poor battery life. Security, health, privacy, and ethical concerns arose too. This example shows the importance of good quality practices to increase the chances of project success.

TOOLS AND TECHNIQUES

Top-down, bottom-up planning

The best and most accurate way to create a plan and establish a realistic deadline is to hold an initial high-level orientation on the best timing to complete the project (e.g., launch date or opening day). Follow that by breaking down the project into activities, then create a bottom-up plan and assess whether the initial deadline is realistic. If not, think of ways to reduce the duration of the project: add resources, work in parallel, or do the project in different phases. When possible, shorten the time allotted by 5 to 20 percent to increase the pressure on the team.

Short deadlines or sprints

Every project manager will tell you projects have a natural flow. There is a relaxed feeling at the beginning of the project, as the end seems distant. Stress starts to hit as the project moves toward the midway point and teams realize that deadlines are coming quickly. Toward the end of the project, everyone is in a mad scramble to get things done. A key job of project managers is breaking projects into smaller deliverables with deadlines to lessen this effect. By breaking the work into the most important things that need to be completed on a weekly or biweekly basis and then having honest conversations about what they accomplished during those periods, teams hold themselves accountable, focusing on what they need to do. Instilling the habit of making and reviewing commitments each week is a great way to focus on what's important and get a clear picture of what's getting done.

Quality control and quality assurance

Achieving success in a project requires both quality control and quality assurance. Quality control is used to verify the quality of the outputs of the project, while quality assurance is the process of managing for quality.[2]

The language itself is a clue: *control* implies checking a component against a defined set of criteria or functionality; *assurance* implies removing the uncertainty or doubt that the project will deliver success.

Testing is about making sure that the deliverable of the project will be satisfactory when presented to the users, clients, and other stakeholders. Years ago, testing was the phase in the project life cycle just before rollout. Because of frequent delays and budget overruns, the step was often cut short or even skipped. Today, the project manager should embed regular tests throughout the entire life cycle of the project. The more uncertainty there is about a deliverable, the more that testing is required, and the more the project plan must include regular quality checks, prototyping, and testing time.

Putting this building block into practice

Every project must have a clear deadline. For the most important and strategic projects, the executive team needs to commit to the deadline and announce it officially. That said, you don't necessarily need to announce the deadline for the project *immediately when it is launched*, particularly if there are elements of uncertainty you need to work through before doing so.

A firm deadline suggests priority and urgency. It helps people keep the end date of the project in their minds at all times, creating the necessary focus that will help them when they have to decide how to allocate their time. On the other hand, if the deadline is unrealistic, it can undermine the project outputs and the eventual success.

Quality has to be embedded in the life of the project. Involve the quality experts—internal or external or both—and make sure they commit time to your project. Quality checks, prototyping, testing, rehearsals, and so on, all have to be incorporated into the project plan and reported on. The sooner potential faults and other deviations in the product are found, the less impact they will have in the project's progress, budget, and timelines.

Key questions you should ask

- Has the plan development been based on the scope and the previously defined WBS?

- Does the plan include milestones on when benefits will be partly and fully achieved?

- Have the expected quality and acceptance criteria of the project been defined?

- Does the project include periodic quality checks, including end customer and stakeholders' feedback?

Change: *How* will we engage stakeholders and manage the risks?

Increasingly, large firms such as QinetiQ are raising the status of their project managers. These companies are using automation, the PMO, and other forms of support to enable their managers to step back from the day-to-day processes of scheduling and reporting and encouraging them (by providing time and development) to focus more on stakeholder engagement and change management.

Change management is about helping the organization and its employees be ready to embrace the changes introduced by a project. Using stakeholder analysis, the project manager, together with communication experts, needs to develop a change management plan that defines the types of information that will be delivered, who will receive it, the format for communicating it, and the timing of its release and distribution. This plan has to be endorsed by the executive sponsor and the steering committee since leadership usually needs to play an active role in leading the change. According to PMI's *Guide to the Project Management Body of Knowledge,* about 75 to 90 percent of a project manager's time during the implementation phase of a project is spent formally or informally communicating.[3] And according to PMI's "Pulse of the Profession 2016" report (an annual global survey about trends in project management), highly effective communicators are more likely to deliver projects on time and within budget.[4]

To advance a project, everybody must get the right messages at the right times. The first step is to find out what kind of information or interventions each stakeholder group will need to embrace the changes introduced by the project. Methods of change management can take many forms, such as written updates, newsletters, face-to-face meetings, presentations, town halls, training sessions, and a project website. Give stakeholders enough information so that they're informed and can make appropriate decisions, but don't bury them in too much information.

The euro rollout

One of the best examples of change management I have observed was the introduction of the euro. On its initial release on January 1, 1999, the euro was an overarching currency used for exchange between countries in the European Union, while each nation continued to use its own currency. Three years later, however, the euro was to replace the domestic currencies of the member states in the Eurozone. During the years before to the introduction, as well as during the transition, almost all European citizens knew about the project and were fully readied for the change. People of all backgrounds, nationalities, and ages knew the key dates and the benefits the euro would bring to them, and they even knew the conversion rate between their existing currency and the euro.

The project had two key success factors. First, getting the population of Europe ready for the change and communication were top priorities for the European leaders. Second, the complicated project was presented in an extremely clear way, so that every single Eurozone inhabitant would understand the purpose, benefits, implications, and timing of the euro conversion project.[5]

Balancing risks

Risk management is an integral technique in project management and an essential duty of the project manager. Bluntly, if a project fails (either because you cannot deliver the project even though the business case remains or because the asset or output, when delivered, simply doesn't provide enough value to have warranted the investment), the failure is related to risk. The project manager or the team neglected to identify or mitigate the project's risks in time.

We must distinguish between project failure and good project governance. The whole point of using a project as a vehicle for investment is to allow you to redirect or cancel the project if either (1) the original benefits are no longer appropriate or offer the requisite level of value or (2) another project comes along and offers a far better return. Consequently, redirecting or canceling a project for these two reasons does not constitute a failure; it represents good project governance. Project failure, on the other hand, means a project has gone to term but did not deliver the required asset or output (because it has delivered nothing at all or something of low value). Think of all the IT projects whose new software is abandoned by users soon after introduction. Or projects that deliver an output or asset that fails to produce anything close to the originally intended value. Remember, the value of a project is related to the costs, so a project that delivers the requisite output but has overrun on schedule, costs, or both is also a failure.

The nature of projects, which is to produce something new and unique, is intrinsically uncertain. Therefore, a central purpose of project management is to identify and manage project risk. The more innovative or uncertain a project, the greater the need for effective and imaginative risk management. What's more, the steering committee must have an appetite for risk, since this group will need to accept the residual risk—the remaining risk that cannot be avoided, mitigated, or transferred.

Many projects fail not because of shortcomings in their risk mitigation, avoidance, or transfer, but because they are hit with a risk that the project team had simply overlooked. Bear in mind that the easiest risks for a project team or steering committee to digest are those for which you have good avoidance or mitigation plans in place. Beware if you find the risk matrix (described later in the chapter) seems too neat or if there appears to be little residual risk in an innovative or complex project. These observations may indicate that the project's initiators considered it easier to shunt what should be classified as risks into a general and undefined pool of "uncertainty." As with everything else in project management, risk identification and mitigation should be a reflective series of trade-offs and conscious, transparent decisions.

Both risk and value are terms to which we like to attach absolute figures, but in fact, both are intrinsically linked to human perception. The value of something is in the eyes of the person who is being asked to pay for it. The riskiness of a project is also associated with organizational and personal perception, in this case *risk attitude*—how you feel or how your organization feels about different types of risk. Assuming that both the organization and the individual are well informed and self-aware, then the greater your capacity for risk, the easier you will find it to include riskier projects in your portfolio. This willingness may stem from confidence in your ability to cover the cost of a risk or to manage a complicated or complex set of circumstances (or, usually, to do both).

When you are managing risk in a project, the first issue is awareness. What are the risks, and how can we mitigate or avoid them by doing something differently or taking out some form of insurance or hedge? The next step is to work together with the rest of the project team to explore and imagine what-if scenarios. Imagination plays a big part in risk management. Rather than trying simply to brainstorm the risks associated with a project, ask those involved these two questions:

1. What could possibly go wrong with the elements of what you are planning, and why?

2. Imagine your project ending in disastrous failure—how did it happen?

While uncertain projects are like driving at night, risk management adds a copilot to the mix, someone who is following a small-scale map of

FIGURE 7-6

Time's relationship to risk

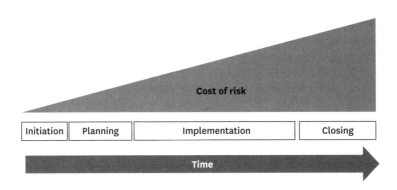

the route ahead and can shout out to the driver to slow down, change gear, or prepare to turn sharply left or right. In risk management for projects, the team looks ahead to see the map of the whole route, seeks expert advice from others who know the route, agrees on options for how the team will respond if the road conditions are not exactly as anticipated. Many project managers rely too heavily on the original plan and struggle to adjust to changes in real time. The most valuable question any project leader can ask of their team is, "Tell me, at this stage in the project, what's the worst thing that could happen next?" Teams working on large, complex projects can use statistical analysis in their risk management to help them understand what level of resources or contingency they should be ready to apply to the project.

As shown in figure 7-6, the sooner the risks are identified and mitigated, the less costly it will be for the project. A great example of this phenomenon of late risk identification is the French railway operator SNCF, which in 2014 ordered two thousand new trains that were too big for many of the stations they needed to visit.[6] The train operator admitted failing to verify measurements before ordering its new stock. Because of the mistake, some thirteen hundred platforms had to be modified, at a cost of €50 million.

One assessment that is often ignored is the additional risk that each project brings to an organization. Projects generate activity, which many organizations incorrectly associate with progress, and this association encourages them to fall into the trap of initiating too many projects concurrently. Adding an extra project to an organization that is already running too many projects increases the risk of companywide failure. In several instances, companies have gone into bankruptcy because of launching too many projects. The collapse of Fortis Private Bank is a notorious example. Before initiating a new project, the leadership team has to make sure that the requisite resources are available without robbing them from other projects. It must also see that any dependencies between the new project and the existing portfolio are addressed (as we will see in chapter 10).

Risk management also involves having a plan B. What if something unforeseen impacts the project just before launch? A typical example is an outdoor event: What is the alternative if it rains?

The first iPhone was famously not fully ready at its launch demo at the January 2007 Apple Convention, but the device looked seamless to the audience. The Apple project team was aware of the shortcomings with the prototype iPhones and mitigated them through detailed risk management. The team designed a plan to use several iPhones, one for each key feature (e.g., making a call, surfing the internet) throughout the demo. The members rehearsed several times so that there would be no last-minute surprises, and they successfully introduced the iPhone.

TOOLS AND TECHNIQUES

Kotter's eight-stage model of change

John Kotter, a Harvard Business School professor and a renowned change expert, introduced the eight-stage model of change in his book *Leading Change*.[7] He developed this framework from his research on one hundred organizations that were going through a process of change. The steps are as follows:

1. Create a sense of urgency.

2. Form powerful guiding coalitions.

3. Develop a vision and a strategy.

4. Communicate the vision.

5. Remove obstacles.

6. Create short-term wins.

7. Consolidate gains.

8. Anchor change in the corporate culture.

Kotter's step-by-step model provides clear descriptions and guidance on the entire process of change and is relatively easy to implement in your projects. It emphasizes preparing and building acceptability for change, as well as the involvement of the employees for the success of the project.

The Kübler-Ross change curve

One model of change was originally developed in the 1960s by Swiss American psychiatrist Elisabeth Kübler-Ross to show how terminally ill patients cope with their impending deaths. Later, the so-called Kübler-Ross change curve was modified to depict how people deal with other loss and grief. The Kübler-Ross change curve gained popularity among corporations and change management experts by the 1980s. The following are the five stages of change (also known as stages of grief):

1. Denial

2. Anger

3. Bargaining

4. Depression

5. Acceptance

The change curve enables us to adapt to change and navigate transitions. It not only helps us deal with change on a personal level but can also be effectively used by businesses to empower their workforce to manage change projects and succeed.

The DICE framework

A tool that measures a project's duration, its integrity, the commitment of the team, and everyone's effort (DICE) was created by BCG to assist project managers in implementing change. Using objective measures, the DICE framework figures the likelihood of a project's success. With enormous pressures on employees' time, this simple tool provides an efficient way to target potential issues before they cause a project to go off course. Here is how these four elements are assessed:

- **Duration (D in the calculations that follow):** the total time, or time between two key milestones. How often does the project review happen?

- **Integrity (I):** the team's ability, skills, and motivation to implement the project successfully. Do the project manager and the team possess the required skills and experience?

- **Commitment (C):** levels of support. Commitment is composed of two factors. First (C_1) is the visible backing from the executive sponsor and senior executives for the project. Are senior executives engaged in communicating the purpose of the project? And second (C_2) is support from those who are affected by the project. Are employees given opportunities to share their feedback?

- **Effort (E):** how much effort the project will require, on top of the business as usual. Are the employees comfortable with the extra work?

Each factor is graded on a four-point scale, where 1 means "best" and 4 means "worst." For example, if you rate duration (D) as 1, it will mean your team is performing excellently on reaching the deadlines and achieving milestones. To calculate whether your project is going to be a success, use the following equation:

$$\text{DICE score} = D + (2 \times I) + (2 \times C_1) + C_2 + E$$

Your DICE score will be between 7 and 28:

- If your score is between 7 and 14, then your project has good chances of being successful.

- If your score is between 14 and 17, then your project is at risk of failure.

- If your score is 17 or above, then your project most probably will fail.

The shadow organization chart

The majority of organizations now make use of both traditional "push" communication techniques such as emails and newsletters and "pull" techniques such as the website or a change dashboard. Communication teams recognize the power of the formal and informal communication networks in organizations or across projects.

In 2015, Carta, an equity management platform, launched an exercise to map its "shadow organization chart." The idea was to create a picture of the informal flow of knowledge, communication, and influence in the business.[8]

Carta asked each of their employees to answer three basic questions:

1. Who energizes you at work? (list four or more people)

2. Who do you go to for help and advice? (list four or more people)

3. Who do you go to when a decision needs to be made? (list four or more people)

Every time an individual was listed counted as a nomination. The Carta team then connected the nominators to the nominees in a directional graph.

The team discovered that the top 10 nominated employees (who didn't include such obvious candidates as the CEO) influenced 70 percent of the company's 250-person workforce.

The communication drumbeat

Think of your communications in terms of a drum kit, each drum with a different resonance and a different purpose:

- **Bass drums** are push communications such as newsletters, reports, videos, and other messages that can be planned and scheduled in advance to build up some expectation of an announcement. Bass-drum beats inform.

- **Side drums** provide the continual background rhythm for your project communications. Schedule these on the same day each week or each month. For example, try issuing a five-minute video once a month featuring someone from the project team talking about the experience of working on the project. If your project is to create a change, try issuing an open challenge to the workforce once a month, inviting them to try a new activity or behavior. Or consider a monthly "open mic" session on Zoom, facilitated by the project director, when project team members or stakeholders could ask questions or share ideas. Side-drum beats engage.

- **Cymbals** are the disruptive elements of the kit, designed to break the rhythm of the other communications. Your cymbals are the stories and events you pick up and share from beyond the project. These might involve news stories about the industry, the publication of reports by government or industry regulators, market or competitor news that has some bearing on your project or the environment in which you are delivering it. Cymbals catch people's attention.

Use your drum kit to establish a regular and consistent rhythm to your communications so that you can build expectations among stakeholders and encourage engagement with the project.

Risk matrix

The risk matrix is the most commonly used tool for assessing the potential risks in a project. Figure 7-7 is an example of a matrix that you can use to evaluate and manage the risks in your project. Start by brainstorming with the key project stakeholders to identify threats that could impede or even bring down the project. You then define the importance of each threat by considering its probability or likelihood (from almost certain to rare) and the severity of the impact (from insignificant to severe). For each risk, identify where it falls on the matrix. The risks that fall in the "extreme" blocks might be those that kill the project and should be mitigated; the risks that fall in the "high" and "medium" categories need to be closely monitored and mitigated if their probability increases. This assessment is not a scientific approach; rather, it is a simple mechanism to increase the stakeholders' awareness of the project's risks. With better awareness, the project leaders can control the major risks and take mitigating actions whenever it is appropriate to do so.

When brainstorming about the level of risk, you and the group should assess a multitude of factors. Consider the amount of innovation required, the level of uncertainty in the project, and the availability of resources. You will also need to look at the capability within or available to the organization, the financial scale of the project, and the amount of financial exposure elsewhere in the organization. Finally, you need to understand the organization's appetite for risk.

FIGURE 7-7

Risk management matrix

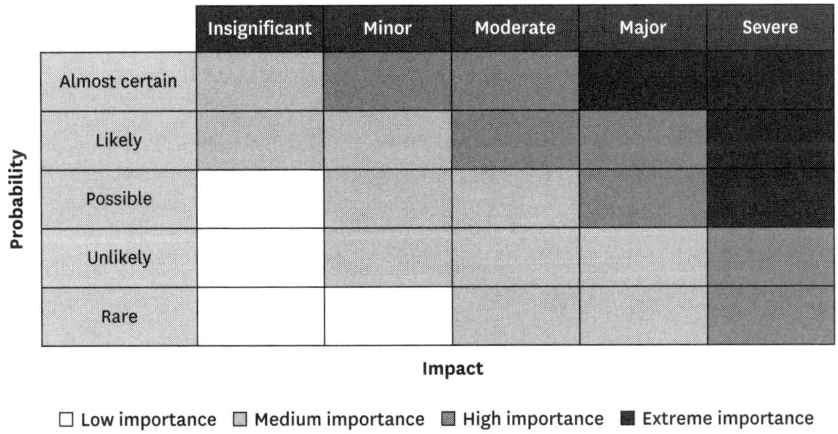

Probability	Insignificant	Minor	Moderate	Major	Severe
Almost certain					
Likely					
Possible					
Unlikely					
Rare					

Impact

☐ Low importance   ☐ Medium importance   ■ High importance   ■ Extreme importance

The risk brainstorm and matrix exercise has two other benefits. First, it will help you build up a picture of the senior team's appetite for risk and under which circumstances the team is risk-seeking or risk-averse. You need this understanding if you are trying to decide how the organization needs to change. Second, simply having a regular conversation about risk will raise risk awareness in the senior team and the organization as a whole.

Putting this building block into practice

All projects require a sound change and risk management plan, but their methods of distributing and communicating the information will differ. Project plans should account for the change management needs of stakeholders, and the plans should specify when information should be distributed and how the interventions will be delivered.

Project leaders must prioritize the change and communication activities and convey the right amount of information. Too much communication can be overwhelming, leading to the loss of important information, and too little communication might not provide a clear enough picture. Project leaders who understand how to send the right amount of information to the right people at the right time will keep things moving smoothly, helping produce a successful project.

Key questions to ask

- Does the project have a communication and change management plan that highlights the expected benefits for the stakeholders?

- Have sufficient communication and change management activities been planned to support the new reality?

- How risky is the project, and can the organization cope with the risk?

- Have major risks been identified and mitigated?

All projects require a careful balance of project control and project management. Project control is part of the old definition of project management, which includes planning, costing, scheduling, and working according to plan to make sure what you deliver is what you originally promised. Modern project management, on the other hand, looks beyond these confines to allow the organization to adapt the plans, the budget, and other project elements, not simply to deliver the project but also to ensure that the project's benefits meet the strategic needs of the organization.

The most challenging element in all this is the organization's strategy, which is sometimes a moving target. Make sure you spend the time defining scope or managing risk wisely. Too little attention to either scope or risk may be a disaster, but too much can waste huge amounts of time and money. Determine the best approach to planning your project, and don't forget to make stakeholders' needs a part of your plan.

Now we have examined in full the three domains of the Project Canvas—the foundation, the people, and the creation—and we have explored the ways they affect the delivery of the project. In chapter 8, we will learn how these elements come together in the Project Canvas and how to use the canvas as a practical tool for project management in your organization.

8.

Putting the Project Canvas into Practice

Adopting the Canvas in Your Organization

In this chapter, we will first learn how to analyze projects through the Project Canvas lens and then how to create a canvas. We will then see examples of the canvas in some real cases and learn how to apply the canvas to programs, agile initiatives, and other projects in our own organizations.

The main purpose of the Project Canvas is to enable you to capture and communicate the key features and drivers of your project. This exercise allows for a common understanding of the project among all stakeholders. It encourages valuable questions and facilitates conversations at any point of the project. In the early stages, you and others are asking questions like these: Does the project have the foundation to be delivered successfully? Is this project the most appropriate way to deliver the desired benefits? Once the project is underway, you will be asking, Are we still likely to generate the benefits we originally identified, and can we achieve them faster? Have any of the initial assumptions changed? On the project's completion, you'll ask, How well did we anticipate the challenges faced, and how effectively did we manage the project?

The following three principles will allow you to better understand the philosophy behind the Project Canvas before you put it in practice:

1. **It is a starting point, not an endpoint.** Just as your business case or benefits map needs to show the reasoning you used to create them, the evidence and assumptions that underpin your canvas must be readily available to your stakeholders. The succinctness of the Project Canvas should not impede clarity but should be a pathway into the data and documents behind it. If the additional project details correspond with the overview presented in the canvas, you enable your stakeholders to drill down and get further detail and evidence.

2. **It expresses the essential principles that guide your project.** The Project Canvas is built on the principles of both explicit and tacit knowledge. *Explicit* knowledge can be communicated in writing. It is supported by the documents and processes that underpin the canvas and can be accessed through it. *Tacit* knowledge is what we know from our own experience, judgment, and learned behavior. This kind of knowledge can't be written down; we need to show it through example or by modeling some behavior. Tacit knowledge is what allows us to take the simple statements expressed on the canvas and use them as a basis to judge the credibility, quality, riskiness, and health of our project.

3. **It communicates with clarity to all your stakeholders.** Any document can be misinterpreted, and you will want to avoid this risk with the Project Canvas. There are four ways to help assure this:

   – Involve your stakeholders in the process of cocreating the canvas. Remember that there is as much value in creating the canvas as there is in its finished outcome.

- Make sure that the way you describe a project or program reflects an outcome or a set of outcomes that can be agreed on objectively.

- Use concrete language. Verbs such as *consolidate, enhance, explore,* and *promote* may sound good but express vague aspirations that are open to different interpretations by different stakeholders.

- Keep the language inclusive and free of strategy and project jargon. The Project Canvas is designed to be an object that both project specialists and decision makers can share.

How to use the Project Canvas

The best time to apply the Project Canvas is after you or your organization has decided to start a project and the project manager has been appointed.

Building, maintaining, and communicating the canvas

The Project Canvas is a shared document—one that needs to work for the project team, accountable senior executives, and other stakeholders.

Build the canvas initially on consensus. The project manager should bring together key stakeholders, experts, the project sponsor, and anyone else who can provide relevant information (customers, suppliers, or others) in a project definition workshop. Don't rush; dedicate two or three hours for this important kickoff meeting. Share the context and any basic details already gathered about the project with the participants. The data you collect can be placed in each building block of the canvas. Print a blank Project Canvas (large poster-sized paper, butcher paper, or a whiteboard) and prepare sticky notes and markers.

You and the other participants may interact with the canvas in any way you prefer. Start with the foundation domain, then move through the other two domains: people and creation. Let each participant brainstorm and post their own views and opinions before summarizing the key thoughts, and iterate if needed.

Once you have completed each domain, be sure that the canvas makes sense as a cohesive whole project. Make sure you're looking at the project from a strategic and organizational perspective. Remember that projects are not islands; they have to be implemented in a fast-changing and multiple-priority environment. Share the Project Canvas with your organization and with other stakeholders, and incorporate their feedback. The canvas will give you a good understanding of the challenges ahead and your readiness for moving forward with the project.

The Project Canvas is a living document. The context and the continued rationale for your project will always be subject to change, so you'll need to revisit your canvas regularly to check whether any original elements have changed and how you should respond. Do so each time you face a major decision. If the project is adjusted after a stage gate, make sure the canvas captures the new assumptions. Use version control so everyone is clear on which iteration of the canvas is current and to capture and archive previous versions; these will become useful tools for analysis and reflection.

Share the latest version of the canvas whenever you make a change, but it's also good practice to send out the canvas from time to time, to remind everyone of the big picture behind the work you are doing.

Finally, you may also want to feature your canvas in your communication drumbeat (see chapter 7). Consider producing a video or an article or facilitating a short workshop around one of the elements in the canvas on a regular cycle—perhaps once a month. This practice will help keep the canvas at the top of stakeholders' minds and will remind them of what underpins the main elements of each domain and building block.

Your Project Canvas is built on the same assumptions as your project's purpose and plan. Senior stakeholders who may wish to understand the certainty or uncertainty related to the project will need access to the fundamental assumptions in the business case, the project's requirements, and the logic behind the benefits strategy or the stakeholder map. The language of the canvas should be reflected in the detailed documents of the business case and the project requirements. There's nothing less convincing than a set of project initiation documents that seem to describe a different project from the version expressed in the Project Canvas.

Writing the Project Canvas block by block

Exactly how you word your canvas hinges on what you need it to do. Depending on your organizational culture, you might use a simple bulleted list of items under each heading, or you might favor longer statements. The following case study example provides a guide for you and your team to better define each building block. The "Helpful" examples are clear, meaningful descriptions for the project team and stakeholders. The "Unhelpful" examples show the most common mistakes people make when describing the key elements of projects.

This real-life project (with the names changed for anonymity) from the travel industry illustrates how you might approach framing the content of your canvas. Travels4You is a Switzerland-based traditional travel business that has been severely hit by the explosion of the internet; its operating revenues have been in continual decline over the past three years. The new CEO understood the severity of the situation and launched the Accelerate project to transform Travels4You into a digital-first tour operator. It was a question of adapt or die.

THE FOUNDATION

PURPOSE: *Why are we doing the Accelerate project?*

Helpful points	Unhelpful points
• Transform our business to become a 100 percent digital company	• Create a website to capture online customers
• Become a leading digital operator	
• Become an attractive employer	

Helpful statements	Unhelpful statements
Become the leading and most valued high-quality tour operator in Europe, 100 percent digital, by end of 2024.	Develop our company website and accept online transactions.

INVESTMENT: *How much will the Accelerate project cost?*

Helpful points	Unhelpful points
• SF 10–12 million investment	• SF 4 million investment
• 1,000–1,200 person-days	• Person-days to be confirmed

Helpful statements

Based on similar transformation projects in the industry, the estimated investment needed to become a fully digital travel agency is between SF 10 and 12 million. We will add a 10 percent contingency for unforeseen matters.

See: Business Case

Unhelpful statements

We have a budget of SF 4 million; let's see how far we can go with that.

BENEFITS: *What benefits and other impact will the Accelerate project generate?*

Helpful points

• Return to profitability in the next two years

• 80 percent of our revenues booked online in two years

• Become a top-ten Swiss employer

Unhelpful points

• New company website

• Increase revenues

Helpful statements

Transform into a new viable business, turning profitable again and bringing 80 percent of our revenues from our new online platform in two years.

See: Business Case and Benefit Card

Unhelpful statements

The main benefits of the project will be the creation of a new company website that will attract new customers.

THE PEOPLE

SPONSORSHIP: *Who is accountable for the Accelerate project?*

Helpful points

- Executive sponsor: Susan Gladby—dedicates one half day per week to the project.
- Steering committee members (see list below) meet once every two weeks.

Unhelpful points

- IT department will carry out the project.
- The executive team will oversee the implementation.

Helpful statements

The Accelerate project is governed by the following roles:

- Executive sponsor: Susan Gladby, vice president of IT [link to page about Susan—her authority, responsibility, and contact details]
- Steering committee [link to committee details with membership, responsibilities, and contact details]
- PMO [link to a page about the PMO and its responsibility toward the project]

See: Project Organization Chart

Unhelpful statements

The Accelerate project is the responsibility of the vice president of IT, Susan Gladby.

RESOURCES: *Who will work on the Accelerate project, and which skills are needed to deliver it?*

Helpful points

- Project manager: Carla Sanchez—full time [link to a page about the project manager and her contact details]
- Representatives from each department and business unit, such as Sales, Marketing, Legal, and Strategy (including senior leaders) to design the new business model
- IT skills required to develop the website
- Acquire external IT competencies if not in-house

Unhelpful points

- Project manager: Carla Sanchez
- IT development skills
- Web design

Helpful statements

Facilitated by the project manager, our entire organization will be involved in the design of the new business model, implications, and transition plan.

We will set up a dedicated team of business analysts and developers to create the new website according to the new business model.

Unhelpful statements

The project will need IT development skills.

STAKEHOLDERS: *Who will be benefit from and otherwise be affected by the Accelerate project?*

Helpful points

- All employees, all departments
- Management
- Owners
- Unions
- Clients
- Partners
- Suppliers

Unhelpful points

- IT department

Helpful statements

The transformation will affect, to different degrees, our entire organization, including our employees, and our clients, partners, and suppliers.

See: Stakeholder Analysis

Unhelpful statements

As we are developing a website, it will mainly affect our IT department.

THE CREATION

DELIVERABLES: *What will the Accelerate project produce, build, and deliver?*

Helpful points	Unhelpful points
• New strategy	• New website and app
• New business model	
• New go-to-market plan	
• Modern, easy-to-navigate website	
• Mobile app	

Helpful statements	Unhelpful statements
The transformation project will produce a new strategy for our new digital business model. It will also create a new go-to-market plan to capture online customers. The new website and mobile app will be the new face and image of our company.	The website will allow us to sell online flights and hotel bookings.

PLAN: *How and when will the work be carried out?*

Helpful points	Unhelpful points
• Traditional approach for the business model; ready in four months	• Project deadline in nine months, sooner if possible
• Agile development for the website and app; first minimum viable product in three months	
• Project completed and going live with our new business in nine months	

Helpful statements	Unhelpful statements
We will use a combination of project management methods. The website and app will be developed using iterative agile methods, and the new strategy and business model will be developed and implemented using a traditional predictive planning approach. The goal is to have our first minimum viable product (MVP; see explanation in text) in three months and be ready to go live with our new business in nine months.	We will use agile development, iterations, and sprints. The MVP should be ready as soon as possible.

See: Implementation Plan

CHANGE: *How are we going to engage the team and manage the risks?*

Helpful points	Unhelpful points
• Address potential resistance from senior employees and unions • Engage early supporters • Involve influencers to encourage change • Communicate the purpose	• Might face some resistance • Change is never easy

Helpful statements	Unhelpful statements
Because of the magnitude of the project impact, we expect serious resistance from senior employees and unions. We will talk to them to understand their needs and persuade them that this is the only option to keep our business alive. We will also develop a change management plan to inform and involve key stakeholders in the project.	We are expecting some resistance from senior employees and unions, but they will certainly adapt.

As we can see from this example, the language we use to define the key elements of our project is not just semantics; we must be clear and concrete. When the Project Canvas uses clear, specific, and concrete language, the project team and key stakeholders are better aligned.

Case studies of the Project Canvas in action

Now let's look at some amazing real-life projects—the creation of the Boeing 777 and the reconstruction of the Notre-Dame Cathedral in Paris—using the lens of the Project Canvas.

The Boeing 777

In the late 1980s, when Boeing announced the development of the 777, the company's 747 had been flying successfully for more than thirty years. Airplane manufacturers, like auto manufacturers, needed to keep innovating by introducing new airplane models if they wanted to survive in the competitive world. Designing, planning, and developing a new aircraft was a huge, complex investment. Boeing, under the leadership of Alan Mulally, adopted an innovative and collaborative designing and development process for the 777 (figure 8-1). The process involved customers, air carriers, technicians, finance experts, computer experts, and even other aircraft manufacturers.

Project Canvas analysis

THE FOUNDATION

- **Purpose:** In the late 1980s, Boeing was under considerable commercial pressure, facing very real competition with Airbus in Europe when Airbus became a major player in the airliner industry. To remain competitive, Boeing needed a new plan, and fast. What was needed to impress the airlines and win their business was a whole new concept—a new way of thinking, a new way of designing and manufacturing airliners.

- **Investment:** The budget was more than $6 billion, and more than ten thousand people worked on the project. The manufacturing facilities covered an area greater than seventy football fields.

- **Benefits:** With this project, Boeing aimed at achieving three strategic objectives: (1) reduce aircraft development time significantly, (2) meet customers' requirements better by involving them in the development process, and (3) eliminate costly modification procedures.

FIGURE 8-1

Project Canvas: The Boeing 777

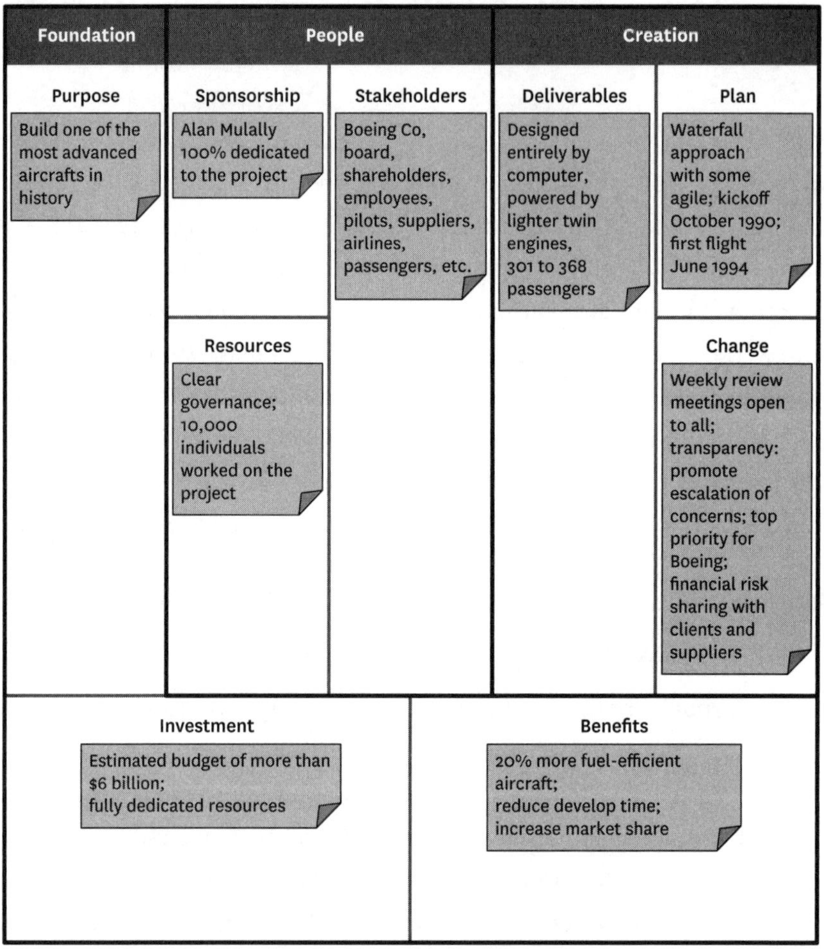

Foundation	People		Creation	
Purpose	Sponsorship	Stakeholders	Deliverables	Plan
Build one of the most advanced aircrafts in history	Alan Mulally 100% dedicated to the project	Boeing Co, board, shareholders, employees, pilots, suppliers, airlines, passengers, etc.	Designed entirely by computer, powered by lighter twin engines, 301 to 368 passengers	Waterfall approach with some agile; kickoff October 1990; first flight June 1994
	Resources			Change
	Clear governance; 10,000 individuals worked on the project			Weekly review meetings open to all; transparency: promote escalation of concerns; top priority for Boeing; financial risk sharing with clients and suppliers

Investment	Benefits
Estimated budget of more than $6 billion; fully dedicated resources	20% more fuel-efficient aircraft; reduce develop time; increase market share

THE PEOPLE

- **Sponsorship:** Alan Mulally served as the Boeing 777 project's director of engineering. He was 100 percent dedicated to the project. In September 1992, he was promoted to lead it as Boeing's vice president and general manager.

- **Resources:** Mulally was determined to introduce new working dynamics in the project. For the first time, eight major airlines had a role in the development. This level of collaboration was a departure from industry practice, where manufacturers typically designed aircraft with minimal customer input. By including all contributors, Mulally changed the way teams were configured. They were open to wider participation and included engineers, procurement staff, manufacturing staff, customers, and suppliers, all working together on design, development, and manufacturing processes.

- **Stakeholders:** A worldwide survey conducted in 1999 and 2000 revealed that the Boeing 777 was preferred by more than 75 percent who flew aboard the Boeing 777 and Airbus 330/340 airplanes. As just mentioned, one of the biggest innovations introduced by Mulally was that he asked some of the key stakeholders to be part of the project core team.

THE CREATION

- **Deliverables:** The new aircraft was produced in two fuselage lengths and, can accommodate up to ten passengers across. It has a three-class capacity of 301 to 368 passengers and a range of 5,240 to 8,555 nautical miles (9,700 to 15,840 kilometers). The 777 was the first commercial airliner to be designed entirely by computer.[1] The plane would be powered by lighter twin engines, the most powerful ever built, and designed to be 20 percent more fuel efficient than its precursors. The frame, some of which was constructed with newly developed materials, would add to fuel efficiency.

- **Plan:** After United Airlines ordered the aircraft in October 1990, the prototype was rolled out in April 1994, and the plane made its maiden flight two months later. United Airlines put the 777 into commercial service on June 7, 1995. In early 2000, Boeing introduced longer-range planes, which were first delivered in April 2004.

- **Change:** An important aspect of the cultural change introduced by the leadership of the project was how the employees were expected to interact with the managers. Team members were encouraged to bring their concerns to management. If they failed to receive an answer, they were encouraged to bring the problem to the next-highest level until they found a solution to their problems. A key innovation introduced in the 777 project was to share the financial risk. Boeing would manufacture the flight deck, the forward section of the cabin, the wings, the tail, and the engine nacelles (casing) in its own plants, while the company would subcontract the rest of the components (about 70 percent) to suppliers around the world.

CONCLUSION: The Boeing 777 project presents an example of good project management practices, for any industry. All nine building blocks were correctly and thoroughly addressed from the beginning of the project onward. Important innovations, such as the involvement of customers and suppliers as part of the design team, were introduced.

The 777 has received more orders than has any other wide-body airliner; as of October 2020, more than sixty customers had placed orders for 2,012 aircraft of all variants, with 1,646 delivered. The 777 has become Boeing's number one best-selling model, surpassing the Boeing 747.

Reconstruction of Notre-Dame Cathedral

Notre-Dame Cathedral in Paris is one the greatest examples of French Gothic architecture. Its construction started in 1163 and was largely completed in 1260. The building was spared during the two world wars, but on April 15, 2019, the roof of Notre-Dame caught fire. The disaster was broadcast live and watched by millions around the world. One day later, French president Emmanuel Macron announced that the reconstruction project would be completed five years to the day later, by April 16, 2024. Many concerns emerged from the architectural community about this short deadline. Let's analyze this ambitious project through the Project Canvas (figure 8-2) and consider the chances of success.

FIGURE 8-2

Project Canvas: The reconstruction of Notre-Dame Cathedral

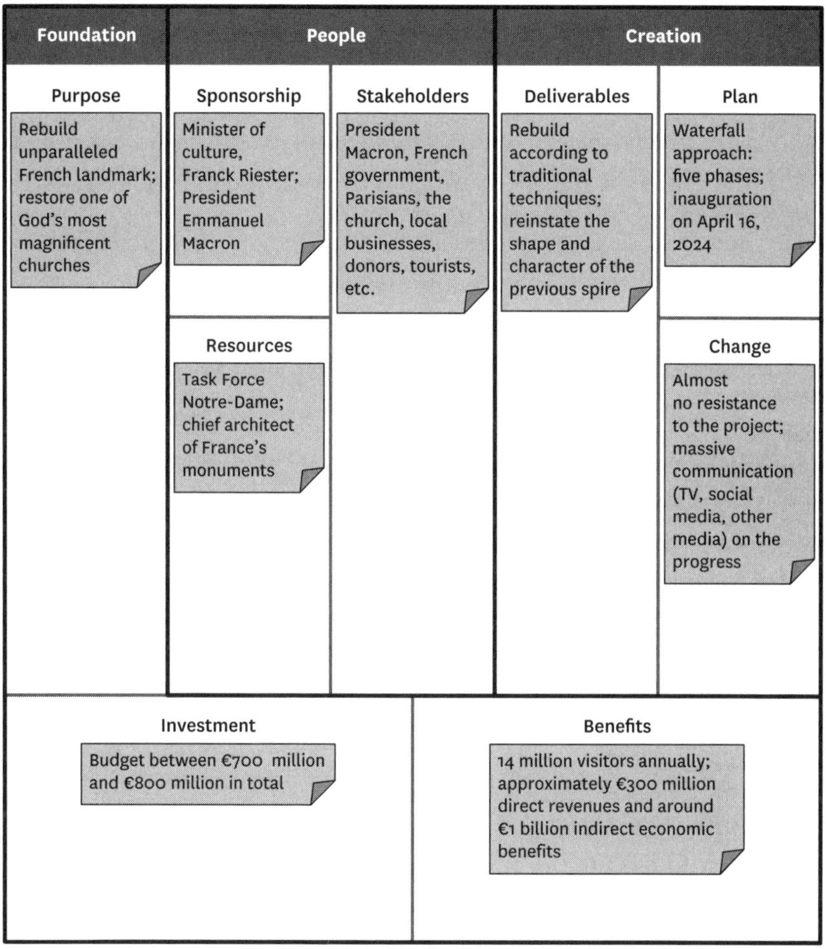

Foundation	People		Creation	
Purpose	Sponsorship	Stakeholders	Deliverables	Plan
Rebuild unparalleled French landmark; restore one of God's most magnificent churches	Minister of culture, Franck Riester; President Emmanuel Macron	President Macron, French government, Parisians, the church, local businesses, donors, tourists, etc.	Rebuild according to traditional techniques; reinstate the shape and character of the previous spire	Waterfall approach: five phases; inauguration on April 16, 2024
	Resources			Change
	Task Force Notre-Dame; chief architect of France's monuments			Almost no resistance to the project; massive communication (TV, social media, other media) on the progress

Investment	Benefits
Budget between €700 million and €800 million in total	14 million visitors annually; approximately €300 million direct revenues and around €1 billion indirect economic benefits

Project Canvas analysis

THE FOUNDATION

- **Purpose:** The purpose of the project is to rebuild France's greatest landmark, an exceptional piece of Gothic heritage of the Middle Ages and part of Paris's identity. For the Catholic community, the purpose is to restore one of God's most magnificent churches.

- **Investment:** The cost of this project is expected to be between €700 and €800 million in total. Securing the structure in and around the cathedral, replacing the roof and framework, and, finally, the consolidation and restoration will consume the largest portions of the budget.[2] Different initiatives have been launched to collect money for the reconstruction. Many stakeholders, with the help of the French government, opened fundraising websites to raise capital safely and transparently. Donations are expected to exceed €1 billion.

- **Benefits:** The reconstruction of Notre-Dame Cathedral will strengthen the French identity and recover an unparalleled wonder of the Catholic and cultural heritage. Seen as a personal bet from President Macron, if the project is delivered successfully by April 16, 2024, it will strengthen his image as an effective leader. In addition to the intangible benefits, Notre-Dame is a profitable tourist cash cow, with an average of thirty thousand visitors per day.

THE PEOPLE

- **Sponsorship:** The official executive sponsor is the minister of culture, Franck Riester, but President Macron is very involved in the project. Both of them are considered accountable for the project's success.

- **Resources:** General Jean-Louis Georgelin is the project manager. As head of the Task Force Notre-Dame, he is responsible for the planning, execution, monitoring, control, and closure of the project. The chief architect of France's monuments, Philippe Villeneuve, provides his expertise and deep knowledge about the cathedral. General Georgelin reports to and is advised by a board, which acts as a steering committee and consists of representatives of several stakeholders, including those from the state, the church, the city of Paris, and the scientific community.[3] The operational teams report directly to Georgelin. The subcontractors are managed by the procurement team, and the foundations collecting the private donations are managed by the finance team.

- **Stakeholders:** The main beneficiaries will be the Parisian citizens, the church, and the tourists who can again visit the cathedral. The key stakeholders are President Macron, the French government, church representatives, local businesses, donors, UNESCO, and others.

THE CREATION

- **Deliverables:** The spire of the cathedral will be rebuilt according to traditional techniques and should reinstate the shape and character of the previous spire. The spire will have the following characteristics: it will be 305 feet high and will use 500 tons of wood (from tall oak trees) and 250 tons of lead. The sixteen copper statues will be restored to their previous position. A modern fire-monitoring system and other prevention technologies will be added, to prevent future accidents.

- **Plan:** The restoration of the roof and spire has to be completed according to the conservation principles accredited by UNESCO and the International Council on Monuments and Sites. Consequently, restorers will use the traditional techniques, guaranteeing 100 percent the stability of the building structure. The reconstruction of the cathedral is split into five phases, beginning with preparatory work in May 2019 and ending with decoration in February 2024.

- **Change:** There is almost no resistance to this project; most if not all the key stakeholders are in favor of it and will support the work within their means to make it happen. Change management activities will focus on massive communication (TV, social media, and other media) about the progress, showing some early wins and, when the project is approaching the deadline, promoting the greatness of the achievement. An important aspect of the project is safety. During the reconstruction, the cathedral is at risk of collapsing, and lead levels around the project are beyond safe healthy limits. The safety of the workers needs to be assured as well as the safety of the surrounding neighborhood.

CONCLUSION: The declaration of a precise date for the inauguration of the reconstructed cathedral is an unusual yet courageous move from President Macron and will exert enormous pressure as that date approaches. Meeting the deadline and striving for reopening before the Olympic Games in 2024 is a priority for this project. On the other hand, the work of this project cannot be rushed. Quality is an equal priority, since the cathedral has to be reconstructed to last for many generations.

As the Project Canvas demonstrates, all the building blocks of the project have been well addressed. Barring some unforeseen circumstances, this splendid project should be completed on time.

Applying the Project Canvas to agile initiatives

As we saw earlier, different types of projects should use different implementation methods. Depending on a project's uncertainty, complexity, and a few other factors, traditional project management methods may not be the best choice. Fortunately, the Project Canvas can be used for projects of any implementation method, including agile approaches. The key success factors, and thus nine building blocks, are the same.

The nine building blocks in agile projects

Let's look at how to read the canvas when applied to an agile project, then learn from a real case study on how to put it into practice.

THE FOUNDATION

- **Purpose:** Any project using an implementation approach needs to have the *why* clearly defined at the beginning. A well-defined purpose is essential for both traditional and agile projects. The one difference between these kinds of projects concerns the ease of definition. It is harder to define a higher purpose for some agile projects, which are sometimes seen as a series of continuous improvements. Nevertheless, project leaders should also think about the higher purpose of their agile initiatives.

- **Investment:** Both types of projects require investments in resources, budgets, and materials. The approach used to develop the estimates is different for agile and traditional projects, but they share the same goal: a clear up-front understanding of the estimated costs.

- **Benefits:** Whether a project is launched because stakeholders want to implement a groundbreaking idea or find the solution to a pain point, the decision to go ahead with the project will likely come down to whether the benefits are worth the investment. Like the purpose, the benefits of agile projects are harder to define, because they are usually a series of continuous improvements. Nevertheless, leaders should think about the broader benefits in agile projects as much as they do for traditional projects.

THE PEOPLE

- **Sponsorship:** In agile initiatives, the executive sponsor plays a similar role as that in traditional projects, but the product owner and team members share ownership of the project. Everyone collaborates to come up with a plan designed to finish the work within the estimated time and cost.

- **Resources:** Instead of a project manager, the person responsible for delivering the agile initiative is the Scrum master. This person works with the product owner (who is responsible for the product backlog) and the development team to build the project.

- **Stakeholders:** Both traditional and agile projects need to identify and assess the impact of the project on stakeholders. In agile projects, stakeholders tend to provide regular feedback to the team.

THE CREATION

- **Deliverables:** Traditional projects focus on the scope and the work breakdown structure to define what the project will produce. Agile projects create a product backlog, which is the single source of requirements. Product backlogs are written in a user story format (e.g., users must be able to register on our website). Agile development uses the minimum viable product (MVP) approach. The MVP is a product with enough features to attract early-adopter customers and to validate a product idea early in the development cycle.

- **Plan:** Instead of planning the entire project beforehand, agile project teams focus on quicker iterations, or sprints. As described earlier in the book, sprints are based on prioritization of features and stories from the product backlog.

- **Change:** Both types of project have to address the needs (and resistance) of the most influential stakeholders through a change management plan.

Project Canvas case study: Creation of a wine e-commerce website using an agile approach

A group of entrepreneurs recognized that online wine sellers typically provide only a catalog—they do not provide accessible information for customers who want to acquire an advanced knowledge of wine and the wine industry. The entrepreneurs decided to address the existing gaps in the industry. For example, the project would help nonexpert customers select quality wines or improve restaurants' expertise when these establishments were dealing with questions from savvy clients. The group decided to create a website for the business using an agile approach.

Let's look at each building block of the Project Canvas to understand if this agile project was well defined (figure 8-3).

Project Canvas analysis

THE FOUNDATION

- **Purpose:** From the height of ancient Greek civilization until today, the world of wine has often been perceived as being reserved only for the elite. The purpose of this project is to break down such barriers globally: to offer a customer-centric online platform for

FIGURE 8-3

Project Canvas: Building a wine website using an agile approach

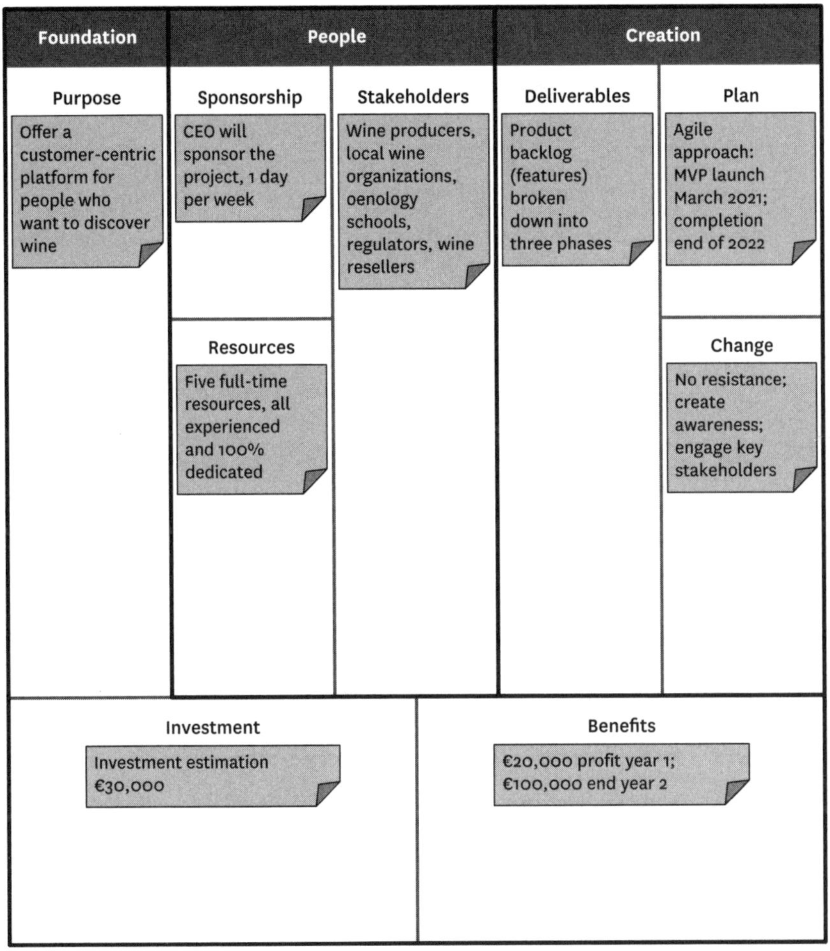

Foundation	People		Creation	
Purpose	**Sponsorship**	**Stakeholders**	**Deliverables**	**Plan**
Offer a customer-centric platform for people who want to discover wine	CEO will sponsor the project, 1 day per week	Wine producers, local wine organizations, oenology schools, regulators, wine resellers	Product backlog (features) broken down into three phases	Agile approach: MVP launch March 2021; completion end of 2022
	Resources			**Change**
	Five full-time resources, all experienced and 100% dedicated			No resistance; create awareness; engage key stakeholders

Investment	Benefits
Investment estimation €30,000	€20,000 profit year 1; €100,000 end year 2

people who want discover, select, and learn more about wines from all around the world.

- **Investment:** The investment required to build the website is an estimated €30,000.

  - Development of the web platform (logo, photos or visuals, web design, coding, etc.): €13,000

- Research and copywriting (drafting of the core text and the scripts of the learning videos, which are necessary to launch the MVP): €10,000

- Preparation of the videos via VideoScribe: €5,000

- Subscription to the content management system Shopify: €2,000 per year

- **Benefits:** The website will not deliver any notable benefits during the first six months. The platform will be offered free for one year, to gain as many subscribers as possible. Revenues will come from advertisements and wine sales through subscriptions. The project will start generating €20,000 in profit by the end of the first year and €100,000 by the second year.

THE PEOPLE

- **Sponsorship:** The CEO of the startup will be the project sponsor. She has a good understanding of e-commerce, wine, and venture capital industries and is committed to dedicating at least one day per week to the project. The steering committee, composed of the executive sponsor, the Scrum master, the product owner, and the lead web developer, will meet once every two weeks.

- **Resources:** The agile team will include five full-time staff: one copywriter, three web developers, and the Scrum master, who will coordinate the team. All of them have experience in developing websites and will be 100 percent dedicated to the project. The product owner and some potential customers will join the team regularly to provide input.

- **Stakeholders:** The main stakeholders of this website project are the owners of the startup. If the project fails, the business will struggle to survive. Other relevant stakeholders include the wine producers, the local wine organizations, the local regulators (sales of alcohol products online), oenology schools, and multinational wine resellers (including supermarkets).

THE CREATION

- **Deliverables:** The backlog of user stories (which will be used as features on the website) has been broken down into three phases:

  - **Phase 1 (MVP):** The team will develop a catalog of six wine regions. Each section will describe the grape varieties in the region, the wine-making methods, and so forth, along with a series of basic teaching videos. Each region will provide a wine learning pack under a monthly subscription that provides six bottles of wine from the region every month. Each pack will include wine "tasting" games and other educational content.

  - **Phase 2 (scaling):** There will be a strong focus on upselling larger quantities of the wines already included in the learning packs and selling similar products through promotions on the website, live meetups, and email marketing campaigns. The company will progressively integrate additional wine regions (and the wine learning packs relating thereto), in light of customer surveys.

  - **Phase 3 (diversification):** The learning packs will include opportunities for customers to visit the winemakers and participate in tastings by enabling people to book thematic road trips to the regions represented on the platform.

- **Plan:** The project development approach will be iterative through two-week sprints, whose overall timing happens in three:

  - **Phase 1:** This six-month development process includes the regulatory approvals, on-site tastings, selection, and contractual negotiations with wine producers as well as the web development and copywriting. This process will end by September 30, 2022. An MVP will be launched in June 2022 to carry out conversion tests and start monetizing the project.

- Phase 2: The scaling phase is an ongoing process that should provide for thirty-day deadlines for the development of each additional learning pack. The creation of dedicated sale channels and email marketing campaigns should be launched by January 2023.

- Phase 3: The website will be launched by the end of 2023.

• **Change:** The most important change management element of the project is creating awareness and engaging the key stakeholders, such as the local wine producers. Unlike other resellers, the goal is not to squeeze their margins but to increase the added value for the customers through innovative features. Traditional wine schools will have an interest in the website through affiliation agreements and partnerships.

CONCLUSION: The wine e-commerce website project has been well planned, using an agile approach for the progressive development of the website with the ambition of having the MVP within six months of the start. The main obstacle to the project's success is the available budget, as the current estimate includes only the cost projected until the creation of the MVP. Another challenge will be the change management aspects of creating awareness and quickly capturing enough subscribers to make the project viable.

Tips for introducing the Project Canvas in your organization

The Project Canvas and other new ways of working can be introduced at different levels of the organization: function, business unit, corporate, country. The larger the scope, the higher the sponsorship level required. Early questions you'll need to consider are how to introduce the canvas in your organization and who is responsible for doing so. Introducing the canvas is a change management project in itself, and the sponsor has to be a senior executive who believes in the new approach, with the director of the

PMO as project manager. Before you can use the canvas with any degree of confidence, you need to establish these key fundamentals:

1. **Define the purpose of the canvas.** Introducing the canvas will build new competencies and will affect your entire organization, its culture, and people's ways of working. Define each of the nine building blocks with the project team, and discuss these elements in the steering committee to ensure buy-in. Use the canvas to communicate widely about the initiative and to gather initial support.

2. **Define the key phases of the change project.** Choose the timing that suits you best; the shorter the time frame, the more pressure and focus it creates. Aim for a three- to six-month project, and consider three phases:

    i. **Developing:** In its essence, the canvas is a tool for building your organization's project implementation capabilities and improving how your organization manages its projects. This means that as simple as the canvas is, it's not a template set in stone. You can adjust it to your own company terminology and best practices. It can also be used as a tool to assess the feasibility of your projects before you decide to invest in them.

    ii. **Piloting:** In this phase, you gather buy-in, adapt the canvas to the needs of your users, and secure some early wins in terms of the impact it has on those using it.

    iii. **Rolling out:** The canvas needs to be integrated into the processes you use for initiating, managing, and reporting on projects. You'll need to adapt such things as the behavior of your PMO and your use of existing project dashboards. If the canvas is treated as simply another thing for people to complete or for sponsors to read *on top of* everything else you already use, it is doomed to failure.

3. **Develop common principles based on the Project Canvas.** While being succinct, the canvas also needs to be broad—a tool that

provides value across all the projects you undertake, no matter their nature or methodology. You will need to create for canvas users a set of principles flexible enough to accommodate a variety of projects. This step means more than merely creating a glossary. When you start using the canvas, take as much time as you need to express the different elements in terms of behaviors and what is your own role. Consider establishing principles around the use of the canvas a key guide for helping your organization prioritize and select projects (described further in chapter 10). The canvas should also be widely embraced by the executive team when this group starts having regular project review meetings.

4. **Offer training on project fundamentals and the Project Canvas.**
    Develop a training program for the entire organization on project fundamentals and the use of the Project Canvas. This handbook provides the basis for both these steps. Training will provide a solid foundation and a common understanding throughout your company. To drive this change from the top, you need to train senior executives especially—many of whom, our research shows, have never been taught how to be a successful sponsor.

5. **Select the most qualified and enthusiastic people to be project ambassadors.** As with any important change, there will be resistance and there will be support. Focus on identifying the most qualified and enthusiastic people, those who believe in the need to do projects better. Train these ambassadors first. Give them the canvas material to allow them to spread the information throughout the organization, converting their colleagues to the new ways of working.

6. **Start with a selection of strategic projects.** The opportunities to learn, improve, and grow a capability are greatest in projects that are the most innovative or the most challenging in terms of uncertainty, budget, schedule, or stakeholders. If you only pilot the canvas on your simplest, least risky, and lowest-value projects, you may never be allowed to apply it to any other project. But you need the

opportunity to do "destruction testing" if you are going to prove the strategic value and resilience of the canvas. Once you have some early wins with the canvas, celebrate these achievements even if they are minor.

Introducing the Project Canvas in your organization requires radical changes in the way projects are proposed, selected, prioritized, defined, planned, and executed. The adoption of the canvas is always easier if your organization is already a project-driven and agile organization (as described in chapter 11) or has adopted some steps toward becoming one.

Example of an organization implementing the Project Canvas

Let's look at a real example of how a global entertainment organization introduced the Project Canvas. The company was experiencing the usual difficulties of the world driven by change: a rapid increase of competition, shorter product life cycles, an urgent need to innovate, and the launch of hundreds of projects in the past few years. All these changes led to a lack of oversight of the projects the company was investing in. It had an acceptable list of corporate projects, although it was missing information like ownership, rationale, and status. The head office had no overview of the projects carried out in the different regions and local sites. The situation became alarming when some of the company's strategic projects missed important deadlines. One of them was the launch of a highly promoted new product, the ability to purchase movies both at its cinema complexes as well as through an app. After this failure, the CEO, Karin, launched an investigation, which revealed that some departments had not been contributing to strategic projects because they were busy with their own unit-level projects they deemed higher priority. Other problems uncovered included a lack of clear governance, the ability of anyone to launch projects with few checks, a failure to examine which resources were needed in the most critical projects, and the absence of a clear, prioritized list of projects.

Recognizing that the situation was urgent, Karin initiated a management framework based on the Project Canvas to evolve the company into a more project-driven organization. She made it clear to her management team and regional heads that this project—transforming into a project-driven, agile organization—was a priority. They all had to commit and contribute to make this approach a success, which they did. It was easy to gain their buy-in, as everyone was struggling with the huge number of projects they and their teams had to deal with, on top of their operational responsibilities.

They set up a project steering committee composed of the management team. Karin delegated the role of executive sponsor to her right hand, Marta, the head of the strategy office. The CEO also appointed a project manager to help the committee design and implement the new approach. The goal was to have the new approach tested and implemented within six months.

The project team, with active participation from the executive sponsor, started by defining the Project Canvas building blocks for the transformation project, which was validated by the steering committee. Among the first solutions introduced was a gate-funded approach to ensure that new projects were launched with consensus. By requiring that a project reach an approval gate before it received further funding, the team could make the entire portfolio of running projects more visible. These gates also helped the group control the project's progress and company spending. Finally, the gate approach ultimately helped keep the focus on the project benefits. One outcome of this step was that the team identified far too many active projects—210 of them.

Before the team started with the detailed analysis, at least 50 projects were canceled because of duplication or lack of clear purpose. Another 100 tasks were deemed inappropriate as projects; they involved small change activities requiring less than fifty days of work. Although these small tasks could theoretically be considered projects, the governance required by applying project management to such endeavors mostly adds unnecessary complexity and bureaucracy. These projects were reclassified as continuous-improvement initiatives and removed from the list. For each of the remaining 60 projects, the team asked the project managers to develop a Project Canvas.

The implementation of the Project Canvas, the development of competencies, and the transformation into a more agile and project-driven organization was deemed a successful project. The CEO and her management team were pleased with the results, and they gained a clearer view of the projects that were being invested in. They were able to better allocate resources to the most strategic projects, which they monitored and supported much more closely. The increase in focus delivered faster benefits as well—time to market for new products fell radically, as did the time it took to implement important changes.

In part 2, we have explored the main framework of the book, the Project Canvas. This new way of looking at projects and project management can help organizations succeed in a world driven by change. You have acquired the tools to define and manage your projects in a more professional way, gained a common language you can use to better communicate the key elements of any project, and learned to apply the canvas in your organization.

In part 3, we will examine three areas essential to project management for both individuals and organizations. In chapter 9, we will look into the competencies required to become an effective project manager and project sponsor and how people in both roles can develop additional competencies to transcend their roles and become true project leaders. In chapter 10, we will focus on the importance of project selection and prioritization and how organizational resources can be allocated to projects effectively. And in chapter 11, we will look at how to adapt the structure and the culture of your organization to become more agile and project based to succeed in our changeable world.

PART THREE

Individual and Organizational Project Competencies

9.

Project Leadership

Competencies for Effective Project Management and Sponsorship

This chapter looks at the competencies required to become an effective project manager or project sponsor. It examines how people in both positions can transcend the customary outlines of these roles to become successful project leaders.

Traditionally, the focus of the project manager role was to develop a detailed plan and to monitor a team of experts who get the work done. These are essentially the hard, technical skills of project management. The project sponsor also had a primary focus on the technical aspects of the project—ensuring that the project manager would deliver the project on time, on scope, and on budget. Both these aspects of project guidance are necessary, especially in the engineering and infrastructure areas. Meanwhile, soft skills—leadership, engagement, empathy, stakeholder influence, and others—were customarily not considered an important part of either role. The *PMBOK Guide*, the global reference in project management, covers ten knowledge areas, yet only three are related to soft skills (HR, communication, and stakeholder management). Of these, stakeholder management was only introduced in the fifth edition of the book, in 2013.[1]

We'll examine how both the roles of both the project manager and the project sponsor are now evolving toward project leadership and beyond. The new roles require a shift from pure technical project management competencies toward a broader understanding of soft skills, stakeholders, strategy, and change management.

The growing need for effective project leaders

In a world with an ever-growing number of projects, the demand for people who can effectively manage projects is increasing just as quickly. A quick search on LinkedIn makes it clear just how many job descriptions require sound project management skills and experience. In two of my previous companies, a major skill gap identified was the ability to lead projects across the organization. Although we pick up some of these skills by intuition and practice, and many people can claim to be de facto project managers already, the reality is that the core competencies of project management require dedicated training.

The same gap applies to effective project sponsorship. Most executives have never been trained in these essential skills and have built their project sponsorship competencies on the job. In our research, only 13 percent of the 566 executives surveyed had received specific training on project sponsorship (figure 9-1).

Quite simply, great project managers and sponsors make their projects more successful. The most effective project manager is like a football coach or an orchestra conductor. As a true team player, this manager can gather a diverse group of people, each with unique expertise, and create a high-performing team out of the different individual talents. Each participant

FIGURE 9-1

Project training among executives

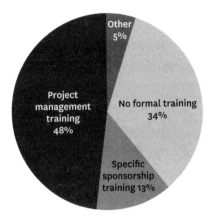

Source: *HBR Project Management Handbook* Executive Survey, July 2020, N = 566

has to have a clear role, feel that they are contributing to the purpose of the project, and be appreciated by the others. A successful project manager will also seek diversity in the team composition and encourage and take advantage of diversity of thought.

The most effective project sponsor will act more like the president of the football club or the opera. The sponsor acts like the ambassador of the project: someone who provides guidance, is personally committed, and unconditionally supports the project and the project manager. The person has to embrace diversity, be accessible to the project manager, and make quick decisions when required. Finally, a successful sponsor must dedicate time to the project. One hour or two hours per month is not enough—and the more important the project, the more time the sponsor should dedicate. The commitment can amount to several full days per week. Worryingly, this level of dedication is not the norm in most organizations.

Anyone can develop into a successful project manager, and any executive can become a good project sponsor. However, the responsibility

A conversation with Alan Mulally on leadership

The following excerpt is from an interview I conducted with Alan Mulally, former CEO of Boeing and Ford Motor Company, and former program director for the Boeing 777. Mulally shares unique insight on some of his upbeat, inclusive ways to lead others.[2]

What kind of project leadership approaches were you applying at Boeing?

Include everybody—it's all about people. Appreciate them so much, because you have all these talented people around the world that are working—everybody needs to be included.

Come together around a compelling vision for what the airplane or the program or the business is, a strategy for achieving it, and also a relentless implementation plan.

Then, of course, there are clear performance goals, having one plan, using facts and data, and the biggest one, probably, is that everybody knows the plan, everybody knows the status, and everybody knows the areas that need special attention.

You engaged the stakeholders from the beginning of the project, including customers, suppliers, and so forth—can you tell us a bit more about that innovative approach?

One of the reasons I believe that Boeing has been successful over the years is that on every airplane program, and especially on the 777, we've always included the airlines in the actual design of the airplane.

requires focus, commitment, determination, personal awareness, eagerness to be a continuous learner, and perseverance during times of failure. As Pamela Gill Alabaster, head of sustainability at Mattel, rightly said, "Continuous learning leads to continuous improvement. Commit yourself to advancing your knowledge, skills, and expertise. The business environment is quickly changing, and your understanding of the leading practices,

They have so much knowledge about how to operate the airplane, how it's going to be used, their reliability requirements, . . . how they're going to take care of it, how they're going to fly the airplane, and how they're going to maintain the airplane. We actually invite the airlines that want to participate in the launch of the vehicle to join the team.

Some of them worry, "If I'm going to share a lot of my knowledge with you in front of the competitor, is that going to put me at a competitive disadvantage?" Then, at one of the early meetings, we had twelve of the world's best airlines in the same room, and one of the airline leaders said, "OK, here's the deal. We want to help Boeing build the best airplane in the world. When we get that best airplane in the world, because we've all contributed to it, then we can compete as airlines."

What was the most difficult part of the 777 project?

I really don't think of it in those terms, because when you operate with these principles and practices, it's all out in the open. So it's not a problem—it's a gem when somebody has an issue.

It's a gem because now you know what the issue is and you're also recognizing that this is an invention, and it's going to be an iterative process, and that's what engineering and design and manufacturing are about, so it's almost like you're legitimizing the process of project management. It's not all going to go right on the plan—it means that you have a process to uncover the areas that need special attention, and you have a culture where everybody is going to share the areas that need special attention, and work together to solve them.

thinking, and emerging tools will help you manage for better results. Be a lifelong student."[3]

Project manager versus project leader

As explained in chapter 2, there is often confusion about the differences between a project manager and a project leader. Here is a reminder of the brief definitions that will clarify the difference and help you understand how these terms are used throughout the book:

- A **project manager** is a role (and often a job title) with a set of responsibilities focused on the technical aspects of the project and with some attention to the softer aspects. The mindset is to produce the deliverables on time, within scope, and within budget.

- A **project sponsor** is a role that executives fill with a set of responsibilities focused on overseeing and supporting the project manager to carry out the project successfully.

- The term *leader* is not a title; it is a set of competencies, a sum of actions, and a special mindset. (For instance, the vice president of sales may be a leader, but that is not on the individual's business card.) Thus, **project leaders** can refer collectively to effective project managers and sponsors who show the qualities of leadership.

Taylor Locke, who interviewed JPMorgan CEO Jamie Dimon in 2020, summarizes his thoughts on these leadership qualities:

> *[Dimon said,]"Management is: Get it done, follow-up, discipline, planning, analysis, facts, facts, facts. . . . But the real keys to leadership aren't just doing that."*
>
> *It's about having "respect for people," not about having "charisma" or "brain power," he said.*
>
> *Having these traits also increases your productivity, along with your success, Dimon said. If you're "selfish" or "take the credit" when it isn't warranted, others are "not going to want to work," which will impact efficiency on your project.[4]*

Both project managers and project sponsors should become project leaders, when the project requires it, by showing the capabilities, competencies, and mindsets of leadership. The most important characteristics of successful project leadership are described in the rest of this chapter.

Project leadership qualities and competencies

I group the main qualities needed to excel as a leader in the project-driven world into six categories:

1. Project management technical skills

2. Product development and domain expertise

3. Strategy and business acumen

4. Leadership and change management skills

5. Agility and adaptability

6. Ethics and values

Another competency—attitude, or a positive mindset—is also a requirement for leadership and has an exponential effect on the other competencies and the project's success. Later in this chapter, we'll examine this attitude and learn why I did not place it as number 7 on the list.

Let's now explore each of these competencies in turn.

1. Project management technical skills

Effective project managers use tools and techniques to determine the rationale and business case of a project. They should be able to work with key contributors and partners in defining scope accurately. The ability to break down the scope into manageable workloads, identify interdependencies, prioritize the work, and translate the activities into a comprehensive, well-defined, and precise project plan constitutes critical technical skills. These skills require a good understanding of details (analytical skills) and the overall picture (strategic skills), as well as the interdependencies and trade-offs between scope, time, and budget. Risk identification and risk management techniques are also essential. Once the project is underway, the project manager needs to establish reporting mechanisms to monitor the execution of the plan and make certain that sufficient quality checks and tests are being carried out. When delays or changes to the plan are foreseen, a good project manager analyzes the consequences and offers viable alternatives to the sponsor and steering committee. A project manager who evolves and gains experience can further develop competencies and grow in related areas such as program management, major projects, project portfolio management, and PMO practices.

To be effective project sponsors, executives, and senior leaders should know the essentials of projects and project management. They should consider these questions:

- What are the key elements that make a project succeed or fail?

- Which questions should they ask to determine if the project's technical fundamentals, such as clarity of the scope, are robust enough to start the project?

- Which characteristics of the project influence the selection of the best project manager?

In addition, sponsors must understand the technical complexity and constraints associated with how sound plans and estimates are developed. A big challenge is the unrealistic expectations that senior leaders have around deadlines, costs, features, and quality; these expectations often bring trade-offs. If you make a plane bigger, then it won't land at every airport and it will cost more to fly, even if you don't sell all the seats. If you make a laptop more powerful, the battery life will suffer. You need to be ambitious, but also pragmatic.

There are plenty of examples of how overreaching or underestimating the complexity of a project has resulted in failure. One is the Myki project in Melbourne, Australia, to introduce a smart-card system to integrate bus, rail, and tram travel throughout the city on a single ticket. Public transport minister Lynne Kosky acknowledged that she was "incredibly frustrated" at the delays that had plagued the project, which was five years late and had required A$350 million in bailout money on top of the original A$500 million price tag. She conceded that in her role as executive sponsor, she had drastically underestimated the complexity of introducing the new smart-card system project across the network.[5] Executive sponsors should understand the basics of designing a solid scope, defining correct time and cost estimates, and the trade-offs between them.

How to acquire these competencies

For project managers, my recommendation, besides reading this book and applying its ideas, is to seek training in the fundamentals of project management. Ultimately, the goal is to obtain a recognized certification that accredits your knowledge. The most common worldwide accreditation is Project Management Professional certification from the PMI. There are others, such as Prince 2 practitioner certification, which is well recognized in the United Kingdom and Commonwealth countries. Praxis is a free framework for the management of projects, programs, and portfolios. It includes a body of knowledge, methodology, a competency framework, and a capability maturity model. A final option comes from the IPMA, which is not as well known but which offers a competency framework (the Individual Competence Baseline, or ICB) that is a good complement to build your technical skills. If you want to completely submerge yourself in training, there are also year-long master's degree programs in project management available.

As a project sponsor, you will almost certainly benefit from training in project management fundamentals for sponsors. You will want to master these fundamentals. You should understand the different types of projects and the methods to implement them, how to select and prioritize projects, and when to consider an idea a project. You should also learn what makes projects successful and some common pitfalls in starting a project. Finally, you should know how to develop a strong business case and purpose for your project.

A better option, which I have assisted many organizations with, is to develop your own in-house training program, specific to your organization's needs and language. That way, you have a consistent way to train all your managers and senior leaders.

2. Product development and domain expertise

Both project managers and sponsors need to have product development skills and domain expertise to lead high-impact projects. They should be proficient in whatever offerings the project will generate: the technology (such as AI or big data), the features, the product, the service, or other capabilities. These competencies give you credibility with the team and the stakeholders. They enable you to communicate in the language of the experts and the product teams, and they give you a good grasp of the project benefits and how and when they will be achieved. Your level of expertise should be overarching rather than detailed. It is not your job to decide on or do most of the work, but you need sufficient understanding to be able to challenge the teams.

With a minimum technical understanding, project sponsors can make good sense of how the project connects with the organization's overall strategy, and they can contribute and challenge the project manager and team on key aspects of the project. A great example of this competency is Steve Jobs's dedication to, and involvement in, the development of the first iPhone project, from 2004 to 2007, Apple's most strategic project at the time. Initially, Jobs knew very little about smartphones, but he soon learned the technology and contributed regularly in design workshops. Executives often struggle to understand new technologies such as blockchain or machine learning; their difficulty contributes to the challenges management teams and boards experience with the implementation of digital transformation projects.

How to acquire these competencies

Be curious and open-minded, both as a project manager and as a sponsor. The bare minimum when starting a project in a domain new to you is to dedicate time to reading articles, watching videos, and looking at analysts' reports. There may be online training via massive open online courses available from many universities and professional business associations. Meet experts if you have access to them. Learn some of the key words in the industry and some of the major challenges it has faced. Summarize of what you find out. Never be afraid to admit that you are new to the industry or the topic—highlight that you are eager to learn, and show your appreciation for the patience of the people who are giving you information.

And take the opportunity to explain to them the project, its purpose, why you need them, and how you will work together to succeed.

3. Strategy and business acumen

A project manager should develop a good understanding of the organization, its strategy, its key competitors, and the environment in which the project will be implemented. For example, if the project's purpose is to increase access to education, an effective project leader will need to appreciate a range of educational systems—which systems are the most successful, why they succeed, and which alternatives best fit the specific needs of the project. Financial knowledge is also a must. The ability to connect the project benefits and purpose to concrete business challenges and priorities is essential for project buy-in and success. Stakeholders, including senior management, will be more supportive if the project manager can make this connection. The most important capability in this category is a strong focus on the benefits and other impacts, even in the early stages. Value creation is a critical and sought-after element in the project-driven world.

Most executive sponsors have already acquired these competencies to reach senior-level positions. As project leaders, sponsors must anticipate trends in the market, spot new opportunities to keep the organization from stagnating, and maintain the project's true raison d'être throughout its entire life cycle. If some of the initial market or customer assumptions need to be addressed, the senior leader, in consultation with the project manager, should intervene to correct course or eventually postpone or even cancel the project.

How to acquire these competencies

While an MBA is still the best way to acquire good business skills, the high cost of MBA programs and the significant amount of time off work they require make this path unavailable to many. Alternative ways to build similar competencies include online courses (some free of charge) on relevant topics (e.g., innovation, finance, and strategy). Some larger organizations have developed their own custom-made master's-level programs. These will not replace the depth of a traditional MBA, but they can provide great value for project managers.

For senior leaders, some of whom already have MBAs, the principles of lifelong learning apply. You will want to continue observing and learning to keep developing your expertise. New technologies and potential disruptors represent great areas for development, so you will want to keep your knowledge up-to-date. Offerings from educational programs like Singularity University and TED Talks, as well as serious business books, can also inspire great leadership.

4. Leadership and change management skills

The increased speed of change, greater complexity, overlapping priorities, the culture of seeking consensus, the multigenerational workforce—all these forces make the implementation of projects much harder than in the past. Although pure managerial skills were largely sufficient for previous generations, today project managers and sponsors must develop strong leadership and sound change management capabilities. From their different positions, they have to provide direction; communicate progress and changes; evaluate, develop, and engage staff; and motivate people even though the managers have no formal authority. They must also develop the skills to confront and challenge others effectively and respectfully. Diverse opinions and different ways of solving problems will lead to potential conflict throughout the life of the project, and misunderstandings will occur— these are a normal part of conducting projects. The best project leaders see these as an opportunity to have a dialogue rather than a debate. A dialogue entails working with others to resolve divergent opinions in ways that all parties can embrace. A debate, on the other hand, is a win-lose scenario where people are more interested in winning personally than they are in being open to alternative solutions to a problem.

The effective project manager should also be able engage the project sponsor and obtain the support of senior leadership and the organization for the project. The ability to understand oneself and effectively sustain working relationships with others—in other words, emotional intelligence—is critical. Both project managers and sponsors have to understand different cultures and how to get the best work from a variety of people; manage and persuade multiple stakeholders, including some who are against the project; build bridges across the organization (which will often be siloed and short on resources); create a high-performing team; and dedicate enough time to develop and coach team members.

Project managers must make effective decisions and be proactive, disciplined, and results-driven. Finally, they have to be resilient—able to bounce back from any difficulties and changes that life throws their way. Resilience is an invaluable leadership skill in projects.

All these skills are situational. Although you can plan your role and involvement to some extent, in the fast-changing, complex environment we have been describing throughout the book, much of your role as project manager is facilitative: anticipating, shaping, framing, and responding. Each project for which you are responsible will require a different approach and emphasis.

Vice Admiral James Stockdale, who survived seven years as a prisoner of war during the Vietnam War, said this about leadership: "Leaders' work is divided into three parts: First, the leader defines the current reality. Then the leader looks at the present but sees a better future. And finally, the leader is the one who, after defining reality and seeing a better future, manages to take the steps and lead the team towards that future."[6]

How to acquire these competencies

Leadership skills are the most difficult to teach and to develop, for both project managers and project sponsors. Some skills, such as communication, are easier to learn than others, but most of them require awareness, time, practice, and perseverance. In a rapidly changing world, leaders need emotional intelligence more than ever.

The first and most important step in acquiring these competencies is self-awareness. Look at yourself honestly, and evaluate your strengths. But even more important, think about your weaknesses. You should also learn to be open and transparent with others. Accept that you are not great at everything, and select one or two areas to improve or develop over the next year. You can work on them alone (self-development), follow a specialized course, or engage a personal coach.

5. Agility and adaptability

In today's world of constant flux, effective project managers need to feel comfortable working in uncertain situations, making plans and decisions with only limited information. When the initiative's requirements are not known in advance, there is much uncertainty about what the outcomes will look like or whether the requirements are likely to change throughout the life cycle of the project. In these situations, the project manager should be prepared to apply some agile methods (or adaptive techniques). Among the many adaptive methods, the most common and most worthwhile are agile project management, Scrum, kanban, and the Scaled Agile Framework (SAFe) (described later in the chapter).

Project sponsors also need to learn to adopt agile methods of working. Traditionally, they were expected to lead according to a predetermined plan and treat decisions as simple and binary activities. Decisiveness and single-mindedness were the preferred character traits of senior leaders. These predictive approaches have now been complemented by a senior management style that involves the ability to frame the future as a series of options that others can understand and then to proceed stepwise: experimenting, then consolidating, adjusting, or stepping back and starting again, depending on the results and other circumstances. Executives must now be comfortable acknowledging that they don't have all the answers but have the courage to change course and cancel projects that are no longer relevant or valuable.

As organizations increasingly sought to become faster and more flexible, they recognized that the agile principles used in software development could be applied much more broadly to organizations as a whole. Leaders focus on creating this agile environment by encouraging everyone to contribute, facilitating joint problem-solving, and encouraging all project team members to take accountability for individual and team outcomes.

Agile leadership is the craft of creating the right conditions for self-organization. Finding the balance between anarchy and an overly strict

Rita McGrath, strategy professor at Columbia University, on adaptability in project management

I think one of the dilemmas with project managers is that they tend to take the projects that they're given as an absolute—"Go break through that wall. . . . OK, I'm going to break through that wall." They don't take a step backward and think about how does breaking through that wall connect with the larger goals. I would encourage project managers to think on the notion of discovery and being discovery-driven. In any context, you have a certain ratio of assumptions that you're making relative to the information that you have; we call it the "assumption-to-knowledge ratio."[7]

For example, you already know quite a bit about the implementation of ERP. You know who the actors are, what needs to happen, and what the outcomes you are trying to achieve are. A very different situation is when you have no idea. For example, "Let's understand how nano-technology is going to influence our cost structure." Those are entirely different kinds of projects, and I think this is where project managers get stuck. They tend to execute everything as though it was that first category—very low assumption-to-knowledge ratio—when in fact, if you're in a high assumption-to-knowledge ratio, it's more about learning fast and at low cost, redirecting and changing the plan, and less about sticking to the plan.

structure is crucial in today's markets. Developing and maintaining this environment is often hard work, requiring you to focus on the needs of others and promote an ownership mindset, feedback, and long-term goals. In this environment, micromanagement takes a back seat to agile teams that collaborate, learn from each other continuously, get quick feedback from users, and focus on quality.

How to acquire these competencies

Although advanced education may not be required to manage an agile project, many available courses and certifications provide a solid knowledge base. PMI provides the Agile Certified Practitioner certification. The Scrum Alliance offers eight professional certification programs, the most popular being Certified Scrum Master. APMG International offers certificate programs for agile project and program managers. The International Consortium for Agile (ICAgile) offers professional, expert, and master certifications covering all disciplines of the agile approach, including leadership, team coaching and facilitation, enterprise coaching, delivery management, value management, development, and testing. Last, Scaled Agile offers several certification programs for those who are seeking knowledge and expertise in implementing the SAFe.

To become agile leaders, senior executives need to develop additional skills in the following areas:

- **Understanding agile fundamentals:** As just described, several online courses provide the basics of agile approaches.

- **Servant leadership:** When leaders practice servant leadership, they put the needs of a group over their own. Servant leadership requires learning how to create trust among employees, help others develop, show appreciation, share power, and listen without judging.

- **Situational leadership:** With this fluid style of leadership, you are always adapting to what the team and the project need as the moment and the environment dictate. It requires you to learn different leadership styles and to assess the emotional states and maturity levels of those you lead. Daniel Goleman, the author of *Emotional Intelligence*, talks about six leadership styles: coaching, pacesetting, democratic, affiliative, authoritative, and coercive. Determine which styles you have mastered and which ones you need to develop.

6. Ethics and values

Ethics play a significant role in day-to-day interactions and behaviors in the world of projects. Project management professionals are held to high ethical standards so that decisions and actions are always honorable and in the best interest of stakeholders. The PMI's Project Management Professionals code of ethics describes the qualities expected of its managers: "Honesty, responsibility, respect and fairness are the values that drive ethical conduct for the project management profession."

Therefore, project leaders' ability to influence others ethically will strongly determine their effectiveness. Project leaders should establish and maintain a psychologically safe, respectful, nonjudgmental environment that will create the trust needed for the team to communicate openly. Demonstrating the courage to make a suggestion, disagree, or try something new fosters a culture of experimentation. Your actions show others that it is safe to be courageous and try new approaches. Team members can then disclose the risks they perceive for the project, express their other concerns, and feel free to share bad news. When ethics and values are made a priority and are respected, projects are more likely to succeed. Both the project sponsor and the project manager should become role models for the team members and the organization.

More than a century old, IBM has sustained its role as a leading business technology vendor by constantly reinventing itself and taking risks, according to Ginni Rometty, IBM's executive chair and former president and CEO. Some 45 percent of the products and services now offered by IBM were introduced in the last two years. Through all this change, however, the company stuck to a set of core values, Rometty said. At IBM, these center on delivering innovative technology for business and society. "Everyone has values," she said, "but it's what you do when no one is looking that matters. We have a dedication to every client's success, to innovation that matters, and to fostering trust and responsibility in all relationships."[8]

How to acquire these competencies

Ethics cannot be acquired—they are part of who we are. However, you can develop a code of ethics that will act as a moral guide for yourself, your project, and the project team on ethical matters. To develop a code of ethics for yourself or the project, look at examples of codes of ethics from other people and other companies. For example, PMI's eight-page "Code of Ethics and Professional Conduct" defines and names "mandatory standards" and "aspirational standards" for responsibility, respect, fairness, and honesty.[9] The IPMA's code of ethics is another good example.[10]

After you have studied these examples, identify your own values: What are my true beliefs? How would I like others to be treated? How would I like to treat others? Share the outcome with your team, and discuss whether the members feel comfortable with these values. Once the project's code of ethics has been approved, it should be applied and followed by every member of the project, starting with you. Nowhere is the aphorism "leading by example" more important than in the area of ethics.

X. *Attitude*

Besides the six key competencies of project leadership, a good attitude is also essential. I label attitude the xth competency and not the seventh, because it has a multiplier effect on all the other competencies and the overall success of the project. Attitude is contagious. As the project manager or project sponsor, your attitude will strongly influence other people around you.

Attitudes are established ways of responding to people and situations—ways that we have learned from our beliefs, values, and assumptions. Attitudes manifest themselves through our behavior and help us persevere through the most challenging moments of the project. Attitude is sometimes more important than facts, the past, and education. A knowledgeable and experienced project manager without a positive attitude will often fail to deliver the project. When choosing a leader for a highly demanding project, organizations are better off with someone who is less experienced or lacks some competencies but who has a strong, positive attitude.

Maintaining a positive frame of mind requires effort. Even when times are difficult, as they often are with projects, look for the bright side of every situation. Spending time with optimistic people will help you stay positive. Expressing gratitude is another powerful way to keep a positive attitude. Show appreciation to your team member and their contributions. They will probably contribute even more to your current project and want to work with you on future projects.

One of the most amazing examples of a positive attitude in a project took place in the Atacama region of Chile in 2010. On August 5, there was a huge explosion, followed by shaking ground and an intense tremble. Deep underground, the San José Mine had collapsed. A group of miners near the entrance managed to escape, but a second group of thirty-three men remained trapped deep inside, twenty-three hundred feet (700 meters) underground and three miles (5 kilometers) from the mine entrance. Emergency officials were unable to communicate with the trapped miners. After two days of searching, the rescuers were not sure if the thirty-three were still alive. The Chilean president, Sebastián Piñera, was informed that the chances of finding the miners were less than 0.00000001 percent. Despite the odds, President Piñera said that he and the government of Chile would put at the rescue teams' disposal all the resources needed to bring the miners back to the surface alive. In an unprecedented move, the mining minister, Laurence Golborne, the project sponsor, began residing full time at the camp to lead the efforts and act on behalf of the president. Despite setbacks, spirits were high among the rescuers and the trapped miners.

The rest is history. Seventy days after the accident, the first miner, Florencio Ávalos, was lifted to the surface in the capsule Fénix, which had been developed with the help of NASA. At a rate of about one miner per hour, all thirty-three men were rescued, safe and alive, as President Piñera, Minister Golborne, and all the families looked on. To date, this is the largest and most successful rescue project in the history of mining.

Strategic projects often require plenty of communication and active leadership, which make project managers and executive sponsors highly visible. Good project leadership not only improves projects but also positively shapes organizational culture as well. In the next chapter, we will see that these leadership traits play a role in how organizations can run hundreds of projects effectively while simultaneously eyeing the future project pipeline for new ideas and opportunities. This process, project portfolio management, will be most successful if the executives responsible apply the competencies and qualities just covered in this chapter. Portfolio management encompasses the selection and prioritization of projects and the governance that helps increase transparency and control in the portfolio.

10.

Selecting and Prioritizing Projects

Managing Your Project Portfolio

Prioritization helps organizations allocate their resources—especially the scarce resources of time, money, management, and employee attention. It allows them to balance their big bets with smaller bets. Effective prioritization sets the agenda for organizations, reflects the organization's short- and long-term strategy, and communicates to managers and employees what really matters to leadership.

Projects that are designated top priorities always have a better chance of being delivered successfully. Most successful companies clearly know what their top projects are and are extremely disciplined in those projects' execution. Take, for example, projects relating to the introduction of the General Data Protection Regulation (GDPR) in 2018, a set of regulations that aim to give European Union citizens control of their data. With a fixed deadline and stiff penalties for nonadherence, GDPR compliance projects were a high priority in most organizations, and managers readily committed resources to them. Something similar happens with large public projects, such as hosting the Olympic Games. These enormous undertakings are almost always delivered on time despite their complexity.

Organizations may be running thousands of projects in parallel, all while endeavoring to stay on top of their pipeline of potential new ideas or project opportunities and the value they might bring. In many ways, managing this pipeline and deciding which projects to invest in or terminate is as challenging as running the projects themselves. In some cases, betting on the wrong ideas, or not betting at all, like the well-known cases of Blackberry, Nokia, and smartphone technology—Blackberry bet wrong on keyboards on phones, and Nokia made no bet at all—can drive an organization to bankruptcy.

This process of keeping abreast of the pipeline of potential projects and deciding to fund, continue funding, or kill numerous projects is called **project portfolio management**.

Why prioritization helps

Prioritization increases the success rate of an organization's most strategic projects and increases the alignment and focus of senior management teams around strategic goals. At the same time, it shifts resources toward projects that address any immediate "burning platforms"—significant threats or opportunities on the direct horizon. In addition, by setting priorities, leaders clear most of the doubts that operational teams face when allocating time to projects. Most importantly, prioritization builds an execution mindset in the organization by clarifying for everyone which projects are the most important (and which are not), thereby guaranteeing close monitoring of the important projects' implementation. Table 10-1 presents some considerations for setting priorities.

Project portfolio management enables organizations to accomplish several tasks that help with organizational strategy:

- Focus on projects that an organization can afford and for which it has (or can access) the requisite resources.

TABLE 10-1

Some key perspectives for managing the project pipeline

Value

How much money will the project generate (and by when)?
What new capabilities will it bring (and by when)?
How critical is it to the realization of strategic objectives?

Risk

How likely is it to succeed?
What happens if it doesn't deliver?
What would happen if we did nothing?

Resources

How much will it cost (and do we have enough money)?
Who will it involve (do we have the right people, or can we get them)?
Do we have the requisite skills?

Balance

What else could we invest in?
What else could our people be working on?
How might this investment in money or people affect other projects?
How risky or uncertain are other projects in the pipeline?
Do we have to do this project now?

- Identify bottlenecks where projects are likely to compete with each other for resources and capabilities unless action is taken.

- Assemble the portfolio to balance short- and long-term objectives and investment; to balance urgent and important change and capability; and to assume an overall risk profile that is in line with the organization's risk appetite.

- Communicate unambiguous strategic intent behind which the senior team and the whole organization can align their efforts.

- Provide a context against which operational teams can plan and make decisions.

- Lay the groundwork for execution. Few things are more debilitating to the pace of project delivery than uncertainty, conflicting demands on time or resources, or an environment in which senior management are required to micromanage because the operational teams are deprived of a clear view ahead.

In most organizations today, PMOs select and prioritize projects. Some organizations have a single corporate PMO that oversees all projects, while others have PMOs at the regional or business-unit level instead (or in addition to the corporate level). The offices' level will determine the scope of the projects they select, prioritize, and oversee. The corporate PMO usually works with the top senior leaders to select the more strategic projects; the business units and regional PMOs will include the strategic projects decided by corporate and will develop and prioritize their own portfolio of projects specific to their needs.

How many projects are we running?

Most organizations and governments struggle to create a prioritized list of their projects. Many lack even a complete list of all the projects they are carrying out. I experienced this problem myself when I started as head of project portfolio management in a large European bank. We didn't know how many projects we were running, and before I could start any analysis and project investment proposals, a team of four members spent six months collecting and clarifying the details of the more than four hundred existing projects. For many reasons, including the following, this problem is understandably widespread:

- You need a critical mass of projects and proposals to make portfolio management worthwhile, but you need portfolio management to obtain a critical mass of projects and proposals. It's a chicken-and-egg dilemma.

- Many established organizations are not conscious of their slow evolution from business-as-usual, operational entities to project-driven organizations. The problems of too many projects, poor results, or competition for resources have crept up on them.

- Western-style management has championed the action-oriented manager, contributing to a culture of presenteeism (working when sick), long hours, and a focus on activity and inputs rather than productivity and outcomes.

- The siloed nature of organizations has enabled directors, divisions, and departments to generate their own portfolio of projects, often undermining corporate projects.

- In some organizations and in government, people tend to downplay a failing project, feeling safe in the knowledge that the project is unlikely to explode until after they have passed it on to their successor.

- Finally, the lack of interest in project management among many senior managers, especially those who didn't come of age in a project-centric environment, has discouraged any detailed reporting or oversight.

Learning to cut, kill, or just say no to projects

Not long ago, I did some work for a leading biotech company. Despite having only seventy-eight employees and seven executives, the company had a list of more than two hundred projects on top of its day-to-day activities. Incredible! Project overload affects almost every organization today, and it creates collateral damage in several ways. Effective prioritization requires saying no to many potential ideas and canceling projects that no longer support organizational goals. It is tempting to say yes and invest in every good idea; in the rosiest scenarios, they all look promising and high potential, and you do not want to miss any of them. But betting on every idea leads to huge amounts of wasted money and resources, the inability to execute the strategy, project failures, and overtaxed, unhappy, and uncommitted employees. Successful individuals are highly focused, and the same applies to organizations.

A great example of prioritization and focus is Starbucks's hiring of Rosalind "Roz" Brewer as COO in 2017. She re-orchestrated the business by eliminating two-thirds of the projects in the corporate office and focused on only three priorities: beverage innovation, store experience, and digital business. Brewer explains her approach: "We just lined everybody up and said if it doesn't fit in these three lanes, we're stopping the work."[1]

From my experience, most organizations could stop between 40 and 50 percent of their projects, and little would change. The Project Canvas is a great tool for finding projects that can be stopped with few conse-quences and whose cancellation would prevent future value destruction. Any project that is missing four or more of the nine building blocks has high chances of failure and should be a serious candidate for cancellation. Assigning the freed-up resources to some of the more strategic projects will accelerate their implementation.

While saying no to some projects and killing others is an essential part of prioritization, these practices introduce some of the conflicts in-herent in projects. Organizations quite rightly insist on a well-conceived business case before a project can be authorized, but unless the selection process and criteria are carefully designed, managers who may have in-vested considerable time and effort in making the case will only associate success with project approval. With this belief (that success means project approval), they frame their proposals in the most positive light. In a similar vein, senior leaders often have difficulty stopping projects in which they have invested time and resources. Because all projects have financial and emotional sunk costs, it is hard to admit publicly that you were wrong. Even so, successful businesses will only invest further in the projects that will build the future and the long-term sustainability of the organization.

Even a well-designed project, particularly one requiring considerable innovation or agility, is still at risk of failure at any stage, and late-stage failure can be both hard to predict and counterintuitive. For example, the Crossrail project in the London area started as an engineering endeavor. Digging the tunnels and laying the track all went according to plan. The project unraveled in the latter stages, however, when the mechanical and electrical systems needed to be installed.

Public companies can face a particular challenge when trying to man-age projects appropriately. The volatility of markets and the fragility of corporate reputations make it difficult to be transparent and honest about challenges and setbacks to much-anticipated projects. This willingness to underplay short-term problems—often quite legitimately if the com-pany is in a position to resolve the impasse—can escalate to encouraging companies to be less than honest about problems that are more serious. Sometimes these behaviors are unconscious or driven by the best of motives, but the results are always the same: cultures that cannot accommodate failure encourage dishonesty up and down the organizational hierarchy.

Nassim Taleb introduced the concept of the **black swan**, a devastating risk that is almost impossible to predict.[2] While the Covid-19 pandemic and other recent upheaval and disasters might suggest that these rarest of birds are becoming more common, the reality is more prosaic, says project management expert Sara Hajikazemi and her coauthors: "What might be a Black Swan to a turkey is not a Black Swan to its butcher."[3] In real life, the causes of project failure are more likely to be what Thomas L. Friedman describes as a "black elephant" in his 2014 *New York Times* article.[4] A **black elephant** is something that has the cataclysmic effect of a black swan but, rather than being unpredictable, is actually the proverbial elephant in the room. In other words, it is a hugely embarrassing issue that everyone tacitly has agreed to ignore because the culture discourages skepticism or suffers from a significant lack of diversity of thinking.

Most companies only prioritize projects when they enter a crisis and are on the brink of collapse. Famous examples of extreme refocus on the core are Apple, the Ford Motor Company, Boeing, Philips, and LEGO. In March 2018, after several years of lower performance and missing sales targets, and having invested more than $30 billion acquiring fifty brands in the past decade, Unilever announced that it was transforming itself into a simpler, more agile, and more focused business.[5] More recently, during the first months of the Covid-19 crisis, organizations kept their businesses alive through extreme prioritization (see part 4 for more on managing projects in moments of crisis).

Often, only when executive teams are pressured to keep the company alive do they make the tough decisions to scrap hundreds of projects and products and to focus their attention, resources, and budgets on the few essential projects. These projects are often in the areas that initially made the company successful.

Knowing when to start a project: Six questions

Successful leaders know when to start a project. And yet this ability is a strategic talent few companies have developed. If you begin a project too soon, chances are high that the project will miss its deadline—if it doesn't fail outright. Using the S-curve learning framework (which recognizes that learning often happens slowly, then quickly, then slowly again over a few years), we can help decision makers envision the right time to initiate a project and thereafter model its progress. The base of the curve represents a period of investigation where relatively few resources have been committed. The purpose of this phase is to ascertain whether there truly is an opportunity in an idea—or not. During this phase, you should seek answers to six foundational questions:

- **Has the project been done before?** The newer the idea, the more time required at the low end of the S-curve to explore it— avoid starting the project right away.

- **Is the project part of your core business, and will it take advantage of your strengths?** The further your project is from the core business, the more time you will need to spend at the lower end of the S-curve. Also, consider the number of projects you already have outside your core business. Too many will jeopardize the project to the point of putting your company at risk.

- **Do you know what the project will produce and look like when it is completed?** If you have less than 50 percent clarity on what the project will deliver, keep exploring and iterating to better define the project or apply an agile approach. Traditional project management theory recommends having 100 percent of the requirements defined at the beginning of the project, but we know this is hardly the case. Aim at having 80 to 90 percent of the requirements defined before moving to the full-blown project stage.

- **What is the investment cost?** Projects are expensive and are likely to cost more than originally planned. Therefore, before starting the project, you must clarify who is going to pay for it. You also need to verify the commitment of the resources, including the time dedicated by executives. All these important decisions should be considered at the initial, lower end of the S-curve.

- **Do you have buy-in from key leaders and the wider organization?** Excellent ideas and brilliant projects have become monumental failures because important stakeholders failed to support the projects. The exploration phase should create a critical mass around the project, enhancing its viability. Are you getting buy-in from crucial stakeholders? Is there movement or inertia around the idea, within the organization? If the institutional will is there, the other necessary resources are likely to be in the pipeline.

- **What is the timeline?** Projects that languish when they should be charging ahead are costly and unlikely to produce satisfactory results. Establish a timeline for the necessary benchmarks. Tight milestones focus organizations and teams, so use them wisely. Beware of project timelines that don't allot time to the exploration phase.

Eventually you reach an inflection point, when it's time to pull the plug on the idea or actively develop it. This point, where the flat growth begins to accelerate, is the place to officially create a project, if you're going to forge ahead. Resources should have been assembled, personnel emplaced, objectives articulated, and a time frame established. The project begins after critical needs have been identified and addressed, not before. The steep part of the S-curve represents a period of explosive growth. When a project launches, it should be ready to go, rapidly ascending this part of the curve.

Benefits of managing a portfolio

A big challenge organizations face today is how to implement their hundreds of projects, agile initiatives, programs, and strategic initiatives while performing their day-to-day activities. Project portfolio management encourages leaders to discuss and agree on the organization's strategic priorities. With a unified approach, leaders can then share these priorities with the rest of the organization and help instill them in corporate culture.

Since the early 2000s, I have held portfolio management executive positions in several organizations: a large telecom operator, one of the largest banks in Europe, and a leading pharmaceutical company. After implementing a portfolio management framework, all these companies have seen major improvements in several areas:

- Increased success rates of the most strategic projects

- Increased alignment and focus of senior management teams around the strategic priorities and the strategic projects of the organization

- Cost reduction of about 15 percent in the area of project management (reduced duplication, consolidated projects, and decreased budget overruns all contribute to these savings)

- Most importantly, an execution mindset and a culture best characterized by language, leadership, and behaviors focused on successful project outcomes

Despite the advantages afforded by project portfolio management, most executives still lack a good grasp of this practice. There is a tremendous opportunity for executives to learn how they can apply this concept to bring focus and alignment, break through silos, and accelerate the implementation of their strategic projects. Project portfolio management provides a frame to help answer the following questions:

- What are the strategic goals of our organization?

- Given these goals, how are we going to achieve them—through projects or our everyday activities?

- Which projects should we invest in for the long-term interest of our company?

- What is the best use of our existing and future financial and operational capacities?

- Do we have the right resources to lead these projects?

- Are there any projects we can stop, suspend, or delay if there is a sudden economic downturn?

- Is the timing right?

- What if the projects fail? Do we have a plan B? And are we learning from failures?

- What value and benefits are we capturing from each project?

Figure 10-1 illustrates an example of a customized project portfolio management framework.

FIGURE 10-1

Portfolio management cycle: Four major steps

Prioritize and select projects and programs (steps 1 and 2):
- Appropriate governance through a monthly investment committee
- A continuous exercise independent from the annual budget process
- Prioritization and selection based on capacity management, decision criteria, risk assessment, and alignment with the organization's strategy

Manage initiative pipeline through the project life cycle (step 3):
- Implementing a consistent and common approach to portfolio management practices
- Gates to reassess and reconfirm the relevance of the project throughout its life cycle
- Splitting funding allocation and commitment to projects by phases instead of full funding

Monitor progress, anticipate risks, and track benefits and closure (step 4):
- Monthly reporting of progress and risks of projects in the portfolio
- Monthly tracking of benefits achieved and formalized project closures
- Adjust project portfolio by closing, delaying, and launching new projects according to new needs

Portfolio must-haves

From the very beginning, you should involve all the key stakeholders (business units, departments, and functions) in the definition of project portfolio management and its application. One great advantage of including stakeholders is that it increases transparency in an area—the change-the-business dimension—where it has not previously existed. Information about the status of priority projects empowers people. You want your major stakeholders to support the project early in its implementation. They need to understand the benefits of the new approach and the mentality of working together as one organization. If only a few departments participate, the selection and prioritization of projects will be flawed. When organizations have project portfolios at multiple levels, the corporate PMO should focus on the overarching strategic goals and companywide projects, while the unit portfolios will cover the projects more specific to their goals and needs.

While every organization should develop a portfolio management framework that fits the needs of its business, the framework must include several elements:

1. A project review board

The project review board decides which ideas and initiatives the organization should invest in and which existing projects should be stopped or delayed. It defines the company's strategic roadmap and oversees the successful execution of it. Both the positioning of the project review board in the organization and the participation of the members will largely determine the impact and success of the entire management framework. Ideally, the chair of the project review board should be the company's CEO, and the rest of the members should be the executive team. The head of the PMO is in charge of preparing and running the cycle of meetings and following up on decisions made.

The project review board should report to the organization's strategic or risk committee and regularly update the board of directors. The business-unit and regional project portfolios should report to the project review board.

Companies struggle to fully manage their project portfolios across all their units; the frameworks are usually implemented through IT, R&D, or supply-chain departments. To work most effectively, the project review board should oversee *all* companywide strategic projects, breaking silos and ensuring that people work more closely together as one company.

The project review board should gather at least quarterly, preferably every month. Once it has established a strategic roadmap, the review board should focus on monitoring the execution of the portfolio of projects.

2. The structured, consistent collection and analysis of new project ideas

Every proposed idea requires a clear rationale and purpose. If the potential project involves a large commitment of financial and other resources, a business case should be developed, including the financial aspects and the qualitative criteria, such as strategic alignment and the acceptable level of risk. Apply the Project Canvas to assess whether all the major elements of an idea can be addressed. Ideas for the most strategic projects, such as acquisitions, will often come directly from the executive team; other more tactical ideas will most likely come from middle management and staff. Everyone can contribute project ideas, and the ideas will undergo the same evaluative process. Projects are not only about business ideas or R&D. They can also address organizational improvements, cost reduction, risk management, regulation, and asset obsolescence, as we have seen in chapter 2.

3. A method for prioritizing and selecting new project ideas

The selection of projects must be fair, transparent, and based on agreed-upon criteria. Some additional criteria for analyzing the new ideas are NPV, ROI, payback period, strategic alignment, risk, complexity, and interdependencies. Ongoing projects must also be ranked, particularly the first time the project review board prioritizes projects in the portfolio. The organization must also keep some good projects in the pipeline rather than launching them right away. The continuous monitoring and managing of project ideas is essential for the long-term viability of an organization.

This practice helps management react quickly to changes in the market in either a defensive or a proactive way.

Project portfolio management requires cross-checking and validating that all the strategic objectives have the means (and resources allocated) to be achieved, in both the short and long term, either through day-to-day activities or through projects. One important selection criterion involves the organization's competencies and capacity. The company must have the right competencies and sufficient available capacity to deliver the project; most organizations struggle to have a comprehensive and up-to-date view of their employees' availability. A simple rule I recommend applying is to finish or cancel at least one project (and preferably more) before launching a new one.

Not long ago, a yearly selection and prioritization round sufficed. However, with the acceleration of changes and the increase in competition, you should revisit the list and new ideas on a quarterly basis.

But do not prioritize merely for prioritization's sake. You should keep the approach focused on only the most important projects and make it an easy process—it should not become heavy or tedious. It is natural to want all the details when dealing with all your projects and investments, but as discussed earlier, obtaining and keeping accurate and updated data related to projects requires significant resources and time. Focus on the most important initiatives instead of trying to cover the whole spectrum of projects. For example, start by prioritizing the twenty most important projects, then assess the rest with a more general level of priority—must do, nice to have, and trivial. Don't try to give 100 percent of your projects an exact ranking; such a list can become cumbersome to produce and to maintain. Remember that some projects will have a top priority at the business-unit level and less so at the corporate level but will still require funding. Also, if the projects are not too complex—they have little uncertainty and need few resources (e.g., less than a hundred person-days)—it is better to handle them as continuous improvements. This treatment will help you clean up a significant part of your portfolio. In my experience, about 60 to 70 percent of projects in a portfolio are of this smaller type.

After leading many prioritization exercises, I came to learn that this exercise is mainly intended to provide managers with different scenarios, encouraging them to make joint decisions through strategic dialogue. Despite most theories asserting that you can produce a complete list of prioritized projects through an automated formula, this practice is not practical. The ultimate decision has to make by the executives using their own human intelligence.

One important last step in the selection exercise is ensuring that each of the organization's strategic projects has a single executive sponsor assigned, dedicated, and accountable to deliver the project.

4. A strategic roadmap

To create a strategic roadmap, make a list of prioritized projects to be implemented by the organization over the next three to five years. The company's strategic objectives and goals should be clearly reflected in this roadmap. The list should reflect the outcome of the prioritization exercise so that the most relevant projects are clearly identified. They will require most of management's attention and preferably the allocation of the best resources in the organization.

Keep in mind that projects are dynamic: as they progress along their life cycle, the initial parameters (costs, benefits, duration, and scope) considered at launch will usually change. These changes may have impacts on the profitability of both the project in question and other projects in the portfolio because of overall budget and capacity constraints. Although changes to the roadmap will necessarily occur, top projects should not change frequently.

At least yearly, the executive team should ask for input and sign-off on the strategic roadmap from the board of directors. Afterward, the team should share and explain the roadmap to all the layers in the organization. The strategic roadmap should be revisited every quarter.

5. A life cycle with funding gates

Installing gates in the life cycle of a project allows the executive team to effectively monitor the portfolio and control project funding. This process consists of establishing three to five standard phases of a project's life cycle— for example, feasibility, initiation, planning, execution, and closing—each of which ends with a gate. At this gate, project feasibility is evaluated on whether the next phase should be begun. If a project is not progressing according to plan, or if the market has evolved, or if the priorities of the organization have changed, the gate system gives top management an opportunity to adjust or cancel the project before more resources are sunk.

6. A method for monitoring the execution of the strategic roadmap

To make sure the strategic roadmap is being executed, the head of the PMO should give top management and the board regular reports on the progress of the strategic projects. The project review board should also have regular deep dives on the implementation progress. The entire list of prioritized projects should be reviewed in depth by the investment committee once per quarter. The PMO should provide a detailed update to the project review board on the roadmap progress, value creation, impact, risks, and most burning issues faced by the strategic projects. The Project Canvas helps facilitate this dialogue. These regular reviews help management quickly react to market changes and supervise the pipeline of new projects.

7. Links to budgeting cycle and enterprise risk management

Portfolio management should always be linked to the organization-wide processes of the budgeting cycle and risk management. Many organizations, including publicly traded ones, operate according to their annual budgeting cycle. Traditionally this cycle doesn't include a dedicated budget for projects, as it is driven from an operational perspective. This focus leads to several challenges for project portfolio management: organizations might start projects at any time, projects are often multiyear initiatives, and so forth. To address this lack of synchronization between projects and the traditional budgeting cycle, more and more companies are starting to split their cycle into one budgeting cycle for running the organization and another for changing it.

Risk management is the other critical companywide cycle that needs to be adjusted for maximizing the impact of project portfolio management. Corporate risk management should evaluate, monitor, and mitigate project risks when appropriate. The most traditional way to manage risk from a portfolio perspective is to consolidate the risks of each individual project on a global level. However, the amount of risk of each strategic project should not be seen in isolation; risks often influence other aspects of the organization, such as operations or compliance. If a strategic project is affected by a serious risk—for example, a delay in the launch of a new system—the risk will have consequences on other parts of the organization. Therefore the risks of strategic projects should be assessed in light of the bigger picture and should be included in overall enterprise risk management.

8. Benefits tracking

Project leaders need to implement a process for tracking the benefits of projects. Take a cue from M&A for this system: during acquisitions, synergies are linked to specific milestones in the integration plans. When a milestone is reached and has synergies attached to it—for example, the closure of some shops—then the benefits can be calculated and compared with the plans. The strategic roadmap for projects should include these synergy-delivering milestones. These give management a method to monitor the benefits of the portfolio of projects.

The increasingly critical role of boards of directors

High-performing boards in particular tend to fall into a complacency trap, relying on past successes without preparing the organization for the future. Such boards often realize too late that their environments have changed, new competitors have redefined industry boundaries, and their offering and business model have become outdated. On the other extreme, excessive change can lead to **organizational burnout**, a situation where managers become preoccupied with change and lose sight of the firm's strategic core. In this respect, the board of directors has a critical role in determining the appropriate timing of change projects to avoid both organizational burnout and complacency over time.

In a world of increasing turbulence, organizational change and digital transformation are major agenda items for boards of directors. The digital age challenges boards to an unprecedented extent and requires them to move beyond their current monitoring duties.[6] As representatives of share-holders, corporate boards need to monitor executive management's strategic actions, including strategic proposals and the portfolio of projects aimed at adapting to the changing business landscape.

Directors have a critical role in project portfolio management. They evaluate and render advice on executives' proposals for transformation initiatives not only about acquisitions or strategic portfolio reconfigurations but also about reinventing their business models. Boards should listen to the different strategic projects and priorities presented by the project review board. After the board's approval, the directors are responsible for overseeing the implementation of the company's strategic roadmaps.

Yet today, few boards assume many aspects of strategic project management, although they would be well advised to do so. Implementation and governance expertise is hardly regarded as a principal skill for directors. Indeed few directors would boast of having this competence, despite the fact that Lou Gerstner considered it critical in his successful turnaround of IBM.[7] This operational capability and know-how in terms of governance and execution of strategic projects is a must-have for boards in the digital age. There are two sides to this coin: on the one side, good governance of strategic projects will prevent serious value destruction, while on the other side, good implementation of strategic projects will enable an organization to navigate effectively in the digital age. The answer to the question of whether success is related to the best governance practices or to exceptional execution capabilities is this: successful organizations must build and must have both.

Boards have to prepare the organization for the future by installing effective governance structures and processes that ensure adaptability over time. Adaptation in the long run has several implications. First, sound project portfolio processes must be established and project management competencies should be developed throughout the organization. Adaptability also means that project managers are nurtured and that executive sponsors are trained and held accountable on delivering the projects and their benefits. Adaptability even sometimes means replacing the CEO and other senior executives when their knowledge has become outdated and new skills are required. Hence, in their succession planning, boards have to assess candidates' competencies that will be required in the future and their ability to navigate an organization through times of change.

———————

Keep your approach to portfolio management simple and pragmatic. Customize it to your organization, and use your own company language. Avoid overengineering the process and making it too abstract. Develop clear instructions for consistency, and be disciplined in the application of new processes. Introducing portfolio management is itself a cultural change project; employees have to understand the purpose of the new process, the ultimate benefits, and what is expected of them. Most likely, there will be resistance at first, so the management team needs to lead by example and be strict in the implementation of the new process. At its best, prioritizing enhances the strategic dialogue at the top of the organization, and the strategic priorities can then be shared with the rest of the organization. Once the executive team understands that prioritization enhances strategic dialogue, prioritization will become embedded in the organization and its corporate culture.

The hierarchy of purpose: A better way to prioritize

Prioritization is vital to individual and organizational success, yet surprisingly, the method of prioritizing is little understood and often neglected. Capacity and gut feeling, rather than strategy and facts, often determine how we prioritize projects. Prioritization sets the agenda in terms of what really matters and, consequently, how resources are allocated—especially the scarce resources of time and money. In my experience, a primary reason that many organizations fail is their lack of a clear sense of what is urgent or simply their selection of the wrong priorities. Get your priorities wrong, and the effects can be calamitous.

Look at two of the classic corporate failures of recent times—first, Kodak. It wasn't that the company didn't foresee the rise of digital photography, but Kodak prioritized the wrong things. In the 1990s, it invested billions of dollars in developing the technology for taking photographs using mobile phones and other digital devices. But in a classic case of Clayton

Christensen's innovator's dilemma, the company held back from developing digital cameras for the mass market because it feared that these new products would kill its all-important film business.[8] Meanwhile, the Japanese company Canon recognized the strategic priority presented by digital photography and rushed in.

Similarly, Finnish company Nokia developed the technology for smartphones earlier than most of its competitors did, yet it decided not to launch projects in this field and prioritized exploiting existing products. If it had chosen different priorities, Nokia could still be one of the leading telecom operators in the world.

And if the executive team doesn't prioritize, middle management and employees will do so on their own. At first, this shouldering of responsibility by the lower ranks may sound like a good practice—after all, empowering people to make decisions has been lauded for decades. Yet without a prioritized set of strategic objectives, the consequences of the selected projects are often disastrous. In a vacuum, the employees will base their priorities on what they think is best for the organization—or perhaps what is best for their business unit, department, team, or just themselves.

To illustrate the problem, let's look at a real example (some details changed for confidentiality). Samantha worked as a teller in a local bank. She loved her job, and her father had spent his entire career in the same bank. However, like many other banks, the company was struggling to survive because of low interest rates, the increase of competition, and the burden of cumbersome regulation. The executive team worked for months to identify a new strategy that would help to turn the company around. The executives identified two strategic priorities that they believed would secure the company's future.

In a series of town hall meetings, the CEO informed the staff, Samantha included, that the new strategy of the bank was based on two priorities:

1. Improve customer experience: increase satisfaction by 20 percent

2. Increase efficiency: serve 20 percent more customers per day

The message was clear: as long as Samantha and her colleagues kept focused and met the two strategic priorities, the company's future and their jobs were assured.

The next day, Samantha was extra motivated, knowing that it was in her hands to save the company she cared so much about. She kept the two strategic objectives in mind and started serving customers as efficiently as possible, always with a smile. This approach worked fine until a customer started to talk about a personal loss and the terrible situation he was going through. He clearly wanted to talk with Samantha, who was initially pleased with the idea, as her attentiveness would significantly increase customer satisfaction.

However, after a few seconds she froze. What about the second strategic objective, efficiency? If she spent a few minutes talking with her customer, her client-servicing rate would suffer. What was she to do? She didn't know which objective was more important, but it was her decision. And every other bank teller was facing the same dilemma every day. The executive team thought that it had clearly communicated the strategic objectives that would turn the bank around, but in fact, the team had created an operational dilemma: two strategic, prioritized objectives can often be contradictory.

A well-communicated set of priorities helps align most projects in an organization with its strategies. This alignment is often championed by business thinkers. But the reality of an organization is much more complex than many of these thinkers suggest. Sometimes, the strategic objectives are unclear, nonexistent, or in conflict. Often, there is a gap or a lack of agreement between the corporate strategic objectives and those from the different business units, departments, or functions.

A popular misconception is that *all* of an organization's projects should be aligned to one or more of its strategic objectives. But because most organizations are multidimensional, it is impossible to match all projects to strategic objectives. For example, continuous process improvement, outsourcing, and regulatory projects keep the organization running efficiently, but they are seldom related to strategic objectives. I recommend that at least the most important projects and programs—let's say the top twenty projects—be fully aligned with strategic objectives.

To prioritize projects effectively, leaders in an organization have to recognize and articulate what really matters most. In my own career, I have tried to apply many theories and prioritization tools, yet none proved to be successful. A popular prioritization technique is to link every project to at least one strategic goal. This approach makes a lot of sense in theory, but in practice, if a company has more than eight hundred projects and more than ten strategic goals, it would need a large team to keep that information accurate.

FIGURE 10-2

The hierarchy of purpose

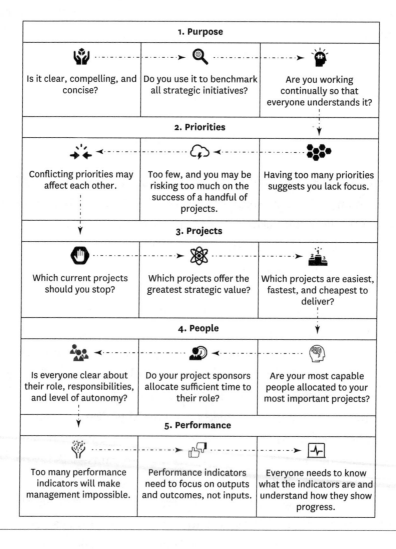

To address the prioritization challenges I have faced over my career, I developed a simple framework called the **hierarchy of purpose**. Boards of directors, executive teams, and even individuals can use the tool to rank priorities and select their most important projects.

The hierarchy of purpose is based on five aspects: purpose, priorities, projects, people, and performance (figure 10-2). Each aspect should be considered in succession, as indicated by the arrows in the figure. Only when an aspect has been pinned down and fully understood should the organization move on to the next.

Purpose

Vision and mission have been popular concepts, yet they tend to be made up of fancy words often developed by consultants. The two terms are often confused, their differences not well understood. Use the term *purpose* instead. State the purpose of your organization and the strategic vision supporting this purpose. The purpose has to be sharp and clearly understood by anyone working for your organization. Amazon's purpose—"to be earth's most customer-centric company"—is compelling enough to avoid any ambiguity.[9] Ryanair, the successful (and controversial) low-cost Irish airline, is very clear about its purpose: "to offer the lowest fares possible and reduce flight delays." Interestingly, the airline puts efficiency and performance—two important objectives that many leaders struggle to prioritize, as we saw in Samantha's case—before customer service. Another remarkable purpose was the one set by Sony's cofounder Akio Morita, when Japan was seen as a country that produced cheap copycat products. He established that Sony's purpose was to "make Japan known for the quality of its products." Notably, he said *Japan*, not Sony. The company's purpose aimed at a higher dimension than its own renown—a bold yet extremely inspiring purpose for its employees.

Priorities

The number of priorities an organization declares is revealing. If the risk appetite of the executive team is low, the executives will tend to name many priorities; they don't want to risk not having the latest technology or missing a market opportunity or other prospects. On the other hand, if the executives are risk takers, they tend to have a laser-like focus on just a few priorities. They know what matters today and tomorrow. As a project leader, you should define what matters most to your organization now and in the future. As the previous example of Amazon showed, its purpose clearly puts the customer in the center. Everyone working at Amazon will know that when they have to make decisions, the ones related to customers will always come first. Or as Emma Walmsley, CEO of pharma giant GlaxoSmithKline, clearly states, "Everyone at GSK is focused on 3 priorities—Innovation, Performance, Trust."[10]

Projects

Strategic initiatives and projects, when successfully executed, bring the organization closer to its purpose and strategic vision. Nowadays, companies run many projects in parallel, mostly because it is easier to start projects than to finish them. Capacity, rather than strategy, often determines the launch of projects. If people are available, the project is launched. If not, it is just dismissed. But which projects should organizations really invest in and focus on? And who wants to risk missing a big opportunity? By uncovering the organization's purpose and priorities, in combination with the Project Canvas, senior executives can identify the best strategic initiatives and projects to invest in. They can also take these steps to identify projects that should be stopped or scrapped. As noted earlier, although some believe these steps can be made into an algorithm, there is no substitute for human judgment.

People

Prioritizing at an organizational level is incredibly difficult. Large organizations are made up of individuals with their own strong sense of what matters. Every individual in an organization has a unique list of priorities. These are by their nature self-serving, informed as much by personal ambition and aspiration as by any sense of alignment with the organization's strategy. Yet, as shown in the example of Samantha, employees are those who implement the company's strategies. They perform the routine business activities and deliver the projects. They also have to make many minor decisions and trade-offs every day. Creating clarity around the priorities and the strategic projects of the organization will ensure that every employee pulls in the same direction. Leaders need to allocate the best resources to the most strategic projects and liberate them from daily operational tasks.

Performance

Traditionally, performance indicators don't measure priorities and seldom indicate the progress made toward fulfilling a company's strategy. Project metrics tend to be lagging indicators and measure inputs (scope, cost, and time) instead of outputs. Inputs are much easier to track than outputs (such as benefits, impact, sustainability, and goals). As you work through the hierarchy of purpose, identify indicators linked to the organization's priorities and to the outcomes expected from the strategic projects. Less is more in this case, so one or two for each area will do the job. When Satya Nadella took the role of CEO of Microsoft in 2015, he announced a new corporate mission: to push productivity, everywhere, across all platforms and devices. Pursuing that mission meant changing the way the company measured success. In an interview in the *Verge*, he explained, "We no longer talk about the lagging indicators of success, right, which is revenue, profit. What are the leading indicators of success? Customer love."[11]

It is better if people can remember by heart how performance is measured. The ultimate goal is to have the few outcome performance indicators embedded in people's minds.

The benefits of the hierarchy of purpose

Organizations that have a highly developed sense of priorities are in a powerful situation and benefit from a significant competitive advantage. By applying the hierarchy of purpose in combination with the Project Canvas, an organization can significantly reduce its costs, because it can stop any low-priority activities that fail to deliver against clearly articulated measures. Through these approaches, organizations can also reduce duplication, consolidate activities, and decrease budget overruns. Overall, prioritizing increases the success rates of the most strategic projects, increases the alignment and focus of senior management teams around strategic priorities, and, most importantly, leads to an execution mindset and culture.

A major hidden benefit I have seen every time I have used the hierarchy of purpose for the first time with top management is that the discussion turns into a stimulating strategic dialogue. For example, the CEO might ask the director of sales, "How are we going to meet that international growth target if currently we only invest in existing markets or if compliance takes up to 60 percent of our project capacity? Is this sustainable in the long term? What would be the consequences of balancing our portfolio and investing more in growth and cost optimization, and less in compliance?"

Think of your organization's purpose and priorities. Are all your employees working according to those priorities? Are the activities prioritized in the best interests of the organization as a whole? How would your priorities change if there were a sudden economic downturn?

If Samantha's executive team had applied the hierarchy of purpose, the members would have had to choose which priority was more important to the bank's strategy: increasing customer service or increasing efficiency. A decision about the top priority would have given more guidance to Samantha and her colleagues when they had to make choices and might have resulted in a very different outcome for the bank.

––––––––––––

Amid the eruption of the Project Economy, every organization in the world will have to implement and include sound project portfolio management as part of its strategic processes and competencies. In the next chapter, we will explore why this change is a prerequisite in a larger organization transformation. We will look at what you and your leadership team need to do to become an agile and project-driven organization.

11.

The Agile and Project-Driven Organization

Building the Structure and Culture Needed for Project Success

Your organization's structure, culture, and ways of working will have an impact on the success of your projects. Traditional, top-down organizations will struggle in the Project Economy—this chapter covers how organizations can adapt to become more agile and project-based to succeed in a turbulent world. It will also discuss the eight most common challenges in project implementation from a cultural, organizational, and work-process perspective and how you and your leadership team can overcome them.

Many Western companies still have a hierarchical structure based on the command-and-control principles of the twentieth century. Budgets, resources, career paths, compensation, KPIs, and decision-making power are "owned" by the heads of business units, departments, and functions. This arrangement was ideal for running daily business activities when efficiency was the name of the game. But there is no doubt that traditional structures are too costly, too slow to adapt, too unresponsive to customers, and too limited in creativity and initiative for the fast and competitive challenges of today's environment. As we will see later in this chapter, many Chinese companies and startups have organizations that are flatter and more fluid, qualities that allow them to react faster. Figure 11-1 shows the evolution of traditional hierarchical organizations toward flatter and more agile ones.

Strategic projects are cross-functional and cross-hierarchical by nature, cutting across organizational levels and requiring resources and input from numerous departments and functions. Cross-departmental projects

FIGURE 11-1

Different types of organizational structures

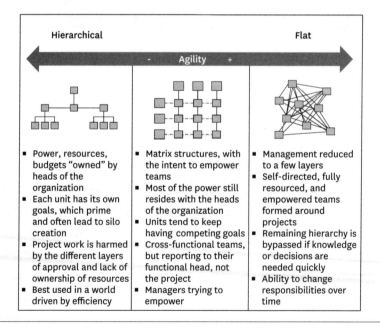

in a traditional organization always face the same difficulties, some of which are linked to the following questions:

- Which department is going to lead the project?
- Who is going to be the project manager?
- Who is the sponsor of the project?
- Who is rewarded if the project is successful?
- Who is the owner of the resources assigned to the project?
- Who is going to pay for the project?

The silo mentality adds to this complexity, with managers often wondering why they should commit resources and a budget to a project that, although important, would not give them any credit if it succeeds. What's more, when individual and team performance is measured with KPIs tailored to each unit or function, conflict may arise between departments.

In a traditional hierarchy, projects cannot be executed quickly. Managing just one project in such a complex structure is a challenge. Imagine the difficulty of selecting and executing hundreds of projects of various sizes. Today's organizations need instead a structure to help people make quicker decisions at the level at which these decisions should actually be made (typically at middle-management levels and below).

How some Chinese companies embody organizational agility

Interestingly, faced with a silo mentality, a lack of agility, an attachment to the status quo, innovation paralysis, and all the downsides of traditional organizational structures, several Chinese companies have managed to reformulate their organizations effectively.[1] Through the lens of three successful Chinese companies—Xiaomi, Alibaba, and Haier—we will learn the best practices on making your organization more agile by applying such concepts as customer-driven projects.

Xiaomi

Xiaomi is a Chinese mobile internet company focused on smart hardware and electronics. It has been included in the *MIT Technology Review*'s list of the fifty "smartest companies," and founder Lei Jun has appeared on the cover of *Wired*, which proclaimed, "It's time to copy China."

The company began in 2010 and has emerged rapidly. It outstripped Apple's smartphone sales in China within four years. Throughout this period, Xiaomi introduced new products to the market at breakneck speed, disrupting or at least surprising market incumbents virtually every time. By 2018, Xiaomi had successfully introduced more than forty products, including smart rice cookers, robot vacuum cleaners, and connected running shoes.

Xiaomi has gained a lot of attention for its unusual marketing strategy, which relies completely on digital technology. It uses low-cost online sales channels and social media platforms to meet the demands of target customers rather than retail shops and distributors. However, the truly innovative aspect of Xiaomi is how its organizational model is driven by projects. Its forty-plus products in the market are not organized in strategic business units; nor have they become part of the organizational hierarchy.

The company has a relatively flat organizational structure—the seven cofounders are only one line of management away from the engineers and sales teams. Sales and engineering make up the largest part of the employee base. Moreover, the cofounders are required to be directly involved with projects and new-product development. They participate in user interaction, such as on Xiaomi's own platform, and keep up-to-date with products and projects. Each Xiaomi employee—including the founders—has a contractual responsibility to deal directly with a certain quota of customer requests. A sophisticated distribution system allocates questions about digital problems to any suitable employee. Customer proximity has not only become a performance assessment criterion for employees but also a requirement for customer-driven projects. The development of each new product *is treated as a project* that can be achieved by mobilizing resources inside and outside Xiaomi. Two features stand out and warrant examination.

Iteration of product development and customer-driven projects

Xiaomi's approach to new-product development focuses on getting proto-types out to the market as quickly as possible with good-enough-quality products. The company actively involves users in fine-tuning and updating the technology and design. Each product is largely codeveloped by the community through an efficient R&D process that could not track any closer to market need. Xiaomi also uses the best-qualified suppliers for components and focuses on integration and design R&D rather than production and hardware R&D. Xiaomi's key competency is a project-driven structure where the business model, marketing, promotion, and design are all centered on the customer interaction. As a result, the company can deliver good-quality products that customers want without the production and R&D investments that a traditional organizational structure would require.

An ecosystem of external resources to speed up project execution

Customer-driven projects gain speed at Xiaomi by exploiting external resources. Following its original three original designs—smartphones, TV set top boxes, and routers—all other Xiaomi products were developed as projects in collaboration with other companies or entrepreneurs. For example, Xiaomi identified a big market need for air purifiers but could not find a suitable producer. The company contacted Su Jun, former associate professor of industrial design at North China University of Technology, suggesting that he develop an air purifier and that Xiaomi invest in the startup. Within nine months, the product was developed and launched, retailing for only one-third of the average market price of air purifiers at that time.

Alibaba

Alibaba Group is among the world's largest and most valuable retailers, with operations in more than two hundred countries. Alibaba's success can be largely attributed to its innovative organizational structure, a business ecosystem that has fostered rapid growth and frequent business transformation since the company's founding in 1999.

Alibaba is widely characterized as a dynamic system of hundreds of companies, ventures, and projects enabled by digital technology. These business ecosystems cut across at least twenty sectors. The majority of the players in Alibaba's system are independently run operations, neither part of strategic business units nor subject to reporting structures, and many of them remain small.

Instead of directing the development of new products and implementing projects from the top down, Alibaba functions as a "gravity provider" and network orchestrator.[2] For instance, Alibaba's core is composed of four e-commerce platforms (Alibaba.com, 1688.com, Taobao.com, and Tmall .com) that are home to seven hundred million users. Moreover, the interdependence between the companies, ventures, and projects is not just based on finance and equity, although these are prerequisites to be part of the business ecosystem. The interdependence is found in growth strategies, investment approaches, and complementarities between offerings, business synergies, and resource sharing. Entrepreneurial projects in this ecosystem are allowed to fail, and failure has few consequences for the sustainability of the whole ecosystem or the careers of top management.

Employees in Alibaba's ecosystem are selected and managed according to alignment of values rather than rules. The company's main values include putting the customer first, teamwork, embracing change, integrity, passion, and dedication. The result of this values-driven approach is the encouragement of risk-taking, a strong organizational culture, and internal competition.

Employees are assessed every quarter and rated on performance and values, both qualities seen as equally important. There is no HR guidebook, only a set of strong principles to help employees operate in a dynamic environment. They can initiate any project they like without regard to their current company or department. In fact, the Alibaba ecosystem provides a safe marketplace of resources that anyone can use to initiate a project. Creators can implement their ideas outside corporate hierarchical boundaries and complex vertical reporting structures.

Alibaba has been, by far, the most active generator of new CEOs in the world. By the beginning of 2016, more than 450 individuals had emerged from Alibaba to start their own ventures. Many of these new projects started within the ecosystem of Alibaba, leveraging its rich resources and opportunities. New project initiatives and implementation stay within the ecosystem and do not suffer from bureaucracy, department silos, or managerial limitations.

Haier

Haier Group is today the world's leading brand of major household appliances. It was founded in 1984 and has been the number one white goods supplier since 2009, with 10 percent of the global market share. In 2016, the company reached revenues of more than RMB 200 billion and acquired GE's appliance division for $5.4 billion, a feat previously unimaginable considering Haier's humble beginnings three decades ago.

Haier is also one of the first Chinese companies to continuously bring new products to the market. The company produces many products that satisfy special needs in China—for instance, washing machines with quick washing cycles and fifteen-minute nonstop washing. Many of the product ideas come from the customer-facing side of the company, such as repair people and salespeople. Haier's Crystal washing machine series represents the outcome of several rounds of user observations and surveys and innovations in spin speed and operating noise.

Since 1998, Haier has been experimenting with self-organizing work units and internal labor markets with the aim of reducing hierarchy and control and increasing autonomy. Then, in 2010, Haier put a unique project organization platform in place throughout the company. The first step was eliminating strategic business units and managerial hierarchies to create zero distance from the users of its products. The company reorganized into three project units:

- One project unit is focused on new-product development, marketing, and production. This unit is closest to the user.

- Another project unit is organized by corporate support functions, such as HR, accounting, and legal.

- The third project unit is executive team. This is the smallest unit and is positioned at the bottom of the inverted pyramid. Its role has been redefined as a support function for the customer-facing, self-organizing project organizations.

Haier now has thousands of work units, more than a hundred of which have annual revenues in excess of RMB 100 million. More recently, the platform has evolved further to allow the work units of noncore products to spin off. Since 2014, external investors have been allowed to invest in promising new products, jointly with Haier's investment fund. For instance, a furniture maker invested in an e-commerce platform (Youzhu.com) that a work unit had developed for home decor. By 2020, forty-one such spin-offs had received funding, with sixteen receiving in excess of RMB 100 million.

The company's project organization platform has had a positive impact on the workforce too. Through measures such as decentralization, disintermediation, and the elimination of internal communication barriers, Haier has decreased its own staff by 45 percent but has created more than 1.6 million job opportunities.

Benefits of a lean, agile, and project-driven structure

Despite being large organizations with strong top-down leadership, these three Chinese companies are highly innovative and adaptive to changing markets through swift project implementation. The cases of Xiaomi, Alibaba, and Haier illustrate how companies can expand their businesses by combining lean, agile, and design thinking approaches with project-driven structures. In 2020, researchers from McKinsey found that "agile organizations responded faster to the [Covid-19] crisis, while those that do not embrace agile working may well forfeit the benefits of speed and resilience needed in the 'next normal' after the pandemic."[3]

The most successful organizations in today's world have adjusted their structure to facilitate and support the execution of projects through a network of teams operating in rapid learning and decision-making cycles. They have become agile and project-driven: resources, budgets, and decision-making power have partly shifted to the project activities, often driven by the implementation of a corporate PMO or strategy implementation office.

Obstacles to becoming an agile and project-driven organization

Agility and a project-driven strategy do not come easily to traditional companies. Changing essential elements of organizational culture or structure requires a sense of urgency and a huge commitment and drive from the leadership team. Organizations will encounter eight common obstacles when striving to become agile and project-driven. Three obstacles are related to cultural matters, two are important organizational design challenges, and three others pertain to implementation and oversight competencies. All eight obstacles are related to the conflicts and challenges of maintaining organizational ambidexterity, as discussed in chapter 1. These difficulties arise as organizations shift their focus from efficiency to change. The barriers must be addressed at the root cause; unless organizations make structural changes, they will continue to struggle to implement their projects successfully, even when projects are well defined and when some of the best practices covered so far in this book are applied. We will look at these challenges one by one and will study examples of how organizations overcame them.

1. Weak accountability for senior leaders and inadequate governance

Today's organizations require governance that includes a body to oversee cross-departmental projects, provides a consolidated view of progress and problems across the portfolio, and takes on accountability for the implementation and value creation of the organization's projects. Because strategic projects require a strong executive sponsor, senior leaders must know precisely what is expected from them in this critical role and must be held ultimately accountable for the success of the project.

Even the most experienced and highly regarded organization can fall foul to problems of accountability and poor governance. The Boeing 737 MAX, for example, was intended to keep the 737 competitive in its market segment and to retain Boeing's strong position in the commercial aviation field.[4]

Despite questions surrounding how well the old design lent itself to new changes, Boeing's 737 MAX took to the air for the first time, in 2016. Sales were strong, and deliveries to airlines started in 2017. Unfortunately, as many readers will be aware, the aircraft suffered a crash in October 2018 (Lion Air 610) that cost 189 lives. Reports indicated that the pilots had lost control of the aircraft because of a sensor failure and the subsequent interventions of the aircraft's systems. Although pilot training issues were initially floated as a primary cause, a second deadly crash (Ethiopian Airlines 302) in March 2019 highlighted potentially deeper issues with the aircraft's design and the entire project.

To prevent any further incidents, the worldwide fleet of nearly four hundred aircraft was grounded later that month. A January 2020 public release of Boeing's internal emails resulted in the project's enduring soundbite: "This airplane is designed by clowns who in turn are supervised by monkeys."[5] Poor accountability, lack of governance, and disproportionate financial considerations in technical decisions all tragically undermined what should have been a world-beating project.

Solution: Assign one strategic project to each executive, and make the person accountable for delivering the benefits

A great example of the increased accountability from senior leaders around strategic projects comes from a leading Swiss biotech company in 2019. Richard, the CEO, set a goal for his executive team to increase revenues by SF 1 billion within three years. In most organizations, the CEO would have to ask each business unit and department to squeeze costs and raise revenues by a certain percentage. However, in a rather unusual move, Richard challenged each of his thirteen top executives to come up with an innovation project that would generate at least SF 100 million in three years. He was going to fund each of the projects if the purpose and initial business case looked positive.

As part of the challenge, his learning-and-development team created a development program for his senior leadership team to teach the leaders the fundamentals of project management and project sponsorship. The learning regimen also included sessions on leadership, finance, team development, communication, the biotech's own business (e.g., new products in the pipeline), and the technological future. The program required strong commitment from the participants, as it consumed three sets of four day-sessions held over the course of a year. It was a huge investment for the company but a great development opportunity. It clearly showed the CEO's firm commitment to investing in talent to deliver his ambition through project excellence.

The participating executives needed to agree to take full accountability of their project, work with their best resources, go through the training, and dedicate enough time to make the project a reality. To monitor the progress, the CEO established a governance committee, with monthly meetings to discuss the status of the projects, and quarterly deep dives to ensure the expected benefits would be delivered. Not all of the projects progressed as planned—by 2020, nine out of the thirteen initiatives were on track and starting to deliver significant benefits—but the company is on course to deliver more than SF 1 billion by the CEO's three-year deadline.

2. Lax discipline and lack of focus

In general, we love to start projects, but we don't like to follow through with them. We need discipline to overcome obstacles, do the difficult work, and drive our projects to the finish. We find it difficult to kill delayed projects or those that are no longer relevant or drifting from their objectives. Without discipline from executives (encouraged by the PMO), the risk is that the number of projects in the organization will continue to increase.

In today's dynamic business environment, the customary methods of deciding which projects to invest in are basically obsolete. According to cognitive psychologist and entrepreneur Gary Klein, the traditional rules and procedures used for making decisions work in predictable, structured situations but fail in unpredictable, fast-breaking circumstances. Klein argues for the value of experience over analysis. "Keep the organization focused," he says. "Don't run away from the 'tough choices,' and follow them through."[6]

Solution: Be clear about the organization's priorities; show discipline by actively participating in and supporting the implementation

Focus imposes order and discipline. It requires energy, work, and some pain, which people often try to avoid. If a company's top management is not focused, it will significantly increase the possibility that the rest of the organization is unfocused. But when top management is extremely focused, this attention is transmitted to the staff, and the increase in performance is huge.

A loss of focus and its recapture is at the center of the fall and rise of LEGO. Once a leading business, the toy maker almost disappeared in the early 2000s because of overexpansion and brand dilution. In the mid-1990s, the company had entered a frenzied state of launching new products to market, going from 109 items in 1994 to 347 just four years later. On the verge of bankruptcy, LEGO hired Jørgen Vig Knudstorp, a thirty-five-year-old former academic and consultant, to become the first externally developed CEO. According to Knudstorp, "the company was struggling because it did too many things at the same time. It lost its focus and its core—and what the capabilities were in that core. What was it really that this company did better than anybody else?"[7] He launched the Fitness Project to turn LEGO around and to recover profitability and growth by refocusing the organization. He wanted the company to become much more customer-centric (selling directly to the consumer through an online shop channel and LEGO-owned stores), cut costs, halt noncore projects, and focus on core products.

3. Low engagement from employees

A major challenge for any transformation project is lack of engagement—and, sometimes, outright resistance—from employees. In its *State of the Global Workplace* report, Gallup concludes that "85% of employees are not actively engaged or actively disengaged at work."[8] That leaves only 15 percent of employees actively engaged. When individuals are disengaged, they experience low levels of meaning, psychological safety, and commitment in their work. Without commitment or meaning, they begin to withdraw emotionally, cognitively, and, eventually, physically from their job. According to Gallup, the economic consequences of this global norm amount to approximately $7 trillion in lost productivity.

With the amount of changes that we experienced in the past in the workplace, many predict that in the next decade, AI will bring about more changes and innovations than what we have experienced in the past 250 years. The Covid-19 pandemic accelerated this trend even further. This constant state of change has led to the idea of **change fatigue:** employees are tired of change after change.

Solution: Identify and talk about the purpose of your projects, look for volunteers instead of appointing team members, let everyone contribute, and recognize people's contributions

To transform your organization to an agile and project-driven one, you must have a higher purpose that resonates with the employees, one that motivates them to participate and contribute to the initiative because they believe in it, not simply because of financial return. When you are selecting champions for the project, look for people who already have influence. They will tend to be natural communicators and will instinctively know how to sell the benefits of the much-needed transformation to their colleagues. Take time to ensure that even the staff members who are not directly involved understand the project and its benefits. Follow up on any suggestions and new ideas that are offered. People are motivated by appreciation, so it's important to share good outcomes with everyone.

Learn about how leading companies engage their employees, and apply the same principles to involve team members in your transformation project. According to Great Place to Work, the top companies in terms of engagement were these three companies:[9]

- **Hilton:** Employees believe the company invests in them and encourages a spirit of entrepreneurship.

- **Salesforce:** According to the company's employees, the firm backs up its talk with action.

- **Wegmans Food Markets:** Its employees praise it as the company where "employees can follow the American Dream" through the many developments and learning opportunities.

There are few lower-cost ways of working in an inclusive, impactful, motivating, and inspiring environment than participating in a project with an ambitious goal, a higher purpose, and a clear, fixed deadline.

4. Overly hierarchical and silo-based organization

Projects are not islands—they cannot be executed in isolation. They are carried out in an organization that often influences their implementation. As we saw in chapter 1, the organizational structure needs to reflect a radical shift from running the business to changing it. More often than not, management underestimates or completely ignores this requirement, organizations fail to evolve (or adapt) as quickly as the business drivers change, and, consequently, many projects fail.

The departments in most hierarchical organizations are not set up to work collaboratively. Instead, they suffer from internal competition and a silo mentality. Department heads invest in building their own little kingdoms and often struggle when they need to share resources, especially their best ones, with strategic, cross-unit projects.

Solution: Establish a flatter organization, and provide full autonomy to strategic projects

The three leading Chinese companies discussed earlier illustrate how to create more-agile and project-driven organizations. There are a few examples in the West, too. In the early 2000s, Siemens, a large German multinational, set out to change its old, siloed organizational structure by providing more power to its internal Management Consulting Group (SMC) under the leadership of Klaus Kleinfeld. The SMC organization was formed to develop and oversee a corporate revitalization and business improvement program. Under Kleinfeld's guidance, SMC transformed from a small corporate cost center into a highly profitable and respected consulting business that established cutting-edge practices in benchmarking, project management, business reengineering, and innovation. Kleinfeld personally led projects for a number of global Siemens industry groups. From these experiences, he gained a broad understanding of Siemens's multiple divisions, often demonstrating his expertise in making things happen. With the success of the unit in transforming Siemens into a more project-driven and agile organization, Kleinfeld was appointed CEO in 2005.

5. A project management office that is not strategic or in charge

The original purpose of a PMO was to support the project leader and the project team in the administrative tasks of the projects, such as tracking time sheets, maintaining issue logs, and chasing down information needed for progress reports. The role has since evolved toward an office in charge of the development and implementation of policies and standards on project management. Ironically, the PMO's focus on controlling and administrative tasks prevented organizations from becoming agile and more project-driven. All this created a negative perception of the value of these PMOs and often led to their dismantlement. These traditional PMOs were also designed to fit into a hierarchical structure; they were another box in the organizational chart. As an organization moves to a flatter and project-based structure, the PMO must evolve as well.

Solution: Transform your PMO into a strategy implementation office, and empower it to be the catalyst for change

My research for this book shows that 52 percent of companies have an established project management department but only 23 percent have a PMO, which is the engine that should coordinate the company's transformation to a project-based organization. The new version of the PMO is linked to the executive team and has a stronger focus on value creation. Its role has evolved and now includes promoting and establishing best practices, building competencies, supporting the top levels of management in prioritizing projects, and executing the most strategic projects. The most advanced PMOs have merged with the strategic planning department and have become what some companies call the strategy implementation office. The most advanced PMOs have a series of project managers, often the best in the company, who are in charge of leading the most complex and transversal initiatives. Often the PMO reports to the CEO, so it is sometimes called a CEO office. Most large organizations today have a CEO office.

6. Inadequate project implementation methods and competencies

For many decades, companies lacked a common and standard approach for managing projects. Projects were often initiated without a detailed business plan. Costs were defined before the project was started and were not properly tracked once it began. Every project manager had their own "cookbook" and way of doing things, generating a lack of agreement on how to implement projects. With no uniform methodology, companies were unable to train their project managers and project teams effectively and consistently.

Later, many organizations developed and implemented a standard, or waterfall, project management methodology, with a one-size-fits-all attitude, meaning that all projects needed to follow the same methodology, the same project life cycle, the same templates, and so forth. From the 1980s until the 2000s, the focus was on these traditional waterfall methods; in the 2010s, it moved to agile methods. Large programs today struggle to balance the need to plan, schedule, and budget with the need to adapt and change as you go. There are also the struggles, thus far, of "agile at scale" (implementing agile practices at enterprise level). Yet as we saw in chapter 3, the right approach depends on the size, complexity, and uncertainty of the project (and sometimes includes sometimes a mix of approaches or a hybrid approach).

Solution: Expand and diversify the project management toolkit with waterfall, agile, and other methods

Today we know that one-size-fits-all does not work; you cannot have just one method to address all the projects and changes you have in your organization. In this decade, we will see the evolution of project implementation into a set of tools that will include agile practices, traditional project management practices, along with some design thinking, innovation, lean startup, program management, and change management. Depending on the type of project, project managers should be able to apply one tool or different techniques simultaneously. Organizations need to build development programs for their managers and employees around this variety of implementation methods.

In a fast-growing market, time to market is of the essence to capture new demand. Proximus, a leading Belgian mobile telecom provider, experienced a significant increase of projects during the decade of the 2000s because of the booming mobile market. It needed eighteen months on average to introduce new products to market, more than double its more dynamic competitors, such as the French operator Orange. The CEO understood the urgent need for something to be done, so the company launched a project to increase its project implementation maturity. Proximus launched a global training program for managers and senior leaders: it was a hybrid project management framework with several approaches and a clear career path for project managers. The project accomplished its mission in a single year, after which Proximus was able to launch new products in less than nine months. Throughout its duration, the project was considered a top priority, and the CEO's involvement and ongoing support was essential to achieve this impressive result.

7. A financial model that fails to reflect project costs and benefits

Probably the biggest shortcoming in project management is the managers' failure to track the benefits delivered by their projects. What gets measured gets done, and what gets measured easily is much more likely to be deemed important. There is no disguising how extremely cumbersome tracking project benefits and costs is in most organizational financial systems; measuring the benefits of investments is also a tortuous exercise. In most businesses, employees spend only part of their time working on projects and the rest continuing their operational work.[10]

What's more, the standard annual budgeting cycles of many organizations simply do not correspond to the needs of their projects, which run for a wide variety of funding periods. Few companies create a budget for companywide change-the-business activities. Some companies forecast project costs by department, but rarely do they develop a budget for projects that are in the best interest of the entire company. Neither of the two most important sets of accounting standards (US Generally Accepted Accounting Principles and International Accounting Standards) clearly specifies how to account for project costs and how to report project benefits.

Solution: Incorporate project investments in your budgeting cycle, and increase your focus on project benefits

A solid project management culture, with a strong focus on tracking project benefits and costs, helps organizations overcome these shortfalls. You should have a formal process to validate the rationale, purpose, and business benefits of the projects to maintain better control over what you are investing in. You can overcome decision-making biases, especially around optimistic business cases, through independent validation. By making project plans focused on when the benefits will be delivered (instead of the traditional deliverables and outputs) and tracking those benefits, project leaders will increase visibility of the value created. Company shareholders, boards, and even financial analysts are starting to demand information about strategic projects and key investments made by the executive team.

French international bank BNP Paribas was an early adopter of important changes to the traditional yearly budgeting cycle. It incorporated the notion of two budgets, one for running the bank and another for changing the bank. Both budgets would be estimated at the same time, but as projects tend to follow their own timelines (most don't finish at the end of the year), this dual arrangement would allow much more flexibility. The adjustment also raised visibility and accountability for costs, investments, and expected benefits.

Additionally, beginning with its 2015 annual report and thereafter, BNP Paribas reported to shareholders on its most important projects. This was a major move in raising the awareness about these projects. At the same time, it greatly empowered the project managers, as their projects' importance was now widely known and external commitments had been made to key stakeholders. No wonder that among the "elder" traditional Western companies, BNP Paribas is one of the most advanced in adapting to the changing world.

8. Inadequacy of systems and tools for monitoring project implementation

Today, most companies have mature systems to manage their day-to-day operations, but they often lack an integrated software to manage their hundreds of projects. Many organizations are still using Microsoft Project or slightly more advanced systems for project portfolio management, often just to describe project plans and their main milestones. Individual projects are not connected, and it is impossible to obtain a consolidated or real-time view of the portfolio of projects, including actual spending, resource availability, or benefits realized.

Consider this real situation: a large pharmaceutical company has 540 current projects costing approximately €256 million and involving 4,780 out of 20,000 employees, but the company has no tool with which to monitor the projects' status, costs, or contributions to the implementation of its strategy. Given that the company has no way of knowing how its portfolio of projects is performing, how can it make good project-related or investment decisions?

Solution: Embrace technology to monitor implementation and capture the benefits of your portfolio of projects

Only with the rise of PMOs and the portfolio management practices described in chapter 10 did some transparency enter the monitoring of project portfolios. In the coming years, this project portfolio monitoring will be followed by a new wave of project portfolio management software.

With the arrival of several major reforms in 2019, such as the examination of the bill on bioethics or the opening of the consultation process for pension reform, the French government, like any other government, is working on thousands of projects. To ensure that progress is made adequately and public money is spent efficiently, President Macron's team developed an application that enables him to monitor the progress of ongoing reforms or their rate of effectiveness in real time.[11] Uses like this demonstrate how combining technology with project management will lead to new organizational capabilities.

———————

In part 3 of the book, we have looked at the individual and organizational competencies that are today's very best practices in project management. We have seen what is needed to be an effective project manager and executive sponsor, including hard work and continuous learning, but anyone who is determined can succeed. We also learned how to select and prioritize projects through the hierarchy of purpose, and how to keep a rich pipeline of ideas while implementing and keeping track of multiple projects in parallel. In this chapter, we have seen how organizational structure influences, for the good or the bad, the implementation of projects. Organizations need to move away from the traditional hierarchal structures and overcome some of the most frequent obstacles to project success. To succeed in a world of transitory circumstances, organizations need to become much more agile and project-driven, like the Chinese examples in this chapter or startup models.

So far, this book has stayed grounded in the present. Each idea presented is one you or your organization can seize on today. In part 4, we will change our viewpoint and look at how project management is continuing to evolve and how it will be reinvented in the future. Examining the themes of crisis management, AI, diversity, and sustainability through the lens of project management, we will discover that the emergence of the Project Economy has only just begun.

PART FOUR

A Better Future through Projects

12.

Project Managing a Better Future

Tomorrow's Innovations and Disruptions in Project Management

Now that we have learned why project management has become a critical discipline in a world driven by change and how you can implement your projects more successfully today, it is time to start looking toward the future. In this chapter, we will learn how projects and project management intersect with four major global trends that are affecting every organization worldwide. These trends will be high on the agendas of senior leaders over the next decade (or are already included on their agendas): crisis management, diversity, AI, and sustainability.

The UK government's National Infrastructure Strategy, launched in December 2020, is an incredible example of how all four of these trends are present in a single strategic, project-driven initiative. The pipeline of more than six hundred infrastructure projects and programs represents an investment of £425 billion, of which £297 billion will be spent over the next five years. The spending includes large-scale housing and regeneration projects alongside key social infrastructure such as schools, hospitals, and prisons. But this massive initiative didn't stop at just implementing the projects; it has addressed the Covid-19 crisis, used diversity to its advantage, introduced new technologies, and enhanced sustainability. "We must build back better, not the same as before," said UK's prime minister, Boris Johnson.[1]

The projects in this strategy will create wealth and thousands of jobs to repair some of the scars that existed before the pandemic. The investment drives a new diversity of thinking and changes the way projects are appraised to favor sustainability elements, such as green energies, to achieve net zero emissions by 2050. The projects include the introduction of smarter technologies to give stakeholders opportunities for a more collaborative approach to measuring and driving improved delivery performance, while reducing layers of bureaucracy. The innovative projects of tomorrow will soon be looking more like this one. Moving past traditional project scopes and goals, the projects of the future will seek to make a better world through broader and more ambitious impact.

In each of the four sections of this chapter, we will begin by looking at these megatrends from today's project management perspective, followed by a prediction of what the future could look like. We will end with the next steps to move into the future.

Crisis management *is* project management

We all remember the terrorist attacks of 9/11 and the 2008 financial crisis that wiped away millions of jobs in a matter of months, yet we had never experienced something similar to the coronavirus pandemic that began in late 2019. Covid-19 was unprecedented in the speed and the severity of the impact it had across the world, not only on the health of millions of individuals and on the health-care systems across the world, but also with tremendous consequences in the global economy and society. Within a matter of weeks after the global shutdown, it became clear that business and the very nature of work would be changed forever.

Another dynamic was at play: there was an immediate, radical shift from running-the-organization activities to changing-the-organization activities. Suddenly, projects were everywhere. At work, at home, and in the news, it became more obvious than ever that crisis management and project management were one and the same. We saw incredible projects, large and small, wherever we looked: hospitals being created in a matter of weeks; schools, universities, and business schools switching to online education; private and public organizations pivoting their entire workforce to remote working; massive production of masks; installation of protective shields in grocery stores, banks, and restaurants; even the project of parents planning their workdays together while educating their children at home.

Now: What the Covid-19 crisis taught us about projects

These projects have also demonstrated some positive aspects of modern project management and exposed the shortcomings of outdated methods. One amazing achievement of the crisis was the development of the Covid-19 vaccines. Typically, the production and launch of a new vaccine takes pharma companies about ten to fifteen years. Most experts were skeptical that a Covid-19 vaccine could be developed faster than that, yet in this case, companies that typically competed fiercely and kept their know-how secret from each other sat together to look for solutions. Important external stakeholders, such as the US Food and Drug Administration and the European Medicines Agency, contributed by lessening the strict requirements for vaccine development. Governments, which rarely support pharmaceutical companies, offered billions in subsidies for vaccine development. Altogether, these developments show that when key stakeholders collaborate on high-stakes projects, combined with an urgent call for action, they can break through the traditional ways of doing things and deliver unimaginable results.

By late 2020, vaccine development seemed like a happy ending. The vaccines were here, and—presumably, life would quickly return to normal.

Yet the vaccine rollout reminded us of another project management lesson: too many governments thought only about deliverables (vaccines) instead of about benefits (vaccinated people) and underplanned and underfunded vaccine rollouts, awareness campaigns, and signup websites. In many countries, rollouts were slow, frustrating, and inequitable. Far too many vials of lifesaving vaccine expired instead of going into arms. Distributing the vaccine should have been the easy part. Instead, many governments fell into the classic problem of assuming that once the deliverables are delivered, the benefit comes out of the black box.

As the section's heading says, crisis management *is* project management, and the major concepts presented throughout this book, including the Project Canvas, remain essential in a crisis. The fast decision-making required in crises must not lead us into our old bad habits in project management. In this case, and in future crises, lives are at stake.

The future: Managing an ongoing series of crises

The post-Covid-19 reconstruction will be unprecedented in human history and may take a decade. According to Ziyad Cassim and his colleagues at McKinsey & Company, governments announced $10 trillion in reconstruction funds just in the first two months of the crisis—three times more than the entire response to the 2008–2009 financial crisis.[2] These funds are earmarked for millions of projects, which will need millions of project managers and executive sponsors.

In addition, there is a consensus that Covid-19 will not be the last global crisis that leaders will need to face in the near future. Recent years have seen dramatic increases in natural disasters, which experts have long warned are the worldwide symptoms of a worsening climate crisis—raging wildfires in California and Australia, heat waves across Europe, fears of a dam collapse in China, and record-breaking hurricanes in the southern United States.

Leaders will need to get used to managing crisis after crisis. The 2015–2018 Cape Town, South Africa, drought serves as an example. Rainfall over the Western Cape during this period was 50 to 70 percent of the long-term average. In 2017, many rainfall records were the lowest ever recorded, and the city faced the very real prospect of running out of water. Population growth and a record drought, exacerbated by climate change, created one of the world's most dramatic urban water crises, coming close to the shutting off of taps to homes and businesses. Citizens were urged to consume less, but more than half of the residents ignored those voluntary restrictions. Officials made an increasingly common mistake: they assumed future rainfall patterns would resemble those of the past or at least would not change too quickly.

Another example is the Texas freezing weather blitz in February 2021. The weather crippled a power system unprepared for frigid temperatures, leaving millions without electricity, heating, and water. These crises offer several pointed lessons to anyone involved in major project leadership during future crises:

- Climate change and the wider issue of sustainability can now cause crises and necessitate change in both government and private-sector projects of all kinds.

- Projects and programs of any scale need leadership that understands and manages through a systems approach that recognizes the complexity and the interconnectedness of people, behaviors, processes, and technology.

- Greater attention should be placed on the importance of social relationships in any system. Partnerships and adaptive management are central to building a robust and flexible system.

- Leaders need to consider more-flexible options that respond much faster to future crises. For example, leaders could provide incentives to customers to reduce consumption so that the system could build up capacity that could be made available on short notice in the event of a crisis.

- Project leaders need to gather and understand data and develop decision-making approaches that are informed by data (as well as the lack of data or the level of uncertainty).

- Leaders should be more conscious when setting project objectives, not always favoring efficiency and low-cost solutions, but instead thinking about building resilience and sustainable solutions.

A common pitfall in crisis management is to become fixated on re-turning to the world as it was before the crisis. Many leaders are unable to anticipate and understand how the crisis changes underlying percep-tions and behavior. In other words, recovery projects need to be oriented toward establishing a new normal rather than returning to life before the crisis.

Recent BCG research shows that most companies responded to the near-term threats—setting up rapid response and business continuity measures, cutting costs in anticipation of a recession, and assessing re-bound scenarios. However, even several months into the crisis, fewer com-panies had taken actions to assess permanent shifts in beliefs and customer behavior and analyze the resulting opportunities.

As we have seen, crisis moments also present great opportunities. New trends emerge, disrupting the old practices, allowing for radical changes, and often introducing sophisticated and a more flexible use of technol-ogy. Smart organizations will seek to seize these moments and select their projects accordingly.

Next steps: Three stages of managing through a crisis

Amid crises, a leader's role is not to simply run the organization; the person must ensure the organization's survival through projects. There are three stages that leaders and project managers should focus on and act on during a crisis. Each stage requires leaders to switch to a project mindset:

1. **Selecting and launching mitigating projects immediately:** Crisis management requires top project leadership.

2. **Stopping, deprioritizing, and delaying projects to shift resources on the critical initiatives:** Stop projects ruthlessly, shift resources swiftly.

3. **Taking advantage of new opportunities, preparing for the new normal, reformulating organizational strategy:** Projects to refocus and reimagine the organization.

Stage 1. Crisis management requires top project leadership

In normal circumstances, management will discuss an idea or a potential project over several months—in addition to taking the administrative steps to prepare a business case—before a project is approved and resources and budgets are allocated.

In a crisis, leaders must think fast and decide even faster. All the stakeholders involved need to be brought together to recognize and acknowledge the reality of the crisis. They need to choose new projects that the organization should launch immediately to overcome, or at least mitigate, the impact of the crisis on their business and employees. With this accelerated timing, especially during a crisis of the magnitude of the coronavirus pandemic, some mitigating projects will probably not succeed; leaders need to adjust course promptly. In an unprecedented situation, where time is of the essence, the longer it takes leaders to intervene, the more severe and costly the impact of inaction will be.

The extraordinary disruption associated with the Covid-19 pandemic has revealed several examples of companies that have launched projects to adapt swiftly to mitigate and, sometimes, to exploit the crisis. Senior leadership at Lin Qingxuan, a Chinese cosmetics retailer, needed to find a solution to engage customers who were no longer visiting its stores. The immediate impact of Covid-19 saw sales plummet by 90 percent, and senior leaders had to find a quick solution to address the massive impact of the sudden crisis. Fortunately, over the previous three years, they had worked hard to embrace digital transformation, building more than six million online followers. On the evening of February 14, 2020, with only a few days' preparation, Lin Qingxuan launched a large-scale livestream shopping event with more than a hundred of Lin Qingxuan's shopping advisers. More than sixty thousand people watched the livestream, and the company sold more than four hundred thousand bottles of its camellia oil. The bold leadership move paid off, sales from this project in two hours ended up equaling the sales of four retail stores in a month.[3]

In just a few weeks in early 2020, worldwide airline travel dropped by as much as 96 percent.[4] Airline leaders needed to find ways to survive.

With few passengers and little baggage being transported on airplanes, there was more capacity for cargo, which goes hand in hand with the increased demand for ordering goods online. Virgin Atlantic leadership rapidly decided to shift its focus to cargo flights, delivering an unparalleled network of cargo-only flying, operating more than fourteen hundred cargo flights in April and May 2020.[5]

Stage 2. Stop projects ruthlessly, shift resources swiftly

To add new projects, leaders must free up capacity and resources as quickly as possible. In normal circumstances, employees and management are fully booked, with dozens or even thousands of projects on top of their everyday business activities. There is no spare capacity. In a crisis, many projects must be stopped to make way for new ones.

In normal times, stopping a project can easily take a few weeks, if not months. In a crisis, shutting down a project should be done almost instantly. While they are selecting mitigation projects, leaders must also decide which ongoing projects to cancel, which to put on hold, and which few should continue.

In my experience, in standard circumstances, an organization can stop about 50 percent of its projects without any short-term impact on the business. In crisis mode, however, leaders should aim at stopping around 80 percent of their running initiatives.

Early in a crisis, leaders must not only show agility, speed, and quick decision-making, but also demonstrate foresight and a steady hand. Teams need to know where the organization's focus will be in the next weeks and months. If leaders struggle to decide or communicate, the whole organization will suffer.

Stage 3. Projects to refocus and reimagine the organization

In the last stage, which should start as soon as the organization stabilizes from the sudden impact, leaders must shift from focusing on disaster response to preparing for postcrisis recovery. This aspect of crisis project management is just as challenging as the immediate response. In addition to all they are doing in the first two stages, leaders must ensure that a smaller group of the organization is working on projects that address new near-term opportunities and longer-term strategy.

Projects that reimagine and refocus the business may involve a return to what made the business successful, but not always. Sometimes it is about reinventing the business, creating a new business model to prepare for a new normal.

The most famous example of refocusing is what Steve Jobs did when he returned to Apple in 1997. He ruthlessly stopped projects and shifted resources. He canceled more than thirty products, refocusing on four (two laptops and two desktops), and withdrew about 80 percent of the company's projects—all those that were not linked to his vision and the new Apple strategy of focusing on its core capabilities. The Jobs approach is what is expected from today's leaders to overcome the global health and economic crisis that will be ongoing features of business in the twenty-first century.

Disney is another great case of reimagining. Before 2020, Disney was not a big player in the streaming world, which had been dominated by Netflix. When the pandemic created an opportunity to rethink its streaming services, Disney merged modern streaming with old-school marketing of concepts. As opposed to releasing a whole series at once as Netflix did, Disney went back to the old concept of spreading the release of episodes weekly, to allow people to talk about it over the weekend and create a buzz. It also released feature films through the streaming platform and introduced tiered pricing—more reimagining. Disney+ subscribers skyrocketed to almost ninety-five million in a little over a year, nearly half of what Netflix had achieved in a decade. Without the crisis, it is unlikely that Disney would have reimagined its business so quickly.

These three stages will guide you as you navigate through any crisis. If you take action, make the tough decisions, communicate, shift resources, prioritize, and focus the organization through effective project management, you and your organization are more likely to get through the crisis successfully. But you need to act immediately. From a project leadership perspective, this is a unique opportunity for leaders to take action, step up, build competencies, and move toward becoming a more agile organization. The best way to do it is through inspirational projects.

Diversity (and diversity of thinking) and project success

There is no doubt today about the importance of diversity. More organizations are recognizing that diversity, inclusion, and equity are matters of ethics that cannot be ignored. For project leaders, promoting diversity on their teams is an essential professional responsibility. There are also business benefits associated with effective diversity and equality practices. Research shows that diverse teams propose and deliver a greater number of innovative solutions than less diverse teams do. According to PMI's Pulse of the Profession research, 88 percent of project professionals say having diverse project teams increases value.[6]

Projects encourage diversity by their very nature: project managers need to work regularly with people with different backgrounds, cultures, genders, and ages. They need to form teams from all these individuals and take advantage of these different experiences and points of view. Less well understood is how the diversity in your project teams—and in the projects themselves—can catalyze diversity throughout your organization.

Now: Encouraging diverse teams and diverse thinking

Divergent thinking is among the most valuable assets for any project and organization. The wider the experience and worldview of those working on a project, the greater the chance of finding imaginative and innovative solutions. Diversity of thinking will lessen the risk that you will find your strategy compromised by groupthink.

Simply put, a diverse workforce is the biggest driver of diversity of thought. This means making sure that your organization is made up of all kinds of people and that it embraces and fosters a culture of inclusion and psychological safety.

Diversity enables any project organization to realize several helpful steps:

- Build rapport and empathy with stakeholder groups that see themselves represented in the organization or its thinking

- Access a wider talent pool of potential candidates

- Develop the full gamut of thinking capabilities: blue-sky thinkers, problem-solvers, completer-finishers, and more

- Build an employer brand as a fair and supportive place to work

- Reduce the risk of groupthink

- Generate wider and more innovative options

Serving a diverse set of stakeholders is impossible with homogeneous project teams. Lenovo, the world's largest PC vendor, focuses on creating programs that embed diversity and inclusion into the company's DNA, and its efforts earned it a perfect 100 percent on the Corporate Index for LGBTQ equality.[7] In the words of Yolanda Conyers, the company's chief diversity officer, serving a global customer base requires "more than out-of-the-box thinking, because it's not just one box. It's a hundred different boxes. A million different boxes. It takes every dimension of our diversity. All our diverse mindsets, skills, and cultural backgrounds, to deliver such a wide array of technology."[8]

Achieving diversity of thinking and behavior is a phenomenon of organizational culture. It's about the way people do things in your organization. In this way, it isn't something that you can simply train your workforce to do or import through recruitment or the use of external consultants. It requires a deliberate intention behind everything you do, and it will take time.

A report by the Work Foundation, a British research organization, advocates three approaches for developing diversity strategy:[9]

- **Inclusive diversity (representational diversity):** Through recruitment strategies, you can ensure that your teams are more representative of the population at different levels. Goals may involve such targets as seating more women on the board or having people with disabilities constituting 5 percent of your workforce.

- **Inclusive processes:** The underlying organizational processes that govern hiring and employed individuals' progression, development, and visibility should enable the organization to benefit from its diversity.

- **Inclusive culture and climate:** This approach creates a culture where people feel comfortable and respected, regardless of individual differences, talents, or personal characteristics.

These three aspects are also applicable to projects. The leaders of Crossrail, the colossal project to create an east–west transport link across London and beyond, were champions of diversity from the early days of the project. In 2013, they introduced their Equality and Talent Strategy, which involved making all the teams accountable for delivering equal and diverse outcomes. At a practical level, this meant that all directors and senior managers had responsibility for equality and diversity requirements in their work area as part of their objectives.

Implementing the strategy involved several steps:

- Monitoring and reporting on the levels of diversity and equality in Crossrail

- Encouraging the Crossrail executive, the Investment Committee, and the Crossrail board to lead and own the Equality and Talent Strategy

- Reworking their contracts and partnerships to embed diversity and equality throughout their supply chain and procurement

- Developing and implementing performance assurance frameworks to assess contractor compliance

- Communication initiatives such as annual Respect Weeks to raise diversity awareness and celebrate workforce diversity

Crossrail found that changing perceptions of diversity took time but had a positive and lasting impact on organizational culture.

Future: Project diversity leads to organizational diversity

All successful projects involve change and development, and many commentators argue that large public projects are engines for social change and improvement. Organizations that seek to make rapid strides on diversity can catalyze their transformation efforts by replicating some ambitious public-sector initiatives. The UK government's National Infrastructure Strategy is unequivocal in its transformational goals: "The projects in this strategy, including £27 billion of public funding next year, will create wealth and thousands of jobs to repair some of the scars from the pandemic."[10]

This investment drives a new diversity of thinking, emphasizing as it does changes in how the biggest decisions are made:

- *Increasing the UK government's ability to invest directly in Scotland, Wales and Northern Ireland through the UK Internal Market Bill;*

- *Changing the way projects are appraised to support levelling up through the Green Book Review;*

- *Expanding devolution within England, and implementing the devolution deal in West Yorkshire;*

- *Relocating 22,000 civil servants out of London and the South East by 2030.*[11]

It is inconceivable that any pipeline of projects can drive radical change of this kind without embracing and creating diverse ways of thinking about project outcomes and delivery processes. The sheer ambition of these project goals in the UK strategy will catalyze this transformation.

Another example of bold moves on diversity through projects is Mindflash, a Silicon Valley company that offers an online training platform for enterprises. Mindflash's CEO, Donna Wells, has a recipe for success that includes diversity as one of the main ingredients for all her strategic projects. Diversity starts at the top of the organization and at the top of projects and includes visionary board members, steering committee members, venture capital investors, and others. "I have hired professional athletes, restaurant managers, and construction workers," says Wells. "Most tech executives wouldn't give these folks a second look. The fact is these are fields that are more diverse, and they also bring a deeper level of diversity when it comes to their personality, upbringing, and personal experience."[12]

In your projects, the team mix not only must look diverse but also must actually be diverse, as shown in the Mindflash example.

You can apply these and other efforts to use projects as a vehicle for your organization's diversity and inclusion efforts:

- Change your portfolio management to select and prioritize projects that enable diversity and innovation. Organizations, like people, *are what they do*. This approach will encourage existing employees to echo the strategic direction of the business in their behavior and will attract candidates who value what you are doing.

- Establish a sense of belonging in all your projects by focusing on diversity and creating an inclusive culture. Having a connection to an organization or a group of people who make you feel that you can be yourself not only spurs greater engagement and creativity in the workplace but also fulfills a psychological need.

- Smaller projects can be more innovative. A recent University of Chicago study, coauthored by Professor James Evans, found that while bigger project teams are important for advancing science, smaller project groups help disrupt it. Think about this when launching initiatives to disrupt your diversity practices.

- Establish metrics, such as gender, ethnic, or minority ratios, and other rules to measure the impact of your projects on diversity. Share progress with the broader organization to make sure diversity stays top of mind for everyone and doesn't become an afterthought.

- Projects with distributed teams can boost diversity, drawing in talent from different locations—with different voices and different ways of working. To make the most of that diversity, project leaders must treat the team as a cohesive and collaborative unit, no matter where individuals are located.

- Use the power that your projects represent in their procurement, recruitment, and selection of contractors and suppliers to build an enterprise organization that is diverse and successful in its inclusion efforts.

Next steps: How to encourage diverse thinking in your projects

As discussed, diversity is reflected not just in the structure of an organization and the people who work there but also in the way that you behave. Here are a few examples of practices that any organization can implement quickly to promote diverse thinking in projects:

- **Reviewing processes that encourage diverse thinking:** Premortems are now an established alternative to postmortems in many organizations looking to encourage learning from projects. Postmortems tend to be ineffective at generating learning from the near misses and might-haves—problems that arose but which the project team managed somehow to sidestep or mitigate. Focusing on the future, that is, where the biggest pitfalls might lie and how to avoid them, can be a far more open process and can build good thinking habits.

- **Mentoring and reverse-mentoring:** When mentoring the emerging generation of project managers, encourage them to exercise their own approaches to problems and to pursue their own solutions with the knowledge that they will have the support of senior managers. Add reverse-mentoring into the mix too, allowing early-career employees to teach new skills and different ways of thinking to senior employees to permeate into the organization's management and even its strategy.

- **Coaching for diversity and gender equity:** GSK's Accelerating Difference program, designed with strong support from senior leaders, aims to increase the career progression of women across the organization.[13] The year-long program is based on three distinct elements:

  - Individual and group coaching

  - Sponsorship and engagement of line managers

  - Open dialogues with sponsors

The group coaching sessions allow participants to explore leadership challenges with peers and give and receive feedback in a safe space.

- **Facilitating diverse thinking in all stages of the project:** Cultivating the conditions for diverse thinking can begin even before any hires are made on a project. In its revamping of the Bank station of the London Underground, the leadership at the UK agency Transport for London (TfL) set up a special procurement process in which any solutions that potential contractors proposed remained their own. TfL surrendered its right to "borrow" their ideas to pass on to whichever contractor was successful in the tendering. This tactic enabled the potential vendors to be more innovative and imaginative in the solutions they proposed than they otherwise would have been, and TfL reaped the benefits.

While the direct correlation between diversity practices and the bottom line may remain stubbornly hard to tease out, look at it from the other end of the telescope. Consider the opportunity cost and the risk to project outcomes of continuing to ignore diversity. Is creating a truly diverse organization challenging? Perhaps. Does it work? Absolutely. And the ROI is the truly innovative, collaborative, and high-performing teams that deliver outstanding value and benefits to organizations and society.

The role of technology

Here's an example of what project management might look like soon. The CEO of a large telecom provider is using a smartphone app to check the value created by her organization's seven strategic projects. She can see that four of them have already delivered more than 30 percent of their expected benefits.

In addition to seeing the overall progress, she can drill down on the project that she is sponsoring. There is no longer a need for separate project charters and project documentation; it is all available at her fingertips. The app informs her of any changes and improvements that the artificial intelligence (AI) tool has automatically introduced to the project, such as new features or the switching of resources. These self-adjustments are based on the parameters agreed on at the beginning of the project with the project manager. She can see project team members' morale levels and the overall buy-in of the critical stakeholders. The app also highlights, in real time, any decisions that she has to make. The tool prioritizes the decisions, provides potential solutions, and includes the recommendations of the project manager. Before making any decision, the CEO schedules a video conference with her project manager.

The project manager now spends most of his time coaching the team, cultivating a high-performing culture, and maintaining regular conversations with key stakeholders. A few weeks previously, he decided to apply some agile techniques to speed up a stream of the project as recommended by the app, in response to evidence that the project was progressing slightly behind plan.

During the virtual meeting, the CEO and the project manager discuss the proposed recommendations and simulate possible paths. They agree on a solution to put the behind-schedule project back on track. The project plan is automatically updated, and instructions are sent to the different teams adjusting the working plans. Everyone working on the team, as well as the stakeholders, receives a message informing them about the changes in the plan and a projection of the expected results.

Thanks to the new technologies and ways of working, a strategic project that could have drifted out of control, perhaps even to failure, is now again in line to be successful.

Now: Lack of technological solutions for projects and project management

Although AI is not yet a standard tool in the world of projects and project management, the technology will no doubt disrupt this discipline soon. According to Gartner, 80 percent of project management tasks will be managed by AI by 2030.

Today, most projects are still managed with Microsoft Project (launched in 1987) or other similar applications. This situation reflects how little the technology has evolved in the area of changing the business.

Can you imagine running your entire business and all your operations with spreadsheets? Traditional project portfolio management software such as Planisware, Planview, or Primavera offer more advanced features but remain far from being the latest technology. More recent applications—LiquidPlanner or Asana, for example—enhance planning and team collaboration but don't bring automation or process improvements to any other critical element of projects.

Radical change will only occur when the next generation of project management software is widely adopted and we start seeing tools that algorithmically predict the success rates of projects, validate the project's scope, and automatically create a well-defined project plan.

Consider the most relevant technologies that will be likely to disrupt project management:

- **AI:** the subset of computer science that deals with computer systems performing tasks with intelligence similar, equal, or superior to that of a human (e.g., decision-making, object classification and detection, speech recognition and translation, and prediction)

- **Machine learning:** focuses on developing predictive algorithms that access and use data on their own, leading machines to learn for themselves and improve from learned experiences

- **Natural language processing:** helps computers process, interpret, and analyze human language and its characteristics by using natural language data

- **Big data:** the practice of gathering and storing large amounts of information and then attempting to make sense of that information

The future: What will AI and other technologies disrupt and improve?

For many project managers, automating a significant part of their current tasks may feel scary, but AI and other digital technology bring vast opportunity along with risk. Successful project managers will learn to use these tools to their advantage, switching their focus away from technical aspects and planning to more value-adding activities and, in doing so, driving an increase in project success ratios.

A handful of researchers, such as Paul Boudreau in his book *Applying Artificial Intelligence Tools to Project Management*, and a growing number of startups, have already developed algorithms to apply AI and machine learning in the world of project management.[14] Which aspects might AI and other technology improve or automate?

Selecting and prioritizing projects

In their essence, selection and prioritization are a type of prediction: Which projects will bring the most value to the organization? AI and machine learning can vastly exceed human accuracy in making predictions and detecting patterns that can't be discerned by other means. The use of new intelligent tools could bring the following benefits:

- Better predictions of project success rates, increasing good investments and reducing bad ones

- Removing human biases from decision-making

- Investment in launch-ready projects that have the right project fundamentals in place

- A better balance in the project portfolio

- A better overview of the risk taken by the organization at any given point

- Faster data collection and improved data quality

Project management office

Data analytics and automation startups are now helping organizations streamline and optimize the role of the PMO. The most famous case is President Macron's use of the latest technology to maintain up-to-date information about all the French public-sector projects.[15] These new intelligent tools will radically transform the way PMOs operate, with a number of benefits:

- Better monitoring of project progress, complementing the input from project managers

- The capability to anticipate potential problems and to address some simple ones automatically

- Improved preparation and distribution of project reports, along with the capturing of feedback

- Greater sophistication in selecting the best project management methodology for each project

- Compliance monitoring for project management processes and policies

- Automation, via virtual assistants, of support functions the PMO provides to project managers, such as status updates, risk assessment, and stakeholder analysis

Project definition, planning, and implementation

As described earlier in this book, a significant challenge when you are starting a project is to define the scope. Several technology startups are creating tools to help with this task. Such a tool reads the requirements and user stories as if it were a human and performs much of the time-consuming analysis work that usually is done by project managers and their teams. It parses, interprets, tests, cross-references, measures, and then reports on many aspects of the project scope. The tool will reveal potential problems such as ambiguities, duplicates, omissions, inconsistencies, and complexities.

Besides scope definition, project planning is the other activity that requires a great amount of effort during the initial phases of the project. New tools can use project data to facilitate scheduling processes and draft detailed plans and resource demand in minutes, with related labor or non-labor costs.

So far, one of the most developed areas in project management automation is risk management. New applications use machine learning models and big data techniques to help leaders and project managers anticipate risks that might otherwise go unnoticed. These tools can already propose mitigating actions, and in the near future, they will most likely be able to adjust the plans automatically to avoid certain types of risks.

Once the project is underway, the project manager must report and maintain the project information (schedule, costs, risks, and so on) through regular project reviews. Project reporting is now a largely manual exercise, involving repetitive tasks such as collecting, challenging, and validating the accuracy of project status information; sending reminders; and consolidating all the information in customized reports for the project team, senior management, or steering committees. Not only is the task time-consuming, but the data and facts presented in the reports are often at least a few weeks old. In the coming years, we will start seeing interactive visual tools that use machine learning models and real-time information to identify project issues before they create problems and to show project status, benefits achieved, potential slippage, and team sentiment in a clear, objective way.

Testing systems and software

Testing is another essential task in most projects, and project managers need to test early and often. It's rare today to find a project that lacks multiple systems and types of software that must be tested before the project goes live. The Crossrail project in the United Kingdom, hailed as a paradigm of good engineering in its early stages, failed in terms of systems integration because of insufficient testing. After the initial failure, the project team developed the Crossrail Integration Facility, a fully automated off-site testing facility that has proven invaluable in increasing the efficiency, cost-effectiveness, and resilience of systems. Systems engineer Alessandra Scholl-Sternberg describes some of the facility's features: "An extensive system automation library has been written, which enables complex set-ups to be achieved, health checks to be accurately performed, endurance testing to occur over extended periods and the implementation of tests of repetitive nature."[16] Rigorous audits can be run at the facility 24-7, free from the risk of operator bias.

Role of the project manager

The changes brought about by technology, some of them significant, will affect and even disrupt the roles of the project manager and project sponsor. If, as Gartner estimates, 80 percent of current project management (and PMO) tasks will be replaced by 2030, then project managers will need to embrace these changes and take advantage of the new technologies. We currently think of cross-functional project teams as a group of individuals, but we may soon refer to them as a group of humans and robots. None of this means that human project managers will be going away. As explored in chapter 9, the project manager of the future will need to develop strong soft skills, leadership capabilities, strategic thinking, and business acumen. Instead of doing administrative work, the manager will focus on the delivery of the expected benefits and their alignment with strategic goals. Managers will also need a good understanding of technology, and some organizations are already building AI into educational and certification programs.

Next steps: The data challenge

AI and machine learning algorithms to manage projects will require large amounts of project-related data to function effectively. Roughly 80 percent of the time spent creating a machine learning algorithm is focused on data gathering and cleaning. If data is available and managed properly, the results will provide enormous value to the organization. If it is not, presumably the AI transformation will never happen at your organization.

Data comes in two main types: structured, which is clearly defined with easily searchable patterns, and unstructured, which lacks easily searchable patterns. The aim of data cleaning is to take the raw and unstructured data and transform it into structured data that can be used by a machine learning algorithm to form a model. Organizations might retain much historical project data, but unfortunately, it is likely to be stored in thousands of documents in a variety of file formats scattered around different systems. The information could be out-of-date, might use different taxonomies, and might contain outliers and gaps.

Natural language processing must be used to convert the words or phrases to usable data; this conversion adds another layer of complexity. Fortunately, there are software tools and specialized vendors capable of scanning databases and finding unstructured data. You can accelerate your AI transformation by structuring data for projects you are running today with a clear and concise taxonomy that any data developer can more easily employ to train future machine learning algorithms.

Before you rush to embrace new data applications, you should take some time to explore a few questions:

1. How much data do you have?

2. How relevant is it?

3. How current is it?

4. How is it validated?

5. In how many formats is it currently gathered?

6. How much of it do you generate, and how much is generated by your supply chain (which may create issues of access and ownership)?

7. Where are the big gaps? (Organizations are usually good at gathering certain, easily generated data but struggle to gather data in other crucial areas.)

8. What are you trying to achieve? (Allowing AI applications to crawl over mounds of data and identify patterns does have value, but in the majority of cases, AI needs to be designed with a purpose in mind.)

9. How fast is the data environment changing, and how can you keep up?

10. How do you anticipate that your access to data, analytics, and automation will change your business?

If you are seriously considering applying AI to your projects and project management practices, the following questions will help you assess your decision. Are you ready to spend time making an accurate inventory of all your projects, including the latest status update? Can you invest several resources for some months to gather, clean, and structure your project data? Have you made up your mind to let go of your old project management habits, such as your monthly progress reports? Are you prepared to invest in training your project management community in this new technology? Are they willing to learn and radically change how they manage their projects? Is your organization ready to accept and adopt a new technology? Are the senior leaders willing to wait several months, up to one year, to start seeing the benefits of the automation? If the answer to all these questions is yes, then you are ready to embark on this pioneering transformation. If you have one or more "no" answers, then you need to work on flipping them to "yes" before moving ahead.

The sustainability revolution

Setting goals around climate change, equality, resource depletion, human rights, and other urgent issues of sustainability is now mainstream in business. The sustainability revolution is another broad-scale transformation that will be implemented through successful projects and effective project management. Now and in the coming decades, project managers and executive sponsors will be the main stakeholders in the adoption of sustainable practices, processes, and outcomes.

Now: An enormous challenge of our time

Marc Pritchard, top marketer at Procter & Gamble (P&G), has recently described some of the profound ways in which the world's biggest consumer goods company is embracing sustainability to transform its brands. Or, as he puts it, to make P&G "a force for good and a force for growth." As part of its new Ambition 2030 plan, P&G has pledged to make all its packaging fully recyclable or reusable by that year. The company also plans to use 100 percent renewable energy and have zero net waste by that point.

Working with the Brands for Good coalition (sbbrandsforgood.com), P&G seeks to use its $7 billion annual advertising budget to educate and inspire consumers to follow a sustainable lifestyle.

P&G is not alone. Sustainability has clearly become one of the most important challenges of our time and a priority topic in every CEO's agenda. No large company seriously debates anymore whether environmental and social issues affect the company's bottom line. Many firms go far beyond that and embrace the triple bottom line of sustainability: economic development, social development, and environmental protection. Organizations around the world—triggered by either their own purpose or that of their shareholders, their regulators, or even their increasingly demanding customers—are setting sustainability ambitions and are adopting several of the UN Sustainable Development Goals as part of their strategic goals.[17]

The future: Sustainable project management

While the relationship between sustainability and project management has been explored by various researchers, the current standards for project management reflect a narrow perception of project success. The *PMBOK Guide* mentions that "the success of the project should be measured in terms of completing the project within the constraints of scope, time, cost, quality, resources and risk."[18] The level of predictability and control suggested by the traditional project management focus on controlling time, budget, and quality is incompatible with global and long-term changes.

The good news is that the number of sustainability resources is growing. Here are a few examples:

- **The P5 standard and methodologies:** According to Green Project Management's Michael Young, P5 is "the world's first standard that brings together projects and their products as well as the sustainability elements of people, planet, and profit. . . . P5 measures project objectives and deliverables, their intended life spans, servicing, and project process for maturity and efficiency perspective against elements based on the triple bottom line."[19]

- **The UN sustainable project alignment tool:** a resource for de-velopment experts to provide real-world and practical actions to ensure the UN Sustainable Development Goals through sustain-able and inclusive projects.[20] The tool currently aims to look at two project types: infrastructure and procurement.

- **Sustainable material exchanges:** Excess Materials Exchange (excessmaterialsexchange.com), a platform showing the financial and ecological value of materials, helps project managers deliver solutions in a more efficient and sustainable manner. The platform also enables projects to trade their by-products or their waste to accelerate the global transition to a circular economy.

- **Major Projects Association sustainability toolkit:** a collection of some of the best information analysis tools, industry thought lead-ership, and guidance resources currently available.[21] The toolkit is designed to help project professionals embed sustainability and circular-economy principles into the delivery of major projects.

Sustainable project management requires us to expand our thinking as project managers and executive sponsors. Jasper van den Brink's chart depicted in figure 12-1 illustrates the broader context of sustainable proj-ect management from the perspectives of local and global society and an enlarged time scale.[22] The context of the project is addressed in relation to the organization's strategy, but also in relation to society as a whole. How far-reaching, in terms of time horizon and scope, are your project outcomes?

Like the AI transformations explored earlier, sustainable project man-agement requires an important investment and willingness to significantly change the ways of working. But the advantage is that sustainability does not need new technology—we are ready to start now!

Next steps: The three imperatives for sustainability

Project management's contributions to sustainable business practices in-volve three areas of focus: (1) using sustainable practices, (2) delivering sustainable outcomes, and (3) designing and executing sustainability proj-ects. We will now examine these three areas.

FIGURE 12-1

Sustainable project management: Broader horizon and larger context

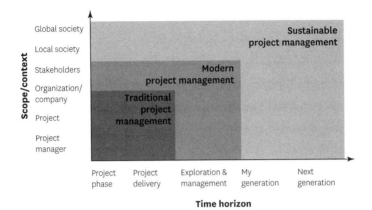

Source: J. Van den Brink, "Duurzaam projectmanagement: verder kijken dan je project lang is" [Sustainable project management: looking beyond the project], *Projectie* 4 (2009). Used with permission.

Employing sustainable practices in projects

Sustainable project management can be defined as "the planning, monitoring and controlling of project delivery and support processes, with consideration of the environmental, economical and social aspects of the life-cycle of the project's resources, processes, deliverables and effects, aimed at realising benefits for stakeholders, and performed in a transparent, fair and ethical way that includes proactive stakeholder participation."[23]

Sustainable project management can be organized with the Project Canvas framework. The following guidance on each of the nine building blocks will help project leaders embed sustainable practices throughout the life cycle of any project:

A SUSTAINABLE FOUNDATION

- **Purpose:** When defining the why of your project, consider whether the purpose can be linked to one or several of the sustainability development goals (see the sidebar "Sustainable Development Goals").

Sustainable development goals

The UN Sustainable Development Goals provide us with a ready framework for understanding the complex levers associated with sustainability. The goals point the way to an important element of sustainable project management: building local capability. Achieving these goals, which were agreed on by all member states in 2015, would "create a world that is comprehensively sustainable," which the UN defines as "socially fair, environmentally secure, inclusive, economically prosperous, and more predictable."[24] There are seventeen global goals:

- No poverty
- Zero hunger
- Good health and well-being
- Quality education
- Gender equality
- Clean water and sanitation
- Affordable and clean energy
- Decent work and economic growth
- Industry, innovation, and infrastructure
- Reduced inequalities
- Sustainable cities and communities
- Responsible consumption and production
- Climate action
- Life below water
- Life on land
- Peace, justice, and strong institutions
- Partnerships for the goals

Like the world, the goals are interconnected, so progress on all of them will have much more impact than achieving only some.

- **Investment:** Resources and budgets are frequently based on a "less is better" model, or MEAT (most economically advantageous tender). But sustainability often comes with a higher short-term price tag and thus requires a different set of criteria. When drafting a business case for your sustainability projects, include the most sustainable elements, such as recyclable products, sustainable vendors, and end-of-life cost—even if their cost is higher than the less environmentally friendly one. This mindset shift is essential to introducing sustainable project management practices.

- **Benefits:** As part of describing the benefits and how the success of your project would look, be sure to link any positive impacts with the triple bottom-line benefits of sustainability: economic development, social development, and environmental protection.

SUSTAINABILITY-CONSCIOUS PEOPLE

- **Sponsorship:** The sponsor should have a strong affinity for sustainability, understand its essentials, and be ready to challenge some of the old ways of doing things and the traditional organizational mindsets.

- **Stakeholders:** Sustainability should be a regularly discussed topic when you are addressing stakeholder needs and expectations. Identify strong advocates for sustainability, and involve them in your project either in the steering committee or on your core team.

- **Resources:** As the project manager, you should understand the essential elements of sustainability, involve sustainability experts, and think about sustainability implications when defining and implementing the project. You can put the social aspects of sustainability (e.g., work–life balance, equal opportunity, and personal development) into practice on the project team.

A SUSTAINABLE CREATION

- **Deliverables:** Apply eco-design principles when defining the scope: the solution delivered is built, used, and discarded in a way that poses no significant threat to the environment. The use of sustainable materials and suppliers is also an important element when your team is designing the project deliverables.

- **Plan:** Sustainable planning means scheduling and sequencing as efficiently as possible, minimizing waste and environmental impact, reducing delivery costs, making better use of resources, finding opportunities to increase labor skills, creating jobs in poorer locations, and considering the economies of mass production. When developing the plan, you need to look at the durability, reusability, and recyclability of all the components at the decommissioning or end-of-life stage of the project's deliverables.

- **Change:** Sustainable projects emphasize the imaginative use of motivation, which includes rewards that are extrinsic (pay and benefits), intrinsic (satisfaction and a sense of purpose that comes from the work itself), and social (the benefit of working collaboratively with others, of belonging). These projects also create a psychologically safe environment that encourages people to speak up and challenge or offer alternative or better ways of doing things. Following the principle of transparency and accountability, leaders of sustainable projects communicate proactively and openly about the project and cover its social and environmental effects.

Delivering sustainable project outcomes

One challenge that leaders face is the inability to choose only projects with exclusively sustainable outcomes. As discussed in chapter 10, organizations typically need a mix of projects to meet their strategic goals. Some resources should be invested in projects that are specific to sustainability, such as eliminating the use of nonrecyclable plastic. At the same time, organizations must continue to invest in product development, reorganizations, acquisitions, expansion, and all the other projects that make up the business's activities. To have a positive impact on sustainability, we need to look to new guidelines for sponsors and project managers to increase the focus of their projects on such sustainable outcomes and benefits as the P5 standard.

Project leaders must recognize that it's not simply the delivery of a project that can have a positive or negative impact on sustainability but also the deliverables produced. For instance, assets we create through projects may be damaging to the environment in their operation, maintenance, or ultimately their decommissioning.

Nor should you imagine that just because something is now digital rather than physical, it no longer poses a threat to the environment. "At 2 per cent of total emissions," says technology reporter Andrew Griffin, "the IT industry's carbon footprint is roughly the same as the entire airline industry. The vast warehouses of data that are dotted around the world can use as much power as a large city."[25] Despite all these challenges, there are ways to make our business-driven projects deliver outcomes and benefits that are more sustainable. Project leaders need to think beyond traditional project benefits. Adding the triple bottom line and the sustainability development goals to your prioritization and project selection discussion is a good starting point. Integrating sustainability requires a scope shift in the management of projects; you move from managing time, budget, and quality to managing social, environmental, and economic impact.

Designing and delivering sustainability projects

Since green and sustainability always cost money, isn't it hard to get business leaders to go along with this kind of spending? This question usually surfaces when people are talking about sustainability in projects. However, the idea that sustainable projects cost extra is more myth than reality. Many projects associated with sustainability save money, even in the short term. For example, some initiatives improve efficiency, save energy, or reduce waste. Of course, some other projects, such as eco-design, sourcing sustainability, or improving the lives and wages of workers in the supply chain, might cost more. But these initiatives, whether offering a quick payback or longer-term value, are investments, not costs. They're no different from the investment choices we make in marketing, R&D, or other areas of the business that require strategic thinking. As Ernst & Young has reported, the walls and silos between people running the numbers and those handling the softer issues around sustainability are crumbling.[26]

Executives are now answering questions from investors (e.g., Black-Rock and Vanguard), both of which are becoming more fluent in sustainability themselves, and those investors want to know, for example, how companies are handling their climate risks.[27] Today, there is no doubt that sustainability projects create business value. Some projects will pay back more quickly than others will, but yes, it's about business value—lower costs and risks, more innovation, and enhanced brand value. It's about building better companies.

The business case for sustainability should no longer be questioned. The UN's Business & Sustainable Development Commission estimated that the Sustainable Development Goals represent a $12 trillion opportunity, combining cost savings and new revenues.[28] According to the commission, "The total economic prize from implementing the SDGs [Sustainable Development Goals] could be 2–3 times larger, assuming that the benefits are captured across the whole economy and accompanied by much higher labor and resource productivity. . . . The overall prize is enormous."

Beyond simply understanding sustainability projects and making the case for them, project leaders must be prepared to deal with their complexity. The Drax Power Station is currently the UK's largest carbon capture project.[29] The station burns biomass (essentially wood pellets), and aside from generating power, it plans to refine the carbon emissions to make a high-grade liquid version of carbon dioxide, which will help make sodium bicarbonate, or baking soda. Unfortunately, the project's green credentials have been severely tarnished even before it has really started to make headway. Accusations suggest that its dependence on millions of tons of wood pellets that are currently imported from forests in the southern United States puts some of the world's most ecologically valuable forests at risk.

———

Every project has an impact, and it is the role of the executive sponsor and the project manager to make it a positive one. The same mindset behind the drive for bottom-line results must also be applied to creating a better world through projects.

The Project Manifesto

The emergence of the Project Economy is an unprecedented transformation with profound organizational and cultural consequences. With project-based work as the engine that drives change and progress, projects are now the essential model for creating value. Project management has been reinvented. It no longer focuses simply on deliverables but now stresses purpose and benefits—and as its purview has grown, project managers and executives needed to work together more closely. Finally, in 2020, projects took center stage worldwide; the pandemic made clear that we are all project managers, and leaders are all executive sponsors.

This book has focused on two goals. First, it has examined the past, present, and future of projects to help you understand how the Project Economy came to be and why it must not be ignored. I hope the book has opened your mind to a new and broader way to think about projects.

Second, the book has given you the practical skills and tools to help your projects succeed. From discussions on better defining a project's purpose, to accelerating benefits, to establishing an organized and disciplined

The Project Manifesto: The guiding principles of the Project Economy

We recognize the significant importance of projects for our society and humanity at large, and that there are better ways of implementing projects successfully and helping others to do so. Through this work:

1. We acknowledge that governments implement policies through projects and that countries develop and societies evolve through projects; we believe that ideas are made a reality through projects and that, if one day poverty is eradicated from the earth, it will be through a project.

2. We believe projects are the lingua franca of governments, businesses, and personal worlds, from the C-suite right through to an individual managing their career and relationships.

3. We are uncovering a vast new disruption; due to the new reality of accelerated change, more and more aspects of our lives are driven by projects, and more and more aspects in organizations are becoming projects; projects are thus becoming an essential element in everyone's professional and personal journeys.

4. In a world that is becoming increasingly automated and robotized, we see projects as the most human-centric way of working.

5. We believe that organizational agility is achieved through projects, which break through silos, reduce management layers, and create high-performing teams.

6. We recognize that startups and organizations innovate, grow, transform, create long-term value, and achieve their visions and strategic goals through projects; founders, entrepreneurs, and CEOs are the ultimate project leaders.

7. We consider our lives to be a set of projects; studies have become projects, and careers have become a series of projects too.

8. Our highest priority is to deliver projects better, to reduce the failure rate, to create more value for individuals and organizations, and to create more sustainable development in our economies and societies at large.

9. We see that projects and project implementation have received very little attention and have been ignored by leading business thinkers, management publications, and business schools; we believe that in the past years, this deficiency is being rectified.

10. We recognize project-based education as the best and most enduring learning experience for students and adults.

11. We seek recognition of projects and project implementation capabilities as essential for all management and leadership positions; we aspire for it to become part of the curriculums of every school and undergraduate program; we aim for it to be taught in every business school and MBA program.

12. We declare that projects and project implementation should be recognized as a profession.

Source: Antonio Nieto-Rodriguez, "The Project Manifesto: The Guiding Principles of the Project Economy," LinkedIn, October 3, 2019, https://www.linkedin.com/pulse/project-manifesto-antonio-nieto-rodriguez.

project portfolio, I hope you have learned the skills you need to succeed as a project leader.

As we reach the end of the book, I will focus on one more aspect: the human and personal elements of project management. Anyone can learn to be a project leader, and people of any nature and background can persevere against the worst conditions to make their dreams a reality through projects. When projects have ambitious goals, a higher purpose, and a defined deadline, people tend to remember those projects more clearly than they remember anything else in their careers. The moments they feel most proud of are the projects they work on—often the successful ones, but also the failed ones. Great projects don't just make the world better—they make *work* better.

With the growing concern around many jobs being taken over by robots and AI, the good news is that project-based work is human-centric. Projects cannot be carried out by machines; they need humans to do the work. Humans must gather around the purpose of the project, dividing the work, bonding, interacting, and addressing emotional aspects to create a high-performing team. Technology, particularly AI, will of course play an increasing role in projects, but instead of stealing jobs, technology will free us from the administrative and mechanical elements of project management and allow us to become better project leaders. It will improve the selection of projects and help us plan our projects better and anticipate potential risks, increasing the chances of success. But technology should remain an enabler and not the goal. People like you, not robots, will lead the project revolution.

My plea for society, and the purpose of this book, is that organizations, leaders, politicians—everyone—build the competencies required to transform and thrive in the new digital and project-driven economy. The potential in increasing the success rate of projects is practically limitless. It could add trillions of dollars' worth of social, environmental, educational, and other benefits to our world.

To expand on this plea, in 2019 I wrote "The Project Manifesto," which has since been endorsed by hundreds of professionals. The purpose of the manifesto is to lay out the guiding principles of the Project Economy. If you also believe that projects are the key to personal development and sustainable value creation and are the only way for organizations to cope with and flourish in today's changing world, the time to act is now. Please abide by the manifesto and share it with your colleagues and people in your organization. You can find it at https://projectsnco.com/blog/the-project-manifesto/.

Ready to succeed with your projects

We have reached the end of this project, but this book is just the deliverable; you are now equipped to succeed in a world driven by change. It's up to you to spread the benefits and to help me meet the purpose of the book: to make you and your organization more successful, as well as to significantly increase project performance rates to generate more value.

By implementing the Project Canvas, your organization will have more clarity on strategic projects and how to implement them. Not only that, but it will also bring the agility you need to react faster to moves by the competition and market opportunities. Your employees will see more possibilities to grow and develop, increasing their engagement and contribution to your organization's long-term success. You and your management team will become leaders in the new Project Economy. As an individual, you now have the tools to turn your ideas into a reality. Make sure you incorporate them into your daily routines. If you do, you'll certainly be more successful with your projects, both professional and personal.

I hope you'll walk the path of becoming a project leader with me.

Good luck with the journey!

The Benefits Card

The benefits card will help both the executive sponsor and the project manager identify the main benefits and key impacts of their projects. As mentioned earlier, each project will bring different benefits to different stakeholders. Project leaders must identify each major stakeholder's expectations of the main benefits of the project early in the process. After formally validating the benefits at the project steering committee, they should agree on the top three benefits for the project.

Benefit	Description	Example	Measure
Increase revenues	☐ New product ☐ New service ☐ New channels ☐ Acquisitions ☐ Expansions ☐ Other	☐ Increased sales ☐ Increased subscriptions ☐ Higher price points ☐ Increased margin	Percentage; financial
Reduce costs	☐ Automation ☐ Technology ☐ Redundancies ☐ Reorganizations ☐ Outsourcing ☐ Other	☐ FTE (full-time employee) savings ☐ Faster processes ☐ Greater accuracy ☐ Reduced fraud	FTE head count; financial
Productivity gains	☐ Efficiency increases ☐ Increased production outputs ☐ Automation ☐ Technology ☐ Default reductions ☐ Quality improvements ☐ Other	☐ Higher production volume ☐ Greater margins ☐ Reduced waste ☐ Lower volume of rework ☐ Greater customer responsiveness	Percentage
Strategic objectives	☐ Contribution to strategy ☐ Other	☐ Market leader ☐ Technology leader ☐ Access to new markets ☐ Introduction of new products or services ☐ Potential to transform or pivot the business ☐ Improved resilience ☐ Greater capacity for change	Percentage; financial; reputation

Reputation and compliance	❑ Stakeholder view of business fitness ❑ Regulator view of business probity ❑ Other	❑ Increased resilience ❑ Increased competitiveness ❑ Increased value and status ❑ Increased contract leverage ❑ Reduced costs of contracting ❑ Greater employee satisfaction	Share price; market reports; regulator reports; internal audit reports; contract terms
Sustainability	❑ Economic, social, and environmental resilience of the organization, its products, and its projects or programs ❑ Other	❑ Improved corporate reputation ❑ Reduced strategic risk ❑ Increased resilience ❑ Greater capacity for change	Percentage; financial; share value
Customer satisfaction and experience	❑ Customer or user attitude toward the business or its products ❑ Other	❑ Improved corporate reputation ❑ Improved competitiveness ❑ Greater resilience ❑ Greater employee satisfaction ❑ Higher price points ❑ Greater repeat business	Percentage; net promoter score; customer conversion rates and churn rates; volume and value of contracts
Market share	❑ Portion of a market controlled by company or product ❑ Other	❑ Greater autonomy of decision-making ❑ Greater production capability ❑ Greater purchasing power ❑ Greater economies of scale	Percentage, financial
Organizational culture	❑ Values and beliefs associated with the organization that drive employee and stakeholder behavior ❑ Other	❑ Greater capacity for, and speed of, change ❑ Greater resilience ❑ Greater productivity ❑ Greater employee satisfaction ❑ Better strategy ❑ Greater capacity for innovation ❑ Increased capacity for risk ❑ Improved communication transparency	Share price, market and regulator reports; employee satisfaction; volume and value of contracts; project performance and benefit realization

continued

Benefit	Description	Example	Measure
Employee satisfaction	☐ Employee attitude to work and organizational environment ☐ Other	☐ Improved employer brand engagement ☐ Improved reputation ☐ Better employee mental and physical health ☐ Reduced level of accidents or near misses ☐ Improved productivity ☐ Increased capacity for innovation and risk ☐ Reduced recruitment costs ☐ Improved supplier and customer relationships	Financial (costs of insurance, recruitment, and employee absences); employee satisfaction surveys
Employee engagement	☐ Employee commitment to the success of employer's business ☐ Other	☐ Greater resilience ☐ Improved productivity ☐ Increased capacity for innovation and risk ☐ Reduced costs of rework and wastage ☐ Greater project maturity ☐ More transparent communication	Employee engagement survey; productivity per employee

The benefits card can also be used as a tracker and communication tool when the project is reporting on benefit progress.

Benefit	Owner	Date	Category	Alignment
Benefit description as easily understood and as quantifiable as possible	Person accountable to deliver the benefit	Date by which the benefit is expected to be realized	Area of the business to which the benefits will contribute—for example, revenue increase	Level of consensus about the benefit among the key stakeholders

Notes

Introduction: Welcome to the Project Economy

1. Ana Terra Athayde, "How Elisa Mansur's Award-Winning Start-up Idea Benefits the Brazilian Families in Greatest Need," BBC, March 7, 2019, https://www.bbc.com/worklife/article/20190307-the-27-year-old-protecting-brazils-hidden-job-economy.

2. Robert J. Gordon, "Revisiting U.S. Productivity Growth over the Past Century with a View of the Future," National Bureau of Economic Research, March 2010, https://www.nber.org/papers/w15834.

3. Association for Project Management, "PwC PPM Global Survey: 'Insights and Trends into Current Project, Programme and Portfolio Management,'" March 27, 2014, https://www.apm.org.uk/news/pwc-ppm-global-survey-insights-and-trends-into-current-project-programme-and-portfolio-management/.

4. Project Management Institute, "US Senate Unanimously Approves the Program Management Improvement and Accountability Act," December 1, 2016, https://www.pmi.org/about/press-media/press-releases/senate-program-management-act.

5. Association for Project Management, "APM Receives Its Royal Charter," January 6, 2017, https://www.apm.org.uk/news/apm-receives-its-royal-charter.

6. Yvonne Schoper, Christoph Schneider, and Andreas Walkd, "Makroökonomische Vermessung der Projekttätigkeit in Deutschland" [Macroeconomic Measurement of Project Activity in Germany], GPM Deutsche Gesellschaft für Projektmanagement, accessed April 7, 2021, https://www.gpm-ipma.de/know_how/studienergebnisse/makrooekonomische_vermessung_der_projekttaetigkeit_in_deutschland.html.

7. Project Management Institute, "Project Management Job Growth and Talent Gap Report, 2017–2027," 2017, https://www.pmi.org/-/media/pmi/documents/public/pdf/learning/job-growth-report.pdf?sc_lang_temp=en.

8. Gavin Gibbon, "Mohamed Alabbar Removes All Job Titles from Emaar Staff," *ArabianBusiness*, July 21, 2020, https://www.arabianbusiness.com/jobs/449829-alabbar-removes-all-job-titles-from-emaar-staff.

9. Burt Helm, "Stan Richards's Unique Management Style," *Inc.*, November 2011, https://www.inc.com/magazine/201111/stan-richards-unique-management-style.html.

10. Lydia Dishman, "Microsoft Says You Will Need These Skills after COVID, and It Wants to Help You Get Certified," *Fast Company*, June 30, 2020, https://www.fastcompany.com/90522593/microsoft-says-you-will-need-these-skills-after-covid-and-it-wants-to-help-you-get-certified; LinkedIn, "LinkedIn's Economic Graph," accessed March 19, 2021, https://economicgraph.linkedin.com/.

11. Shane Hastie and Stéphane Wojewoda, "Standish Group 2015 Chaos Report: Q&A with Jennifer Lynch," *InfoQ*, October 4, 2015, https://www.infoq.com/articles /standish-chaos-2015.

Chapter 1: Projects Everywhere

1. Daniel A. Levinthal and James G. March, "The Myopia of Learning," *Strategic Management Journal* 14 (1993): 95–112.

2. Concept coined in Antonio Nieto-Rodriguez, *The Focused Organization: How Concentrating on a Few Key Initiatives Can Dramatically Improve Strategy Execution* (Burlington, VT: Gower, 2012).

3. Manuel Hensmans, Gerry Johnson, and George Yip, *Strategic Transformation: Changing While Winning* (London: Palgrave Macmillan, 2013).

4. For details on Western Union's circumstances, see Antonio Nieto-Rodriguez, "How Can a Company Survive for More than 100 Years?," *Today's Manager* 2 (2015).

5. Ingo Bögemann, "Product Life Cycles Are Getting Shorter, Your Development Times Too?" *MB Collaborations*, January 15, 2018, https://blog.mb-collaborations.com /en/shorter-product-life-cycles.

6. Yvonne Schoper, Christoph Schneider, and Andreas Walkd, "Makroökonomische Vermessung der Projekttätigkeit in Deutschland" [Macroeconomic measurement of project activity in Germany], GPM Deutsche Gesellschaft für Projektmanagement, accessed April 7, 2021, https://www.gpm-ipma.de/know_how/studienergebnisse /makrooekonomische_vermessung_der_projekttaetigkeit_in_deutschland.html.

7. Project Management Institute, "Latest Findings Show Project Management Professions in High Demand as Industry Job Growth Accelerates," https://www.pmi .org/about/press-media/press-releases/latest-findings-show-project-management -professionals-in-high-demand.

8. Roger L. Martin, "Rethinking the Decision Factory," *Harvard Business Review*, October 2013, https://hbr.org/2013/10/rethinking-the-decision-factory.

9. Roger L. Martin, personal communication, 2019, https://www.linkedin.com /pulse/least-80-activities-white-collar-workers-projects-1-nieto-rodriguez/.

10. UK Cabinet Office, "Successful IT: Modernising Government in Action," accessed September 20, 2020, https://ntouk.files.wordpress.com/2015/06/successful-it -modernising-government-in-action-2000.pdf.

11. UK Institute for Government, "Specialisms in the Civil Service," updated August 8, 2017, https://www.instituteforgovernment.org.uk/publication/whitehall -monitor/whitehall-explained/specialisms-civil-service.

12. David Gelles, "The Husband-and-Wife Team Behind the Leading Vaccine to Solve Covid-19," *New York Times*, November 10, 2020, https://www.nytimes .com/2020/11/10/business/biontech-covid-vaccine.html.

13. US Department of Defense, "Coronavirus: Operation Warp Speed," accessed April 7, 2021, https://www.defense.gov/Explore/Spotlight/Coronavirus /Operation-Warp-Speed/.

14. Eddie Obeng, "Smart Failure for a Fast-Changing World," TEDGlobal 2012, June 2012, https://www.ted.com/talks/eddie_obeng_smart_failure_for_ a_fast_changing_world.

15. Bernard Marr, "10 Amazing Examples of Robotic Process Automation in Practice," accessed September 20, 2020, https://www.bernardmarr.com/default .asp?contentID=1909.

Chapter 2: What Is a Project?

1. Naomi J. Brookes and Giorgio Locatelli, "Power Plants as Megaprojects: Using Empirics to Shape Policy, Planning, and Construction Management," *Utilities Policy* 36 (October 2015): 57–66.

2. Various studies have shown that mergers have failure rates of more than 50 percent. One recent study found that 83 percent of all mergers fail to create value, and half actually destroy value. See, for example, Robert W. Holthausen and Mark E. Zmijewski, *Corporate Valuation: Theory, Evidence, and Practice*, vol. 2 (New York: McGraw-Hill, 2010).

Chapter 3: What Project Management Is Now

1. Duncan Haughey, "A Brief History of Project Management," Project Smart, January 2, 2010, updated December 24, 2014, https://www.projectsmart.co.uk /brief-history-of-project-management.php.

2. Project Management Institute, *PMBOK Guide: A Guide to the Project Management Body of Knowledge*, 6th ed. (Newton Square, PA: PMI, 2017).

3. Jeff Sutherland, "Takeuchi and Nonaka," *Scruminc* (blog), October 22, 2011, https://www.scruminc.com/takeuchi-and-nonaka-roots-of-scrum/.

4. Karoline Thorp Adland, Michael Ehlers, Niels Ahrengot, and John Ryding Olsson, *Half Double: Projects in Half the Time with Double Impact* (Copenhagen: Implement Press, 2018).

5. Nadim Matta and Ron Ashkenas, "Why Good Projects Fail Anyway," *Harvard Business Review*, September 2003, https://hbr.org/2003/09/why-good-projects -fail-anyway.

6. Shane Hastie and Stéphane Wojewoda, "Standish Group 2015 Chaos Report: Q&A with Jennifer Lynch," InfoQ, October 4, 2015, https://www.infoq.com/articles /standish-chaos-2015.

7. Full research and more details can be found in my book, Antonio Nieto-Rodriguez, *The Focused Organization: How Concentrating on a Few Key Initiatives Can Dramatically Improve Strategy Execution* (Burlington, VT: Gower, 2012).

8. Queensland Government, "The 7 Ps of Marketing," Business Queensland, updated June 21, 2016, https://www.business.qld.gov.au/running-business/marketing -sales/marketing-promotion/marketing-basics/seven-ps-marketing.

9. Christina Garcia-Ochoa Martin, "The Sidney Opera House Construction: A Case of Project Management Failure," *Escuela de Organización Industrial* (blog), January 14, 2012, https://www.eoi.es/blogs/cristinagarcia-ochoa/2012/01/14 /the-sidney-opera-house-construction-a-case-of-project-management-failure.

Chapter 4: Introduction to the Project Canvas

1. "Porter's 5 Forces," *Investopedia*, February 22, 2020, https://www.investopedia .com/terms/p/porter.asp; "Porter's Value Chain," University of Cambridge Institute for Manufacturing, accessed October 2, 2018, https://www.ifm.eng.cam.ac.uk /research/dstools/value-chain-.

2. Martin Reeves, Sandy Moose, and Thijs Venema, "BCG Classics Revisited: The Growth Share Matrix," Boston Consulting Group, June 4, 2014, https://www .bcg.com/publications/2014/growth-share-matrix-bcg-classics-revisited.aspx.

3. Strategyzer, "Business Model Canvas," accessed March 24, 2021, https://www .strategyzer.com/canvas.

Chapter 5: The Foundation

1. Simon Sinek, *Start with Why: How Great Leaders Inspire Everyone to Take Action* (New York: Penguin, 2011), 45.

2. Jim Collins and Jerry I. Porras, *Built to Last: Successful Habits of Visionary Companies* (New York: HarperBusiness, 1997).

3. Antonio Nieto-Rodriguez and Daniel Evrard, "Boosting Business Performance through Programme and Project Management," PricewaterhouseCoopers, 2004, https://mosaicprojects.com.au/PDF/PwC_PM_Survey_210604.pdf.

4. Mark Bonchek, "How to Create an Exponential Mindset," *Harvard Business Review*, July 27, 2016, https://hbr.org/2016/07/how-to-create-an-exponential-mindset.

5. Jeroen De Flander, personal communication, summer 2015.

6. Anders Inset, personal communication, spring 2019.

7. Ian MacDonald, Catherine Burke, and Karl Stewart, *Systems Leadership: Creating Positive Organizations*, 3rd ed. (Oxford: Routledge, 2018).

8. UK Office for National Statistics, "Measures of National Well-Being Dashboard," October 23, 2019, https://www.ons.gov.uk/peoplepopulationandcommunity/wellbeing/articles/measuresofnationalwellbeingdashboard/2018-04-25.

9. Tom Gilb, "Quantify the Un-Quantifiable: Tom Gilb at TEDxTrondheim," TEDx Talks (video), November 3, 2013, https://www.youtube.com/watch?v=kOfK6rSLVTA&t=3s.

10. HM Treasury, *Guide to Developing the Project Business Case* (London: HM Treasury, 2018), www.praxisframework.org/files/guide-to-developing-the-project-business-case.pdf.

Chapter 6: The People

1. Ron Ashkenas, "How to Be an Effective Executive Sponsor," HBR.org, May 18, 2015, https://hbr.org/2015/05/how-to-be-an-effective-executive-sponsor.

2. Project Management Institute, *PMBOK Guide: A Guide to the Project Management Body of Knowledge*, 6th ed. (Newton Square, PA: PMI, 2017), 81.

3. Colin Marshall, "How David Lynch Got Creative Inspiration? By Drinking a Milkshake at Bob's Big Boy, Every Single Day, for Seven Straight Years," *Open Culture*, August 16, 2018, www.openculture.com/2018/08/how-david-lynch-got-creative-inspiration.html.

4. Marshall Goldsmith, personal conversation, January 2020.

5. UK Government Project Delivery Profession, "Project Delivery Capability Framework," November 2018, https://assets.publishing.service.gov.uk/government/uploads/system/uploads/attachment_data/file/755783/PDCF.pdf.

6. European Commission, Centre of Excellence in Project Management, *PM²Project Management Methodology Guide 3.0.1* (Luxembourg: Publications Office of the European Union, 2021), https://op.europa.eu/en/publication-detail/-/publication/b8458be2-821d-11eb-9ac9-01aa75ed71a1.

7. Charles Duhigg, *Smarter Faster Better: The Secrets of Being Productive* (London: Cornerstone Digital, 2016).

8. Jose Maria Delos Santos, "Understanding Responsibility Assignment Matrix (RACI Matrix)," Project-Management.com, January 28, 2020, https://project-management.com/understanding-responsibility-assignment-matrix-raci-matrix/.

9. R. J. Sendt, "Auditor-General's Report, Performance Audit: The Cross City Tunnel Project," Audit Office of New South Wales, May 2006, www.audit.nsw.gov.au /sites/default/files/pdf-downloads/2006_May_Report_The_Cross_City_Tunnel _Project.pdf.

10. Louise M. Worsley, *Stakeholder-Led Project Management: Changing the Way We Manage Projects* (New York: Business Expert Press, 2017).

Chapter 7: The Creation

1. Project Management Institute, *PMBOK Guide: A Guide to the Project Management Body of Knowledge*, 6th ed. (Newton Square, PA: PMI, 2017).

2. ISO 9000, clause 3.2.10, defines QC as "a part of quality management focused on fulfilling quality requirements." ISO 9000, clause 3.2.11, defines QA as "a part of quality management focused on providing confidence that quality requirements will be fulfilled." International Organization for Standardization (ISO), Online Browsing Platform, accessed April 7, 2021, https://www.iso.org/obp/ui /#iso:std:iso:9000:ed-3:v1:en.

3. Project Management Institute, *PMBOK Guide.*

4. Project Management Institute, "Pulse of the Profession 2016," 2016, https://www .pmi.org/learning/thought-leadership/pulse/pulse-of-the-profession-2016.

5. For the transition to the euro, the European Commission developed a detailed change management plan, in every language of the EU. The plan included information packs, visuals, commercials, toolkits, and so on. See European Commission, Directorate-General for Economic and Financial Affairs, "Preparing the Introduction of the *Euro*: A Short Handbook," 2008, ec.europa.eu/economy_finance/publications/ pages/publication12436_en.pdf; and European Commission, "Communication Toolkit," accessed April 7, 2021, https://ec.europa.eu /easme/en/section/communication-toolkit. These two resources will give you a good overview of what is needed to prepare an effectual and successful change management plan for your project.

6. Kim Willsher, "French Railway Operator SNCF Orders Hundreds of New Trains That Are Too Big" *Guardian*, May 21, 2014, https://www.theguardian.com /world/2014/may/21/french-railway-operator-sncf-orders-trains-too-big.

7. John P. Kotter, *Leading Change* (Boston: Harvard Business School Press, 1996).

8. Henry Ward, "The Shadow Organization Chart," Carta, September 12, 2017, https://carta.com/blog/the-shadow-organizational-chart/.

Chapter 8: Putting the Project Canvas into Practice

1. Wikipedia, s.v. "Boeing 777," updated March 31, 2021, https://en.wikipedia.org /wiki/Boeing_777.

2. Lyndsey Matthews, "Notre-Dame Cathedral Will Be Rebuilt the Way It Stood before the 2019 Fire," *Afar*, July 10, 2020, https://www.afar.com/magazine/what-will-it -take-to-rebuild-notre-dame-cathedral.

3. Francesco Bandarin, "Notre Dame Enters a New and High-Risk Phase in Its Restoration," *Art Newspaper*, December 30, 2019, https://www.theartnewspaper .com/news/notre-dame-enters-a-new-and-high-risk-phase-in-its-restoration.

Chapter 9: Project Leadership

1. Institute of Project Management Ireland, "PMBOK #5 Promotes Stakeholder Management," July 3, 2013, http://projectmanagement.ie/blog/pmbok-5-promotes -stakeholder-management.

2. The Project Economy by Antonio Nieto-Rodriguez, "ANR Interview #4: The Project Revolution with Alan Mulally—Former CEO of Ford Motor Company & Boeing" (video), June 20, 2018, https://youtu.be/pXkABzHYaV0.

3. Jené Luciani, "28 Powerful Women Share Their Best Advice," *Shape*, August 13, 2013, https://www.shape.com/celebrities/interviews/28-powerful-women-share -their-best-advice.

4. Taylor Locke, "JPMorgan CEO Jamie Dimon: People with These Traits Succeed—'Not the Smartest or Hardest-Working in the Room,'" *CNBC Make It*, November 18, 2020, https://www.cnbc.com/2020/11/18/jpmorgan-ceo-jamie -dimon-on-what-makes-the-most-successful-leaders.html#close.

5. Paul Austin, "State Tips Another $350M into Myki Debacle," *The Age*, May 27, 2008, https://www.theage.com.au/national/state-tips-another-350m-into-myki -debacle-20080527-ge74cr.html.

6. James Bond Stockdale, "The Principles of Leadership," *American Educator* (winter 1981).

7. This excerpt is from Rita McGrath, interview with the author, June 1, 2018.

8. Nadia Cameron, "IBM's Ginni Rometty: Comfort and Growth Will Never Co-Exist," *CMO*, November 9, 2017, https://www.cmo.com.au/article/629768 /ibm-ginni-rometty-comfort-growth-can-never-co-exist/.

9. Project Management Institute, "PMI Code of Ethics and Professional Conduct," accessed April 7, 2021, https://www.pmi.org/-/media/pmi/documents/public /pdf/ethics/pmi-code-of-ethics.pdf.

10. Integrated Project Management Association, "IPMA Code of Ethics and Professional Conduct," 2015, https://www.ipma.world/assets/IPMA-Code-of-Ethics-and -Professional-Conduct.pdf.

Chapter 10: Selecting and Prioritizing Projects

1. Rosalind "Roz" Brewer, quoted in Beth Kowitt, "How Starbucks Got Its Buzz Back," *Fortune*, September 24, 2019, https://fortune.com/longform/starbucks-coo -roz-brewer-sales-retail/.

2. Nassim Nicholas Taleb, *The Black Swan: The Impact of the Highly Improbable* (New York: Random House, 2008).

3. Sara Hajikazemi, Anandasivakumar Ekambaram, Bjørn Andersen, and Yousef J-T. Zidane, "The Black Swan—Knowing the Unknown in Projects," *Procedia—Social and Behavioral Sciences* 226 (2016): 184–192.

4. Thomas L. Friedman, "Stampeding Black Elephants," *New York Times*, November 22, 2014, https://www.nytimes.com/2014/11/23/opinion/sunday/thomas-l -friedman-stampeding-black-elephants.html?_r=0.

5. Unilever, "Building the Unilever of the Future," March 15, 2018, https://www .unilever.com/news/Press-releases/2018/building-the-unilever-of-the-future.html.

6. For a good exposition of this new reality, see Liri Andersson and Ludo Van der Heyden, "Directing Digitalisation: Guidelines for Boards and Executives," INSEAD Corporate Governance Initiative, 2017, https://boardagenda.com/resource /directing-digitalisation-guidelines-boards-executives.

7. Louis V. Gerstner Jr., *Who Says Elephants Can't Dance? Leading a Great Enterprise Through Dramatic Change* (New York: Harper Collins, 2002).

8. See Clayton M. Christensen, *The Innovator's Dilemma: When New Technologies Cause Great Firms to Fail* (Boston: Harvard Business School Press, 1997).

9. Amazon Jobs, "Earth's Most Customer-Centric Company," accessed October 7, 2018, https://www.amazon.jobs/en/working/working-amazon.

10. Emma Walmsley, GlaxoSmithKline annual report, 2017, https://www.annualreports.com/Company/glaxosmithkline-plc.

11. Verge Video, "The Future of Microsoft with Satya Nadella," interview by Nilay Patel (video), *Verge*, October 7, 2015, https://www.theverge.com/video/2015/10/7/9473677/microsoft-windows-10-device-event-satya-nadella-interview.

Chapter 11: The Agile and Project-Driven Organization

1. This section draws on insights from a decade-long research program at Zhejiang University (2007–2017). The research included interviews with hundreds of local Chinese entrepreneurs and investors, as well as executives in large Chinese firms, and focused on the status and development of dynamic capability by local Chinese firms. Specifically, the program conducted research on the digital ecosystems of Alibaba, Baidu, Tencent, Xiaomi, and LeEco, and a proprietary database on their expansion activities is summarized in Mark J. Greeven and Wei Wei, *Business Ecosystems in China: Alibaba and Competing Baidu, Tencent, Xiaomi, LeEco* (London: Routledge, 2017). Research on pioneering Chinese companies and hidden champions is summarized in Mark J. Greeven, George S. Yip, and Wei Wei, *Pioneers, Hidden Champions, Changemakers, and Underdogs: Lessons from China's Innovators* (Cambridge, MA: MIT Press, 2019). See also Mark Boncheck and Sangeet Paul Choudary, "Three Elements of a Successful Platform Strategy," HBR.org, January 31, 2013, https://hbr.org/2013/01/three-elements-of-a-successful-platform; Antonio Nieto-Rodriguez, *The Focused Organization: How Concentrating on a Few Key Initiatives Can Dramatically Improve Strategy Execution* (Abingdon, UK: Routledge, 2016).

2. Boncheck and Choudary, "Three Elements of a Successful Platform Strategy."

3. Nikola Jurisic, Michael Lurie, Philippine Risch, and Olli Salo, "Four Global Success Stories Offer Insights and Lessons Learned on Achieving Organizational Agility," McKinsey, August 4, 2020, https://www.mckinsey.com/business-functions/organization/our-insights/doing-vs-being-practical-lessons-on-building-an-agile-culture.

4. Calleam Consulting, "Boeing 737-MAX," *Why Do Projects Fail?* (blog), accessed June 12, 2020, http://calleam.com/WTPF/?p=8802.

5. Natalie Kitroeff, "Boeing Employees Mocked F.A.A. and 'Clowns' Who Designed 737 Max," *New York Times*, updated January 29, 2020, www.nytimes.com/2020/01/09/business/boeing-737-messages.html.

6. Gary A. Klein, *Streetlights and Shadows: Searching for the Keys to Adaptive Decision Making* (Bradford, PA: Bradford Books, 2011).

7. BCG, "At Lego, Growth and Culture Are Not Kid Stuff: An Interview with Jørgen Vig Knudstorp," February 9, 2017, https://www.bcg.com/en-be/publications/2017/people-organization-jorgen-vig-knudstorp-lego-growth-culture-not-kid-stuff.

8. Gallup, *State of the Global Workplace* (New York: Gallup Press, 2017), https://www.gallup.com/file/workplace/238079/State%20of%20the%20Global%20Workplace_Gallup%20Report.pdf.

9. Great Place to Work, *"Fortune* 100 Best Companies to Work For, 2019," accessed April 7, 2021, https://www.greatplacetowork.com/best-workplaces/100-best/2019.

10. The exceptions here are organizations such as consulting firms, which make a living completing projects, or companies that dedicate resources full-time to one specific project.

11. Camille Langlade, with Jules Pecnard, "L'application qui fait trembler les ministres: comment Macron mesure en temps réel leur efficacité" [The app that makes ministers tremble: how Macron measures their effectiveness in real time], BFMTV, September 16, 2019, https://www.bfmtv.com/politique/gouvernement/l-application -qui-fait-trembler-les-ministres-comment-macron-mesure-en -temps-reel-leur-efficacite_AV-201909160021.html.

Chapter 12: Project Managing a Better Future

1. HM Treasury, "National Infrastructure Strategy," November 2020, https:// assets.publishing.service.gov.uk/government/uploads/system/uploads/attachment_ data/file/938049/NIS_final_web_single_page.pdf.

2. Ziyad Cassim, Borko Handjiski, Jörg Schubert, and Yassir Zouaoui, "The $10 Trillion Rescue: How Governments Can Deliver Impact," McKinsey, June 5, 2020, https:// www.mckinsey.com/industries/public-and-social-sector/our-insights/the-10-trillion-dollar-rescue-how-governments-can-deliver-impact.

3. Alibaba Cloud, "How Did Alibaba Help Retailer Lin Qingxuan Cope with the Coronavirus Outbreak?" March 5, 2020, https://www.alibabacloud.com/blog/how-did-alibaba-help-retailer-lin-qingxuan-cope-with-the-coronavirus-outbreak_595950.

4. Gregory Wallace, "Airlines and TSA Report 96% Drop in Air Travel as Pandemic Continues," *CNN*, April 9, 2020, https://edition.cnn.com/2020/04/09/politics /airline-passengers-decline/index.html.

5. James Asquith, "Commercial Airlines Are Now Operating Cargo-Only Flights," *Forbes*, March 28, 2020, https://www.forbes.com/sites/jamesasquith/2020/03 /28/commercial-airlines-are-now-operating-cargo-only-flights/#5202969b6f0e.

6. Project Management Institute, "The ROI of Inclusion on Project Teams," June 8, 2020, https://www.pmi.org/learning/library/case-diversity-teams-11998.

7. "Lenovo Scores 100% on 2018 Corporate Equality Index," Lenovo, November 9, 2017, http://news.lenovo.com/pressroom/press-releases/lenovo-scores-100 -on-2018-corporate-equality-index.

8. Yolanda Conyers, "Diversity," Lenovo, accessed April 9, 2021, https://www.lenovo .com/gb/en/lenovo/diversity/.

9. From Alexandra Jones, "Rising to the Challenge of Diversity: A Discussion of the Business Case," Work Foundation, January 2006, http://multifaiths.com/pdf /DiversityReportWorkFoundation.pdf.

10. HM Treasury, "National Infrastructure Strategy."

11. HM Treasury, "National Infrastructure Strategy."

12. Woody Woodward, "Firm Aims to Disrupt Silicon Valley Diversity," *Fox Business*, June 6, 2016, https://www.foxbusiness.com/features/firm-aims-to-disrupt-silicon -valley-diversity.

13. GSK, "Inclusion and Diversity at GSK," accessed April 9, 2021, https://www.gsk .com/en-gb/responsibility/our-people/inclusion-and-diversity-at-gsk/.

14. Paul Boudreau, *Applying Artificial Intelligence to Project Management* (Paul Boudreau, 2019).

15. David Doukhan, "Découvrez l'application smartphone secrète qui place les ministres sous la surveillance de l'Elysée" [Discover the secret smartphone application that places ministers under the surveillance of the Elysée], *Europe 1*, September 16, 2019, https://www.europe1.fr/politique/information-europe -1-lapplication-smartphone-secrete-de-lelysee-qui-fait-trembler-les-ministres -3919812.

16. Alessandra Scholl-Sternberg, "Crossrail Integration Facility and Test Automation: Improving Resilience with Automated Testing," Institution of Railway Signal Engineers, 2019, https://learninglegacy.crossrail.co.uk/wp-content/uploads /2020/10/7G-017-IRSE-News-Crossrail-Integration-Facility-and-Test -Automation-20200915.pdf.

17. United Nations Department of Economic and Social Affairs, "The 17 Goals," https://sdgs.un.org/goals.

18. Project Management Institute, *The Project Management Body of Knowledge (PMBOK)*, 6th edition (Newton Square, PA: PMI, 2013), 35.

19. Michael Young, "7 Ways for Project Managers to Make Your Projects Sustainable," Green Project Management, July 6, 2016, http://www.blog.greenprojectmanagement. org/index.php/2016/07/06/top-7-ways-that-project-managers-can-incorporate -sustainability-into-their-projects/.

20. UN Office for Project Services (UNOPS), "Sustainable: Designing Projects with Greater Impact," accessed April 9, 2021, https://sustainable.unops.org/.

21. Major Projects Association, "Sustainability and Circular Economy Resource Guide," accessed April 9, 2021, https://majorprojects.org/sustainability/.

22. J. Van den Brink, "Duurzaam projectmanagement: verder kijken dan je project lang is" [Sustainable project management: looking beyond the project]. *Projectie* 4 (2009).

23. A. J. Gilbert Silvius and Ron P. J. Schipper, "Sustainability in Project Management: A Literature Review and Impact Analysis," *Social Business* 4, no. 1 (2014): 63–96.

24. Business & Sustainable Development Commission, "Better Business, Better World."

25. Andrew Griffin, "How Using the Internet Damages the Environment," *Independent*, July 12, 2019, https://www.independent.co.uk/environment/internet-environment -data-climate-change-global-warming-servers-centre-a8968296.html.

26. Ernst & Young, "How Sustainability Has Expanded the CFO's Role," 2011, https://www.sustainabilityexchange.ac.uk/files/how_sustainability_has_ expanded_the_cfos_role.pdf.

27. Brian Tomlinson, "How Long-Term Investors Influence Corporate Behavior," *Sloan Management Review*, March 23, 2018, https://sloanreview.mit.edu/article/how -long-term-investors-influence-corporate-behavior; Ross Kerber, "Vanguard Seeks Corporate Disclosure on Risks from Climate Change," Reuters, August 14, 2017, https://www.reuters.com/article/us-vanguard-climate/vanguard-seeks-corporate -disclosure-on-risks-from-climate-change-idUSKCN1AU1KJ.

28. Business & Sustainable Development Commission, "Better Business, Better World" (executive summary), January 2017, www.un.org/pga/71/wp-content/uploads /sites/40/2017/02/Better-Business-Better-World-Executive-Summary.pdf.

29. Jillian Ambrose, "UK's Biggest Carbon Capture Project Is Step-Change on Emissions," *Guardian*, June 26, 2019, https://www.theguardian.com/environment /2019/jun/27/uks-biggest-carbon-capture-project-is-step-change-on-emissions.

Index

Acknowledgments

Writing a book is a complex, purpose-driven project. The pressure escalates when the deadline is approaching and you still have many pages to write. It's like running a marathon—constantly on your mind for months and sometimes years—but when you finally cross the finish line you have the great satisfaction of seeing the outcome of your dedication and hard work.

It is impossible to accomplish such an endeavor without the support of the family. Thanks to my exceptional wife, Clarisse; my amazing children, Laura, Alexander, Selma, and Lucas; my caring parents, Maria Jose and Juan Antonio; and my brilliant brothers, Javi, Iñaki, and Jose Miguel.

I want to especially thank my editor at Harvard Business Review Press, Dave Lievens, for his fantastic advice and guidance throughout the book development process and for pushing me to get the best out of myself and make this my best book yet. Thanks also to Jen Waring for her great proofreading skills. And of course I want to thank Jonathan Norman for his invaluable support, which started in 2012 with my first book, *The Focused Organization*. Thanks also to Richard Pharro, Stuart Crainer, Judy Miao, Ron Ashkenas, and Ray Sheen, who kindly volunteered to review the manuscript and provided valuable insights and recommendations.

Even so, this book will not accomplish its purpose and deliver any benefits unless people read it, learn from it, and apply some of the concepts to make them more successful. For that I want to thank the extremely supportive marketing team at the Press, led by Sally Ashworth.

Finally, I would like to thank the editors of *Harvard Business Review* for giving me the opportunity to write the *HBR Project Management*

Handbook. It is the perfect culmination and recognition of a quest I started in 2004 to elevate project management from a tactical topic to the new lingua franca of business. It also confirms the importance of projects and the project management profession in our new world driven by change. Therefore I would like to also dedicate this book to the millions of project managers who, with their hard work—often unrecognized—contribute to making this a better world.

About the Author

Antonio Nieto-Rodriguez (www.antonionietorodriguez.com) is the global champion of project management. His work focuses on advising senior leaders on how to lead transformational change, prioritize and implement strategic initiatives, build high-performing teams, work across silos, and become a learning organization. He was the Global Chairman of the Project Management Institute, where he launched the Brightline Initiative. He is the founder of Projects & Co., a global consulting firm of implementation experts. He is also the cofounder of the Strategy Implementation Institute.

Antonio's research and global impact in modern management has been recognized by Thinkers50 with the prestigious Ideas into Practice award and is ranked in two of the Global Gurus Top 30 lists, on management and education. He is part of Marshall Goldsmith 100 Coaches. He has presented at more than five hundred conferences around the world, including the Business Summit, the Strategy Leaders Forum, Gartner, TEDx, and the EU Cohesion Conference.

He was the Director of the Program Management Office at GlaxoSmithKline Vaccines. Previously he worked as Head of Project Portfolio Management at BNP Paribas Fortis. Prior to these positions, he was Head of Post-Merger Integration at Fortis Bank, leading the acquisition of ABN AMRO bank, the largest acquisition in financial service history. He also worked for ten years at PricewaterhouseCoopers, becoming the global lead practitioner for project and change management.

Antonio is the author of *Lead Successful Projects*, *The Project Revolution*, and *The Focused Organization*. He has contributed to seven other books. A leading authority in teaching and coaching senior executives the art and science of strategy execution and project management, he is currently visiting professor at Duke Corporate Education, Instituto de Empresa Business School (Madrid), Solvay Brussels School of Economics and Management, Vlerick Business School (Brussels), and Skolkovo Moscow School of Management.

Born in Madrid and educated in Germany, Mexico, Italy, and the United States, Antonio is fluent in five languages. He is an economist and holds an MBA from London Business School and INSEAD's International Director Program.

He can be reached via email at antonio.nieto.rodriguez@gmail.com.

Invaluable insights
always at your fingertips

With an All-Access subscription to
Harvard Business Review, you'll get
so much more than a magazine.

Exclusive online content and tools
you can put to use today

My Library, your personal workspace for sharing,
saving, and organizing HBR.org articles and tools

Unlimited access to more than 4,000 articles in the
Harvard Business Review archive

Subscribe today at hbr.org/subnow

The most important management ideas all in one place.

We hope you enjoyed this book from *Harvard Business Review*. For the best ideas HBR has to offer turn to HBR's 10 Must Reads Boxed Set. From books on leadership and strategy to managing yourself and others, this 6-book collection delivers articles on the most essential business topics to help you succeed.

HBR's 10 Must Reads Series

The definitive collection of ideas and best practices on our most sought-after topics from the best minds in business.

- Change Management
- Collaboration
- Communication
- Emotional Intelligence
- Innovation
- Leadership
- Making Smart Decisions

- Managing Across Cultures
- Managing People
- Managing Yourself
- Strategic Marketing
- Strategy
- Teams
- The Essentials

hbr.org/mustreads